The Harper's Forum Book

The Harper's Forum Book

◆

What Are We Talking About?

◆

Edited by Jack Hitt

Introduction by Lewis H. Lapham

A Citadel Press Book
Published by Carol Publishing Group

A Citadel Press Book
Published by Carol Publishing Group

Editorial Offices: 600 Madison Avenue, New York, N.Y. 10022
Sales & Distribution Offices: 120 Enterprise Avenue, Secaucus, N.J. 07094
In Canada: Musson Book Company, a division of General Publishing Co., Ltd., Don Mills, Ontario.

Queries regarding rights and permissions should be addressed to Carol Publishing Group, 120 Enterprise Avenue, Secaucus, N.J. 07094

Carol Publishing Group books are available at special discounts for bulk purchases, for sales promotions, fund raising, or educational purposes. Special editions can be created to specifications. For details contact: Special Sales Department, Carol Publishing Group, 120 Enterprise Avenue, Secaucus, N.J. 07094

Manufactured in the United States of America
10 9 8 7 6 5 4 3 2 1

Library of Congress Cataloging-in-Publication Data

The Harper's forum book : what are we talking about? / edited by Jack
  Hitt : introduction by Lewis H. Lapham.
      p.   cm.
  "A Citadel Press book."
  ISBN 0–8065–1230–X
  I. Hitt, Jack. II. Harper's.
  AC5.W42   1991   91–9092
  051–dc20   CIP

Contents

Acknowledgments

The *Harper's Forum*, like the *Index*, is a magazine feature that is conceived and executed at the office. The ideas often arrive by afflatus, but when that fails, I am fortunate to have my colleagues. All of them have pitched in on one Forum or another, but I would like to thank especially Gerry Marzorati and Michael Pollan. Special thanks also goes to Paul Tough, who for reasons known only to himself and God, has come into my office from time to time with great ideas and volunteered to take on the burdens of this section.

The work of putting together a *Forum* is sometimes simple—nothing more than writing a few letters. Other *Forums*, the majority of them, are nightmares, with tasks ranging from reimbursing the expenses of, say, the head of the Crips in Los Angeles (cash only, hand delivered) to realizing (at the last minute) that all the food at a gathering of animal-rights advocates was not altogether considerate. It will not be easy to forget the look on the faces of the waiters at the Union Club in New York City during the murder-mystery *Forum*—in which five crime writers and I sat at a table plotting in detail the perfect murder of my hypothetical wife. As the waiters would come in every fifteen minutes to refreshen our food and drinks, they grew increasingly alarmed as five of us would listen to someone such as Sarah Caudwell, while smoking her pipe, explain, "When he returns to his dimly lit bedroom, there, crawling on his bed, is this gleaming and horrible snake. And he strikes out at it wildly, bludgeoning and bludgeoning until by the time he's finished, there isn't much left of Linda."

The young men and women who were always there to help me pacify a freaked waiter or to arrange to chopper someone in at the last minute were the *Harper's* interns. Since I began this job, there have been thirteen assistants who have had to withstand the caprices of my moods and the eccentricities of this job. I would like to thank them all: Jennifer Barton, Lynne Bertrand, Michael Boxall, Matthew Butcher, Dorothea Herrey, Richard Hicks, Chris Horymski, Diedre McFayden, Chuck Oldham, Patricia Pearson, Joe Tabbi, Mark Warren, and Jonathan Zarov. Finally I have to thank Lewis, who trusted me when I suggested we write a sequel to "The Tell-Tale Heart" or figure out the economics of selling human body parts or plan the media campaign of Christ's Second Coming.

Introduction

The American Dialectic

*H*arper's Magazine is the oldest of America's monthly journals for the oldest of American reasons—because it has retained both the willingness to experiment and the wit to change with the times and make a new deal in a new line of country. On the first page of the first issue, published in June of 1850 (the same year that Horace Greeley first went west across the Great Plains and James Fenimore Cooper published The Deerslayer), the magazine announced its intent to address what was known as "the general interest" and to inform its readers across a broad and shifting spectrum of political, literary, cultural, and scientific affairs. The general interest also happens to be the public or common interest, which, in a country as multi-faceted and in as much of a hurry as the United States, is never easy to discover, much less define.

By 1984, the magazine had passed through at least three extensive revisions (in the 1890s, in the 1920s, in the 1960s), but the general interest was still as elusive as always, and in some quarters of society it had become an object of both suspicion and scorn. The times, it was said, were too complex. The best critics bemoaned the loss of a common language in which the numerous American publics could exchange signals or greetings. Bond salesmen presumably could speak only to bond salesmen, weapons analysts only to weapons analysts, novelists only to novelists. Communication by means of the mass media too easily deteriorated into slogan, and in the more rarified atmosphere of the technical and policy journals, the correspondents spoke only in code. Besieged by data of all denominations and surrounded by a din of images, we seem to know less than we did when we sealed our letters with wax and waited two months for a reply from Philadelphia. The mass of facts overwhelms and puts to rout the phalanx of thought.

Not only literary critics but also presidents of multinational corporations remark on "the interconnectedness of things" and "the interdependence of the global community," but what do the phrases mean, and who can translate them into an idea that people can grasp? How is it possible to conduct a general discourse in a universe of specializations that recede from one another literally at the speed of light?

Given the prevailing tendency to hide from yet another barrage of incoming paper, the task of editing a magazine directed to the general interest assumes a degree of foolhardiness that would do credit to a trapeze artist attempting a triple somersault without benefit of a net. Even to propose something so gauche as a generalization invites the condescension of specialists who prefer the safety of jargons and footnotes and polls. And yet it is precisely the lack of meaningful generalization that defeats the hope of republican government and makes nonsense of the American dialectic.

Democratic government is a purpose held in common, and the enterprise requires the collaboration of all present. If democracy can be understood as a more or less unified field of temporary coalitions between people of different interests, skills, and generations, then everybody has need of everybody else. The structure of the idea resembles a suspension bridge rather than an Egyptian tomb. Its strength, which is also the strength of the democratic discourse, depends upon the stress and balance struck between the public and the private interest. The idea collapses unless enough people have enough courage to sustain the argument between government and the governed, between city and town, capital and labor, matter and mind, time past and time future.

Even as recently as twenty years go, it was necessary to send out for the news. Now the news beats on the doors of the media, and the media have no choice but to perform the acts of exclusion and interpretation. Much to everybody's surprise, the circumstances favor the smallest instruments of the media. The diminishing audience for network television news proves the post-modernist rule of mass communication—i.e., the larger and more expensive the technology, the smaller and poorer the meaning. Partly this is because so much of the media has become an institutional Wizard of Oz. The functionaries who operate the machinery come to imagine that they already know all the answers worth knowing, and they tend to choose the texts and photographs that confirm their theories of the world.

Because *Harper's Magazine* addresses a relatively small and coherent audience (i.e., 200,000 readers who can be counted upon to think for themselves and make the implied connections between disparate sectors of experience), it could afford to follow rules of journalistic procedure precisely opposite to those of the mass media. When the magazine was revised in 1984, the editors assumed that they knew a good deal less than a lot of other people who weren't confined to the editorial cloisters of New York or Washington, and they proceeded on the premise that it was their business to open things out, not to wrap them neatly up. The magazine set itself the task of asking questions. Instead of attempting to provide ready-made answers, the magazine said, in effect, look at this or imagine that—see how much more beautiful and strange and full of possibility is the world than has been dreamed of by the mythographers at *Time* or NBC.

The editorial premise allowed for a redesign of the magazine that accorded with the ways in which people talk to one another. We belong to a literate but not a literary society, and we express our thought in notes and memoranda as well as in telephone conversations, legal briefs, tax laws, letters of credit, and advertising promotions.

Not everybody knows, or cares to know, how to write a magazine article, but they know what they have seen and thought, and so it was the magazine's task to discover forms convenient to the vernacular habits of speech. The redesign hit upon the devices of the *Index*, the *Annotation*, the Summary of *Readings* and the *Forum*. Each of the forms conveys a concrete sense of the world's ambiguity and size, but it is the *Forum* that most dramatically embodies the spirit of the American dialectic.

As opposed to the attenuated debates conducted on the Op-Ed pages of maybe three or four of the nation's better newspapers (which never achieve critical mass because of their brevity and because the argument trails off over a period of days into the corrections of the letters column), the *Harper's Forum* encourages loud and extended disagreement. The magazine's editors bring together individuals of many talents and points of view and set them talking on a subject of general interest (the schools, men and women, racial discrimination, crime, the media, biotechnology, etc.) and offer those present time enough and space enough, as well as the chance to complete their lines of thought, amend or revise their dearest prejudices, and maybe come to a conclusion they hadn't brought with them from Washington or Chicago. The resulting conversations comprise what can be fairly construed as the only audible debate in the country.

The discussions take both oral and written forms. Sometimes the respondents sit around a table and talk not only to each other but also to a stenographer. The abridged transcript of their remarks constitutes the substance of the debate. On other occasions the respondents submit manuscripts assigned as improvisations on a topical theme, and it is the anthology of their collected writings that makes up the weight of argument. The volume in hand presents *Forums* conducted in five of the most common variants (*Writing at the Table, Improving on a Theme, Promoting a New and Improved Product, Listening at the Margins,* and *Arguing from Principle*), but no matter what the device or the occasion, all of the *Forums* accept the premise that the society stands in need of as much doubt and as many questions as it can muster. A democracy proceeds on the assumptions that nobody knows enough, that nothing is final, that the faith in human reason promises neither comfort nor immortality. To the extent that democracy gives its citizens the chance to speak their minds and come to their own conclusions, it gives itself the chance not only of discovering its multiple glories and triumphs but also of surviving its multiple follies and crimes.

LEWIS H. LAPHAM

1

Writing at the Table

One side effect of our increasingly visual culture is that we have all become amateurs of plot structure. Who talks about a film or television program without critiquing the architecture of the narrative? After any movie in any city, one is likely to hear small groups expressing their admiration—"I loved the part when . . ."—or their unwillingness to suspend their disbelief—"That part wasn't realistic," or if you are a teenager, "Too fakey." The demand for verisimilitude, originally applied to theater and literature in centuries past, survives in popular culture.

This development coincides with a fundamental shift in the way a story is written in media controlled by technology. Today's writers, in Hollywood especially, are no longer (and perhaps never were) left alone to write a great story on a piece of paper. Instead, the careful turns of a plot are the subject of a half dozen meetings that take place long before the typewriters begin to clack. These gatherings are called "story development meet-ings," and in them are discussed every tic in a character's development and every twist in the plot line. The story development meeting has be-come an institution and a useful construct in order to examine the way in which writers assemble the pieces of a contemporary narrative. From time to time, *Harper's Magazine* asks writers from different genres to hold a story development meeting and to allow us to sit in on it.

In Pursuit of Pure Horror

Judging by the success of the horror story in all of its forms, it appears that Americans crave few sensations as much as the shudder of dread. Other societies fear monsters or vampires or inexorable plagues. But we seem to be most terrified by the spectacle of a seemingly ordinary character—whether presented under the name of Roderick Usher, Norman Bates, or Jason—driven to the point of grotesque crime. What does it suggest that during the 1980s this Ur-character almost exclusively has pursued partially clad, cowering young women? Perhaps we are not as reconciled to the ambitions of feminism as we had thought.

Now that the popularity of the slasher film is waning, Hollywood and the publishing syndicates are testing new narratives, hoping to discover the way the all-American murderer will be dressed for the 1990s. To assist in this effort, *Harper's Magazine* asked four masters of horror to convene a story-development meeting and plot an updating of the earliest incarnation of this character: the edgy killer of Edgar Allan Poe's masterpiece "The Tell-Tale Heart." Were he to reappear among us today, what would he be like? What would goad him to murder? On what victims would he prey?

3

◆
---

*T*he following forum is based on a discussion held at 60 East Fifty-fourth Street. Near here, in 1934, one of New York City's most frightening murderers was apprehended. Albert Fish, an old man described in a contemporary newspaper account as an "undersized, wizened house painter with restless eyes and thin, nervous hands," confessed to eating more than a dozen young children "by the light of a full moon." During his trial, one of Fish's own children testified that his dad was given to reading the Bible while setting fires in the family bathroom and to eating raw steaks by moonlight. During his cannibalistic binge, Fish indulged in severe mortification of the flesh: He inserted sewing needles into his abdomen until they disappeared—after he was captured, X rays revealed twenty-nine of them—and he regularly beat himself with a paddle or tree branches. Fish especially horrified the public with a creepy cheerfulness that he maintained right up to the end. Minutes before his execution, Fish observed how eager he was to try out the electric chair. "What a thrill that will be," he told his guards. "The only one I haven't tried." Jack Hitt served as moderator of this forum.

JACK HITT
is a senior editor of Harper's Magazine.

ROBERT BLOCH
is the author of many books, including Psycho *and* Lori.

SUZY MCKEE CHARNAS
is a Nebula Award-winning science-fiction and fantasy writer.
She is best known in the horror genre for her novel
The Vampire Tapestry.

HARLAN ELLISON
is the author of dozens of books, teleplays, and motion-picture scripts.

GAHAN WILSON
is a cartoonist whose work appears in The New Yorker *and*
Playboy *magazines and is the author of* Eddie Deco's Last
Caper. *He is also the author of the unillustrated novel*
Everybody's Favorite Duck.

I

JACK HITT: I want to talk about Edgar Allan Poe's "The Tell-Tale Heart," and how we might recast that story for a modern audience. Assume that Poe's narrator has been released. To make the story truly contemporary, let's say he gets off on a Fourth Amendment technicality. He's out. It's "The Tell-Tale Heart, Part II." How would we open the story for today's audience?

HARLAN ELLISON: Here's what I'd do. What if the "killer" in Poe's story didn't actually kill the old man? What if he only *thought* he'd done it? What if the old man had died of a heart attack? Our guy gets out because he confessed to a murder he didn't commit! The old man was dead before our guy ever cut him up. What could they arrest him for?

ROBERT BLOCH: Maybe make a cardiac arrest?

HITT: Doc Severinsen, a rimshot, please?

ELLISON: Okay. So let's put him in a large city, maybe Detroit. He's been relocated. Now, not only has he been let out but—because he's innocent—he has inherited the old man's money. His picture has been in the paper. Open the story with the old landlady realizing who it is that's living in the back apartment. Also in the area is, perhaps, a Hispanic street gang. They say, "This guy up there, he's got a lot of money." And you reverse the situation. They come after him. So you open with a completely crazy character who believes he's murdered somebody, and you've got these kids who are trying to take him out. I would make *him* the victim.

GAHAN WILSON: I think you're throwing away a great villain.

ELLISON: Now he's a victim *and* a villain. Because eventually he starts taking out the kids.

5

SUZY MCKEE CHARNAS: I would pick up on Poe's theme of sound. I like the idea of somebody who's supersensitive to sound, going back to the heartbeat in Poe's story. Suppose, in his new life, he can't get away from the noises of everyday life. They drive him crazy.

So maybe he locks up a fire station and torches the place, with the firemen inside, because he can't stand sirens. Maybe the gang members have boom boxes. And he can't stand it, so—an ice pick through the ears! You did it to my ears; now I'm doing it to yours.

WILSON: Sweet.

CHARNAS: Our guy should work in a very quiet place. Maybe in a beautiful, ornate library.

BLOCH: Where the rule is silence, quiet. Very nice.

CHARNAS: Exactly. It's a safe place. But it gets invaded by noisy people, and so he goes for them. Eventually, he gets into a situation where everything backfires, and he ends up paralyzed. He's trapped in a wheelchair, and there are noises all around. He can't get away. He opens his mouth and screams, and the scream begins to crack the wall and break the place apart: He's got a sound inside him that is *that* destructive. That's why sound was so integral to him.

ELLISON: I love the library idea. Maybe he hollows out books. And one day somebody picks up a copy of Halliburton's account of his adventures, opens it, and finds a piece of a face in the book.

BLOCH: And maybe the book is Conrad's *Heart of Darkness*?

HITT: Okay, if this were a movie, what would be the opening scene establishing that this is Poe's character and grabbing the audience?

WILSON: I like Suzy's idea. The overriding obsession of this guy is that life is intolerable. Poe would love this. In "The Fall of the House of Usher," one encounters this supersensitivity. Our guy can't stand the world. It is *too* painful.

I'd kick it off with his release. He is marched out of prison, and he winces frightfully at all these new sounds.

Every noise pains him. You could have a short comic scene in front of the judge, and it's a quiet discussion among lawyers. Then the judge finally hits the gavel. And our guy's face is an explosion of tics.

CHARNAS: Say he worked in the prison library, so we can segue our guy straight into a real job when he gets out.

ELLISON: I would start on a long shot—simple credits with white on black. Then you see a little square light, with the camera dollying in smoothly. You begin to hear the voices of a coroner's inquest. You hear a voice saying, "He clearly could not have done it." Another guy says, "But he *thinks* he did it. What's the difference? He's dangerous." Another says, "We can't legislate that. The old man died of a heart attack." "Yes, but he cut the old man up." "All right. That's desecration of a corpse at most, and he's been in prison for three years already."

As the square of light gets closer, you realize that it's a window, and, closer, it's a madhouse. The camera moves through the window, and he's down below. You shoot straight down on him, and he looks up at you, and you hear the voices say, "We have to let him go."

Then quick cut to a mundane building, a brownstone. You come in on the window, and he is making himself tea on a little hot plate. Then banging on the door. It's the landlady, shaking a newspaper and saying, "I knew there was something about you. Your name isn't Thomas, your name is, uh, uh, Kropotnik! You're the guy who murdered that old man. I want you the hell out of here." The idea is to establish all of the backstory as quickly as possible so that you can get into the new material.

CHARNAS: I'd open on a dark street, with the sound of a heartbeat. His heartbeat. My experience with movies is that the visual is not scary. *Sound* is scary. That's why I like this idea. The times I have walked out of movies are when I can close my eyes but not my ears. In *Bonnie and Clyde*, when Gene Hackman has been shot in the head and he's making grotesque sounds, I had to leave. And at the end of Lina Wertmuller's *Love and Anarchy*, a prison official types, "He died by banging his head against the wall." And you know what's going to happen. They grab this guy with his hands tied behind him, and they start banging his head against the wall. I couldn't stand the sound.

WILSON: I agree. I remember Arch Oboler, the guy who did horror radio shows. One time there was the problem of someone being thrown out a window and landing—swack!—on the sidewalk. So they built a marble slab, miked it, and then the soundman climbed a stepladder and heaved a grapefruit straight down and—swack! The sound was an initial splitting, then a squirting, and then—this is the beautiful part—it made this hideous little slurp as the grapefruit resumed its regular spherical shape, sucking in air. It was a fine, fine sound.

HITT: Has what scares us changed over time?

ELLISON: Everything that scares us today dates back to Jack the Ripper. He is still the operative icon of terror. He may be small potatoes by current standards—a guy mowing down twenty-five people in McDonald's with an Uzi—but the Ripper started it. He created the form.

WILSON: Just as no one paints landscapes the same way since Turner, a creative monster like the Ripper changed the landscape of what scares us. He inspired generations.

ELLISON: He had all the appurtenances of show biz: a name, a style, a media approach. He once mailed a piece of a victim's kidney and claimed that he had eaten the other half.

WILSON: Or he signed his notes, "From hell, Mr. Lusk"—Lusk being the head of the London Vigilance Committee.

ELLISON: "Yours truly, Jack the Ripper" is how he signed the notes that went to the London *Times*. Or when he wrote, "My next victim—to be sure you know who I am—I'm going to nick her ears good and proper." That kind of charming behavior gets you media attention.

WILSON: The prettiest murder he did had a *horse* as a witness. As the murder was occurring, this horse sensed it, reared up, and scared Jackie off. You just don't get details like that too often.

HITT: "Jackie"? That's somewhat familiar, isn't it?

WILSON: He gave himself that name. Jackie was very droll, and that's the point. He *changed* the way we were scared. There had been horrible murders aplenty, but he pioneered the grotesque dismemberment of the victim, always with overtones of sexual violence. He culminated one killing by decorating the victim's apartment with her viscera. He set the standard.

ELLISON: At a place called M'Carthy's Rents, he removed the fetus of a pregnant victim and hung her veins on picture hooks. Hardened members of Scotland Yard vomited on the spot.

WILSON: Another aspect of horror that has changed is the extent of documentation in the papers. I remember Ed Gein, on whom Bob based *Psycho*, in the fifties. When his activities were first reported, the newspapers told you everything: A piece of liver was found in a frying pan, or whatever. Then suddenly this kind of detail stopped, and we got very circumspect announcements.

ELLISON: "The woman was defiled."

WILSON: Or "A body was discovered." Now it's gone full circle, and you have a quickly published pocketbook that lovingly retells all.

BLOCH: Okay. Where were we in our story? We've gotten to the point where he is living in this rooming house, and we have introduced the gang menace. The landlady has discovered his identity. Now, in order for the plot to advance, we first have to dispose of the landlady as a menace. I'm talking in technical, workshop terms: Since he lives with her and would be immediately suspected if she died, *he* cannot be the one who kills the landlady. So one of the gang members is after him and kills her by mistake. That takes her out and leaves him where he is.

With Suzy's idea of sound as the principal leitmotiv and

harking back to the original story, it's the heartbeat that sets him off. He removes the hearts of the kids—in different ways—one by one. In the end, of course, after multiple killings, he realizes that the sound that has driven him crazy all this time is the sound of his *own* heart, and he must stop *it* as well.

CHARNAS: Lovely. I would like the venue to be the library and not some spooky house. The library is his kind of place—quiet. Then it's invaded by these kids.

WILSON: The sequence I see is one in which these kids are doing their damnedest to sneak around, but they can't sneak quietly enough because our guy hears everything.

HITT: Maybe you have a scene in which he stabs through the wall, nailing the kid perfectly.

WILSON: Exactly. When the kid is creeping along, you—the viewer—can't hear a thing. But cut to our guy's point of view, and you hear the crunch, crunch, crunch of someone walking.

ELLISON: Yeah. The kids think he's got this money. That's what is motivating them. One of the toughs says, "You guys have been trying to take out one guy! What's the matter with you?" And they say, "Go ahead and do it." So the gang member knocks out the light bulbs in the hall, thinking this will put our guy at a disadvantage.

The kid is coming down the hall for him in the dark of night. The kid takes off his shoes so that our guy won't hear him. But, of course, our guy can hear everything and has planted razor blades in the floor.

CHARNAS: Aaah. Pretty farfetched.

ELLISON: Getting cut is one of the most terrifying things. Have you ever gotten a paper cut in the soft folds between your fingers?

CHARNAS: Definitely the worst.

ELLISON: So let's cut the soft folds of his toes. What could be worse? Then our guy is on top of him.

WILSON: What if the kid breaks the bulbs, but our guy, like so many Poe characters, is meticulous and prissy. Somehow he knows the bulbs are broken, and he has gathered them up neatly, old-maidishly. He knows the kid is coming and scatters the broken bulb glass in the hall.

ELLISON: Except bulb glass won't cut you that well.

WILSON: In my film it will.

ELLISON: One has to strive for verisimilitude.

CHARNAS: Harlan, our guy shouldn't start out as a cut killer. Remember, he *smothered* the old man. What I'd like to see him do is take on a dog. Barking is an effective sound. He's got to get rid of it, but he doesn't know how.

ELLISON: He smothers him in a garbage can?

CHARNAS: I was thinking of drowning.

ELLISON: In a dumpster full of rainwater?

CHARNAS: It could be. It should be a physical thing. That's where he gets his taste for actually doing it with his *hands*, not just using a pillow.

ELLISON: First of all, make it a little rat dog. Everybody despises those things—the only animals in the world that go through menopause their entire life. He starts to kill the little rat dog, and our guy's wearing a leather vest. So you hear the dog's paws scrabbling against the vest.

WILSON: No. No. The dog is scratching the wall; that's what sets him off.

CHARNAS: No. You've got to have the dog facing him. What sets him off is the yap-yapping.

ELLISON: You've got to get that scrabbling sound against the guy's clothes.

WILSON: I think you're right, Harlan. He grabs the dog and holds it. The dog's going yap, yap, yap. He clamps the dog's mouth shut with one hand; the other hand holds the dog in the air by the neck. You still hear the dog's muffled yaps. So he just takes two fingers, and he slowly and easily pinches the dog's nostrils and suffocates him.

ELLISON: That's horrible, Gahan!

CHARNAS: But so delicate. Very nice.

WILSON: And as the dog's muffled yaps die down, you see our guy, and an expression of relief, of bliss, blooms on his face.

II

BLOCH: It's interesting how easily we have moved from the quill pen to the camera. There is no question at this table that this story should be done for the big screen. Cinema is where the enthusiasm is these days. Visualizing. It's much simpler that way. You easily overcome problems that Poe didn't overcome in the original: motivation, rationale—

CHARNAS: —and who tells the story.

HITT: If you wrote this story, who *would* tell it?

CHARNAS: Well, it couldn't be Poe's narrator. He's such a blithering psychotic that you can stand him only for the three pages it takes Poe to tell his story. But for something the length we're talking about, he would drive you crazy. You'd have to go to third-person omniscient.

HITT: If you were writing it for today's audience, what events drawn from reality might you use?

WILSON: I think of New York, with those kids who just wander around and go wilding. You haven't got a specific villain; you can't track down the killer; and there's no geographical fix. These mobs just suddenly emerge from a subway or spring up in the park.

CHARNAS: That's a monster story, essentially. A monster is a juggernaut.

WILSON: But this is such a contemporary monster: It comes right out of the new chaos theory of the physicists. Out of the general tumult of urban life, this thing suddenly takes form, coalesces—a mob, gathering like a storm.

CHARNAS: Always terrifying is the dead, a fresh corpse. In fact, many cultures so feared lifeless flesh that the burial customs were designed to keep a corpse confined and harmless until the flesh had decayed. Then the bones were dug up and removed to an ossuary. In some cultures, you actually received a second, "final" burial. In other cultures, there existed a special caste of people whose duty was to strip the flesh from the bones of the recently deceased. No matter how sophisticated we have become, we fear few things more than a lifeless body.

WILSON: One of the most horrific things of late involved the serial murderer Ted Bundy. Do you remember a journalist who quit interviewing Bundy several years ago because he thought that everything Bundy uttered was a con? The journalist said, "This son of a bitch Bundy is going to die *conning* someone right up to the end."

Now, do you remember the last interview Bundy gave to that preacher, just hours before his execution? Bundy, with a straight face, blamed everything he did on reading pornography—porn would make Bundys of us all!—and the preacher ate it up. Meanwhile, everyone's waiting for the governor to call and say "halt" or "proceed." Bundy is working his con on this preacher—minutes from death— and the phone rings. You can see this on the tape: Bundy locks momentarily in mid-sentence, trembling slightly. But does he turn to look at the guard who answers the phone? To discover his fate? No, he doesn't even glance over, but rather he *carries on* with the con! My blood ran cold when I saw that. It's straight out of Poe.

BLOCH: I think the most horrifying thing that most people can imagine is persistence: something you can't stop, that inexorably continues. In Poe's story—after all, conscience doth make cowards of us all—the heart's beating was what forced the protagonist to confess. Jack the Ripper captured that essence: When would these murders ever end? That's what scares us.

WILSON: The persistence of our protagonist is thematically related to the original: It's the heartbeat that drives our guy mad. In each scene, he is driven to *muffle* his victim.

ELLISON: So if he kills the kid in the hall—

WILSON: —he rolls the kid in a carpet!

ELLISON: Or he grabs the landlady's cleaning bucket from the hall closet and stuffs the kid's head into a bucket filled with rags redolent of English polish and carbolic acid. The tools he uses should always be things at hand. That's where you find terror. You're not going to find terror with *Dr. No* superweapons.

WILSON: Maybe he's grabbing a shawl from the table to kill one of the kids and he inadvertently knocks over a bust of Napoleon. It crashes, and he halts momentarily—winces at the noise, furious that he made this sound—and then resumes his killing.

BLOCH: Everything should be done manually. Even in the end, he should use the Aztec technique—in which you cut open the chest with an obsidian knife and scoop out the heart—to cut out his own offending heart!

ELLISON: Have you ever tried to rip a heart out?

BLOCH: Only halfheartedly.

HITT: All right. What about locations? *Alien* took place in deep space—where "no one can hear you scream"— essentially resetting the little-girl-gets-lost-in-the-woods story. And *Psycho* made brilliant use of the shower, that last sanctuary, sensual, private, and safe.

WILSON: What about the toilet?

HITT: Well, a shower is sublime; a toilet is farce.

WILSON: I disagree.

HITT: You think a toilet is sublime?

ELLISON: I disagree with you both. *Alien* is terrifying because of the sets—purely sexual images. You enter the ship; you enter a vagina—

WILSON: —it did look like someone's guts.

ELLISON: Remember how the ship was always wet and moist? And the reason Bob's shower scene works so well is because it is so mundane. When you take an ordinary object—say, a spoon—and suddenly this ordinary object is cutting someone's heart out, then it becomes horrible.

HITT: Is there any longer a place like Bob's shower?

ELLISON: There's the confessional, the bed, the bathroom. They've all been done.

CHARNAS: That's why I like the library. Like Bob's shower, it's peaceful, safe, and controlled.

WILSON: The charm of our movie is not visual but aural. We should be thinking about sound.

ELLISON: You know how one scene might work? He's sitting behind the checkout desk in a two-story library with a wrought-iron balcony inside. It's very mundane. You've got two guys—avoid the cliché of two high-school kids giggling and tittering—a couple of professorial types. They are softly whispering and flipping through the card catalogue. That's reality. Then you cut to his perspective. And the voices are thundering throughout the place, and the riffling cards sound like the wind.

But you have to build it as the film goes. You cannot start at that pitch.

WILSON: One nice touch might be that he moves very quietly. Everything he does is quiet. When he removes his keys, it is done carefully.

CHARNAS: Or he wraps them in a handkerchief; or he has each key wrapped separately. Wait a minute, Harlan. You want to start off slowly. What if he's taking medication in the institution? We know he has to take certain drugs. As the plot develops, he stops taking these drugs, and his senses begin to heighten.

ELLISON: I've got a great scene. He's sitting at the desk, and there's a pile of books to be checked out. Instead of stamping them, he rests the stamp gently on a book and then presses quietly.

Suddenly there's a sh-sh-sh. He doesn't know what it is. But it's something very commonplace. It's, maybe, a cricket in the wastebasket with a half-dozen popcorn balls of paper.

WILSON: Yeah. First he picks up a ball of paper and slowly squeezes it until he can't squeeze anymore. But he still hears the sound. So he does this a couple of times, until he squeezes one ball of paper and the cricket's chirping stops. And that smile plays across his face.

BLOCH: Let me play devil's advocate. If all sounds cause such a reaction, we might lose the significance of *why* he is killing off these tormentors. Let us say that his rage to suffocate occurs only when he gets extremely annoyed. Take the cricket. It's a beautiful thing. This is an introduction. This is what tells the audience that when he hears a certain kind of sound, he kills the source. It's like *Jaws*. Only we don't need the rinky-tink music. When he hears the sound that upsets him, the audience will know.

HITT: Are you saying that only *rhythmic* sounds reminiscent of a heartbeat set him off—the rhythmic chirp of the cricket or a song on the boom box that has a heartbeat-like bass or the yap-yap of the dog?

WILSON: You're right, Bob. He can't be perpetually pissed off at this painful, noisy world.

CHARNAS: I think we have another problem, though. I'm concerned about this gang of kids as our victims. I'm fed up with women and kids always being the victims, even though that reflects reality. I would like to see, well, one of your professors get it, Harlan. Some comfortable, secure, white, rich male. Harlan's right that there are no safe places—no showers—left to violate. But there are *people* we think of as safe—like white guys with property.

ELLISON: And that's a person we all know—arrogant, supercilious beyond belief.

CHARNAS: I was thinking of Bill Buckley.

WILSON: Would you like to snuff Bill?

ELLISON: Absolutely. I've always hated his nostrils. Have you ever noticed them? Terrible nostrils, like Judd Nelson's. Roomy enough to take in boarders. True horror for me is a Judd Nelson movie with a tight close-up of his face.

HITT: This might be off the subject.

ELLISON: Actually, it isn't. Everything is grist for a good writer. If Suzy's supercilious character is a victim, then one of the sounds the professor makes constantly is that disdainful sniff-sniff characteristic of Buckley. Maybe our guy is driven crazy by this rhythmic sniffing.

HITT: Not too comical?

ELLISON: Why not have fun? Something commonplace but irritating that activates his rage.

BLOCH: What do you do if this guy walks down the hall and encounters a grandfather clock?

CHARNAS: It's not alive.

BLOCH: We have to establish that difference, because that relieves the story of so many questions. He goes off only when the sound comes from the living.

ELLISON: We can make the psychosis affect him any way we want. It's easy. He's coming down the hall, and the clock is ticking. He stands and listens. It's metronomic; in fact, he likes it.

CHARNAS: And then you hear the little dog yapping in the distance, and he starts to twitch.

WILSON: Wait, I want to kill the professor. How do we do it? Pile pages of paper over his face?

ELLISON: Bludgeoned by books?

WILSON: No, he must be smothered.

HITT: Press his nose into the spine of an open book?

ELLISON: That's ridiculous. You couldn't really kill someone that way. You don't need reality, but you must strive for verisimilitude.

WILSON: Come on, gang, let's kill the professor. How would we do it?

ELLISON: We pull his tweed jacket up over his head and tighten it. It's muffling; and it kills him.

WILSON: Tweed is good.

ELLISON: And what if he's carrying his tweed, fresh from the dry cleaner's? It is covered in a plastic bag.

WILSON: Our guy takes the plastic bag and pops it over the professor's head. His gasps are a grotesque version of his sniffing. And we've cast this professor to look as much like Buckley as possible—those bulging eyes looking out of the bag coming into view when he sucks in the bag for air, sniff-sniff, and the bag blowing out, sniff-sniff.

III

HITT: We've wiped out the professor, the kids, the old lady. Now, it is often said that the response of fear is related to the sexual response. Is it? And should there be any sexuality in our story?

ELLISON: It's always there.

BLOCH: The Marquis de Sade made that connection; so did Jack the Ripper.

WILSON: The profile of these killers is always one of an enormously sexy person. Ted Bundy. Robert Chambers.

BLOCH: The sexual component operates on several levels. I was robbed in Paris once by Gypsies. They came out of nowhere; it lasted thirty seconds. I felt I'd been raped. This fear, the victim's fear, is sexual. The aggressor—with all the symbols of knives, guns, what have you—is, of course, phallic; he is violating you.

ELLISON: That's one thing the cops, particularly, never understand. They dismiss burglary as nothing too traumatizing since it's only a stolen stereo. What they do not understand is that for most people crime operates on the level of personal revulsion you describe, Bob. It's not your stereo or silverware you care about. It's that they came into your home. They looked in your drawers. They *felt* your underwear.

WILSON: A lot of burglars understand this notion of violation. Many of them physically or biologically violate the place after the burglary. Often they urinate, or defecate, or masturbate.

ELLISON: Or it's banal. They eat half a candy bar and put the other half back in the refrigerator.

HITT: Just to terrify you? Sort of a signature?

ELLISON: Absolutely. Mercenary commandos in World War II used to sneak into German camps in sub-zero temperatures. The soldiers would be sleeping together, two guys in one bag, to keep warm. They would cut the throat of *one* guy but leave the other guy alive. If they killed both, they're both dead. But if they left one alive, that guy would need fifteen people to handle him after he wakes up next to his dead buddy. It's the same impulse with burglars. There was one recently in L.A. who would use your toothbrush and then leave it for you with toothpaste on it. And he would prove that he had used it by spitting and leaving a gobbet in the sink.

WILSON: I know this fascinating guy, a Brit. He was with the OSS and the French Resistance. They had a piano wire tied to little sticks, and they'd almost decapitate a guy with this thing. *Then* the violation part came. Because collaborating officers all carried these little dandy hankies in their cuffs—an Erich von Stroheim touch—the members of the Resistance would wipe their piano wire off on this hankie and leave it.

ELLISON: Sometimes they would stuff the hankie into the mouth and out through the neck opening. Sex, religion, and death: They all aspire to the same physical response.

Remember Angela Cartwright in *Alien*? In one scene she is trapped between two corridors with Yaphet Koto, and the alien is coming after her. The shot is low, from behind her, and she's standing with her legs apart. The beast is suddenly in front, hovering over her. The camera shows that scorpion tail coming around and striking up between her legs. Death, terror, and sexuality—all in one.

BLOCH: This connection between fear and sexuality is very physical. Go to your nearest slaughterhouse and watch the cattle being pushed down the ramp to their doom: They will couple. The realization of imminent death evokes sexuality the same way a man has an orgasm when he is hanged by the neck. I believe the reaction is psychological as well as physical—not that I'm personally all that eager to find out.

CHARNAS: The feeling is a physical excitation; whether it's fear or sexuality or whatever, they are biologically related.

BLOCH: I'd like to draw a distinction between these killers and burglars we've been talking about and great horror. What is truly monstrous about any monster is a total innocence of what he is doing, an ignorance of his own monstrosity.

WILSON: That's right. You have to be totally unaware, you have to be solipsistic.

CHARNAS: In *Silence of the Lambs*, one psychiatrist says, "These serial murderers treat people like dolls. They are not real people."

WILSON: One of the Ripper's letters to the commissioner of police has this incredible line in it: "Saw you, box of toys."

HITT: What does that mean?

WILSON: He considered people a box of toys.

ELLISON: These attitudes are no different in depth and kind from those of the Ayatollah, who thought nothing about saying, "I'll kill that man; he said something bad." Or kids you see walking the streets who pull out a shake knife and do you for your pocket change.

WILSON: Bundy hardly ever had sex with a living victim. He had to turn this person into an object by killing her. Then he would have his way with her. He said, in much filthier language, "They're not really mine until I've killed them." In other words, he had to remove this distracting element of their being human beings.

BLOCH: You know what he was trying to remove, I think? The judgmental element. That's one of the reasons child molesters go for children. Their sexual performance will not be judged.

ELLISON: There's another great case in L.A. A man and a woman who killed. Carol Bundy is the woman's name— no relation to Ted. It's so horrific, it makes Ted look mild by comparison. After the guy killed one woman, who had been one of his lovers, Carol Bundy put the head in her freezer. To Carol, the dead woman had caused the guy to kill her. So every day Carol would remove the head and cry sentimentally over it. She would kiss the head's lips and cry over it.

WILSON: Sentimentality, of course, is a perverse emotion. It takes something real and renders it artificial.

HITT: Let's discuss the end of the story for a minute. How would we actually pull this off? What would be the final gripping scene?

BLOCH: When our guy realizes the sound is coming from within.

CHARNAS: For that scene I want to put him in the library— that safe place he has cleansed of the maddening noise caused by others.

ELLISON: You have to build logically to this conclusion, when he actually tears out his own heart. You have him holding the thing, and it's still attached and beating. He's still alive and he says, "Now it will be quiet." And you hear "bump-bump," and you pull back, as the camera—bump-bump— tightens to an iris, and—

WILSON: —a saintly peace comes over his face as he looks at his heart, and his coloration grows paler and paler, and more blissful—

ELLISON: —and the camera irises in—bump-bump—and closes tight on full-screen black and—bump. The end.

HITT: If you knew that this book or movie was going to do quite well, could you end it in a satisfying way that still leaves the door open for *The Tell-Tale Heart III*?

WILSON: The sequel starts with the doctor finishing the last suture, biting the cord and saying, "I think he'll live." Bump-bump. Bump-bump.

ELLISON: I would nail the story shut.

BLOCH: It was a black day in Hollywood when producers discovered Roman numerals.

WILSON: You don't have to worry about it, because Hollywood could resurrect this guy no matter what you did to him. You crush him with a cement truck and roll him flat. You could burn him alive. Whatever you do, next year you'll have *The Tell-Tale Heartbreaker*!

ELLISON: *The Beat Goes On*?

BLOCH: *The Tell-Tale Heart Transplant*?

ELLISON: I hate the idea of sequels. As Samuel Johnson said, "What we cannot resist, we must at least attempt to palliate." I won't even discuss it. This story ends right here.

◆

Lay Pipe, Add Heat, Get Laughs!

Television entertainment has often attracted criticism—"chewing gum for the eyes," "the bland leading the bland," "summer stock in an iron lung," "the longest amateur night in history"—but such confidently bookish dismissals are heard less frequently these days. Now that a generation raised on television is seizing the controls of popular culture and writing its history, the medium is acquiring an inchoate respect. When Jackie Gleason died in 1987, *The Honeymooners* was suddenly vaulted to the status of art; its thirty-nine episodes were reborn under the rubric "television classics." Sooner or later, and probably sooner, *The Beverly Hillbillies* can expect the same treatment.

The situation comedy has emerged as a genre as peculiar to the American character as the short story or the sermon. What defines the Seventies better than *All in the Family*? Or the Eighties better than *The Cosby Show*? One wonders what new situation might capture the nation's TV viewers in a post-Reagan, post-yuppie era. To find out, *Harper's Magazine* invited five members of the latest generation of television writers to a story-development meeting and asked them to create a series that will keep Americans laughing into the Nineties.

◆

T*he following forum is based on a discussion held at Michael's restaurant in Santa Monica, California. Jack Hitt served as moderator.*

JACK HITT
is a senior editor at Harper's Magazine.

PAMELA EELLS
is a co-producer of the program Family Matters.

MAXINE LAPIDUSS
is a stand-up comedienne who appears regularly at Caroline's, Catch a Rising Star, and the Duplex in New York City, as well as the Improv and Igby's in Los Angeles. She has written for the programs Dr. John *and* The Tracey Ullman Show. *She is a producer on the program* Baby Talk.

SALLY LAPIDUSS
is a co-producer of the program Family Matters.

KARL SCHAEFER
is a television producer and was the creator of the program TV 101.

DONALD TODD
was the producer who created The Van Dyke Show. *He is currently writing for the program* Good Grief.

24

Stanislavskian Hotcakes

JACK HITT: If television both shapes and reflects our popular culture, I wonder what kind of situation comedy you think audiences will laugh at in the post-Reagan era. What would you pitch to the networks if they gave you free rein?

MAXINE LAPIDUSS: Everybody wants to do something a little different, a little progressive, a little controversial. But there are only a few basic jokes, a few basic concepts, and they've all been done before.

HITT: Such as?

M. LAPIDUSS: Take Garry Shandling. His show was praised as original because it broke the fourth wall—that is, he talked directly to the audience. But that was done by Burns and Allen thirty years ago. Shandling's show is great because it has good writing that is suited to his personality.

PAMELA EELLS: Another example is *The Cosby Show*. It's a great show, which is driven by the star's personality, but in genre, it is basically a black *Father Knows Best*. Networks are always looking for a tried-and-true formula that has a slight twist.

SALLY LAPIDUSS: Something different but not too different. You might pitch it this way: *All in the Family*, only the wife's the bigot.

DONALD TODD: Well, then, first we need to figure out what *kind* of comedy we want to do. Should it be a domestic comedy, like *The Cosby Show*; an arena comedy, like *WKRP in Cincinnati*; or a romantic comedy, like *Duet*?

HITT: Which do you think would be most appropriate?

TODD: It might be a good time for a romantic comedy. I think people are tired of arena comedies like *Taxi* and *Cheers*, where all the action takes place in a taxi stand or a bar. And no one wants to watch another domestic comedy right now.

S. LAPIDUSS: Max and I were talking about this a while back, and we considered what's on TV and what isn't. And one thing we noticed was that everybody on TV has money. They all have beautiful clothes. They're not worried about where their next check is coming from. But a lot of real people are living check to check, job to job. What about a character—

HITT: Ralph Kramden redux?

S. LAPIDUSS: Exactly. Ralph Kramden. You don't see characters like that anymore.

M. LAPIDUSS: Money has to be an issue. Not that every week you want to tune in and hear people crying about their lack of funds. But for Ralph Kramden it *informed* his life. That doesn't mean there wasn't humor. Lots of other things happened on *The Honeymooners*, but that stratum is one you never see on TV today.

TODD: Working-class comedy doesn't interest me. It's impossible not to talk down to the audience. Most television producers and writers are not working class. It's very easy to condescend: "Let's talk about the little people."

M. LAPIDUSS: That's crazy. Nine-tenths of the public are working class and nine-tenths of our viewers are. There's too much fantasy out there as it is. Shows such as *Dynasty* and other prime-time soaps are popular because the audience thinks "If only my life was like that." And they lose themselves in it for an hour.

KARL SCHAEFER: I don't know if the attraction of watching *Dynasty* nowadays is wishing "my life was like that" as much as the thrill of watching rich folks get screwed and be miserable. If the country's attitude keeps changing, we may see more shows that bash wealth rather than celebrate it. *Miami Vice* did that—in reverse. The early shows were about cops disgusted by the wealth and stylized squalor of rich drug dealers. As the Reagan "me first" decade developed, the show came to symbolize the wealth and style that it had so much contempt for originally.

TODD: But our job is not to make jokes about the lives of blue-collar workers. When I try to think of a working-class comedy that audiences have accepted, I can't.

EELLS: How about *The Honeymooners, All in the Family, Cheers,* and *Roseanne*? Even *Cheers* is a working-class show, although it has its resident pseudo-intellectual.

SCHAEFER: There's no realism in *Cheers*; there isn't a drunk in the place.

TODD: *Cheers* shies away from blue-collar hardships on purpose. If you're dealing with the working class, you *have* to deal with economic realities.

HITT: But couldn't the working-class aspect of the comedy just be the backdrop? Wasn't that the way *The Honeymooners* worked? The comedy in the show wasn't derived from their modest paychecks.

TODD: Backdrops don't matter. The viewer has to be able to relate to the characters. Can you think of a successful working-class comedy that hasn't had such characters?

SCHAEFER: *Green Acres is the place to be.*

TODD: Don't put down *Green Acres.*

HITT: I will defend *Green Acres.* It's a kid's worldview: the central character is constantly frustrated because he's surrounded by lunatics who all make sense to one another but not to him.

EELLS: I see *Green Acres* as another manifestation of the American pop-culture mythology of utopian communities.

S. LAPIDUSS: From *Walden* to *Petticoat Junction.*

EELLS: No, really. I once read an apologia for *Green Acres* that explored the coherence behind the seeming illogic of the show. It beautifully plumbed the profundities of Sam Drucker's general store.

s. LAPIDUSS: I remember that: one passage noted the truly Stanislavskian intensity with which Eva Gabor flipped those hotcakes.

EELLS: Can I back up for a second, Jack? What recent shows can you think of that have been emblematic of their time?

HITT: There's *All in the Family*, a show that came on the air just after the civil rights movement had peaked and been assimilated into the American zeitgeist. So television comes along and creates a racist who is a buffoon: Archie Bunker, the incarnation of all that we hated about ourselves in the 1960s. And we comfortably laughed him out of our lives.

Then, what replaces *All in the Family* as the top show in the country? *The Cosby Show*—a sitcom that taps into the Reaganesque reaffirmation of the American Dream. The show is a symbolic welcome by the middle class to a historically oppressed group, blacks. We laugh while we think: this really is a great country.

s. LAPIDUSS: It certainly is Reaganesque. America can deal with a black family only if it poses no economic, social, or racial problems.

EELLS: I agree with Jack, in part. I think one of the reasons that *The Mary Tyler Moore Show* did so well in the 1970s is because of the women's movement. The timing was ideal. The three women on the show—Mary, Phyllis, and Rhoda—all represented different types of women at different stages. That was brilliant.

M. LAPIDUSS: Do you know what the next sitcom might be? A yuppie couple who climb to the top and suddenly lose everything. The driving force in the show could be the battle to get back up but—

EELLS: —they don't get back up.

TODD: The struggle of the human spirit to obtain goodness through adversity. I like it.

M. LAPIDUSS: Or the struggle to obtain a cheap apartment.

S. LAPIDUSS: Especially in New York.

M. LAPIDUSS: To adapt, to be faced with what might happen if Wall Street really takes a plunge. Nobody has any money. Everybody buys on credit. They're broke and suddenly struggling for basic necessities. That's a potential fact of life for most people.

EELLS: And as more families become homeless, people are afraid of losing what they have.

TODD: But you show people that it's okay. You're not going to die; it's all right. You play into the basic-human-values-are-solid theme. That's what people have to fall back on.

M. LAPIDUSS: I like the working-class scenario because when Sally and I were growing up our parents were always struggling to stay in the middle class. So turn that on its ear. Make it a working-class couple that momentarily succeed during the Reagan era. When the economy slows down, they are forced to return to blue-collar life. That might be fun.

S. LAPIDUSS: Some major catastrophe rips the plush pile out from under them.

TODD: Fine. But you can't do *The Thorns* kind of thing. You can't make the characters unlikeable. You have to make them decide to persevere—not just whine and complain each week. You can't get comedy out of whining characters.

M. LAPIDUSS: But you could have them hauling hay or doing something menial; combine the fish-out-of-water thing with the urbanites-in-the-country shtick. That could be funny.

TODD: Either they kill themselves or they keep going. If they kill themselves, it's ground-breaking TV but a creative error. If they decide to keep going, then they have to make the best of it. That theme has always appealed to me.

S. LAPIDUSS: And if the couple still see their friends from the old days, show how they handle that. You can imagine the gaffes at dinner parties and the great setups.

EELLS: Show their new friends meeting their old friends.

HITT: And how do their children deal with it?

M. LAPIDUSS: No children, please.

EELLS: Slap a child-buster logo on this show.

TODD: I don't like children on TV either.

HITT: Why not?

M. LAPIDUSS: They have to be likeable too much of the time. A writer is always worried that a character will not be likeable. You can have rotten adults like Danny DeVito in *Taxi*, but America is not ready for *Bad Seed: The Sitcom*.

EELLS: Actually, if you did this the way it often happens, it would be a woman who's just divorced, who's on her own—

TODD: *Who can turn the world on with her smile?*

EELLS: Mary Tyler Moore wasn't divorced on her show, and she didn't have children. But the idea that a woman's income declines by 73 percent after she's divorced, and that a man's income shoots up by 42 percent, is—

TODD: Is that true?

SCHAEFER: Well, Joanna Carson throws the curve off a bit.

HITT: Declining income—can that be funny?

EELLS: It could be. At least it's grounded in reality.

S. LAPIDUSS: The question is, do people watch TV to see reality or to escape it? Both, I think, if it's entertaining.

TODD: I think you have to worry about the characters first. How old are they?

M. LAPIDUSS: I would like them to be past their thirties, not yuppies. You'd feel a little more for them if they were older. Fifties, perhaps. Maybe Dick Van Patten is available.

EELLS: This is getting pathetic.

TODD: I agree. Fifties is different. You're talking "the golden years," the last desperate fling. But I can say that because I'm twenty-seven.

EELLS: What if the characters were in their forties?

M. LAPIDUSS: Fine. I hate it that everyone on television these days has to be in their thirties.

S. LAPIDUSS: That's because they're the people who buy the products.

TODD: You have to appeal to a market segment, or so I read somewhere.

M. LAPIDUSS: So if you're not thirty-five, you don't buy anything? Someone buys Geritol.

EELLS: But not in prime time.

S. LAPIDUSS: It's actually good to have older characters on a show. *The Golden Girls* is hot, and it reflects the fact that the population of America is getting older. But for our show, if the couple is in their fifties, it takes on the wrong tone.

TODD: A forty-year-old man is fundamentally different from a man in his fifties. Make him thirty-eight, thirty-nine.

M. LAPIDUSS: I'll compromise.

EELLS: What about the woman?

TODD: She's part of the conflict. Maybe she's been raising a family and she needs to reestablish her career, so now we have a one-career traditional family that must adjust to a two-career family life. And the kids are latchkey kids.

M. LAPIDUSS: What if the kids are twenty-five?

TODD: And Dad's thirty-eight? What are they? Southern?

HITT: My mother in South Carolina thanks you.

M. LAPIDUSS: Older children are moving back to the nest. Young adults—people who are twenty, twenty-five, thirty—are moving back home because they can't afford their own apartments. Maybe we could work that in.

EELLS: A couple thrown out of work, out of their house, and now their children want to move in? What do we call this series?

TODD: How about *Margin Call?*

EELLS: Or *What a Week. Oy!*

HITT: Maybe the kids move back in a later episode.

TODD: No kids.

EELLS: What about a post-feminist woman, who is not all that interested in going out and getting a job but would rather stay home and be supported. That's happening a lot among my friends. Maybe her husband says, "But, honey, work will fulfill you." And her reaction is "Well, I already am fulfilled."

SCHAEFER: Maybe she's not married but keeps meeting liberated guys who won't support her. That's her main problem.

TODD: Don't we box ourselves into a corner after the third episode? We end up with a standard domestic comedy.

M. LAPIDUSS: Depending on what her job is. Maybe she *gets* a job and that's the focal point.

TODD: Then you've lost the concept of this couple trying to adjust to their new life. After four episodes, they adjust.

SCHAEFER: Send them off in a trailer across the country.

EELLS: And get sued by Albert Brooks.

S. LAPIDUSS: Cue the banjo music.

SCHAEFER: *Rolling, rolling, rolling, keep this trailer rolling!*

TODD: How about using the trailer and creating a serial anthology? That's something I've never seen. A half-hour comedy serial anthology.

HITT: What's a serial anthology?

TODD: *The Fugitive* was one; it centered on a fixed character who went from place to place and encountered different people, different situations. Most half-hour comedies have the same set—a little couch with table and chairs in a living room downstage. And all the stories take place there.

SCHAEFER: A half-hour comedy with a different set each week?

TODD: The trailer could be one set. But you could also have swing sets, new sets that you've never seen before.

SCHAEFER: Maybe the diner they pull into every once in a while is a set, and you could use it for a great gag. It's the same people, the same basic table, the same blue plate specials, but a different restaurant each time. One week it's the "Holy Tortilla"; the next it's "Tiki Acres."

TODD: But the same characters always work there?

A TV Writer's Glossary

Act: all half-hour sitcoms are divided into two acts, each lasting approximately eleven minutes.

Arc: the course of a character's development during a half-hour show.

Backstory: the prior circumstances that set up the overall premise of the series, often depicted in the opening of an episode; in *The Beverly Hillbillies,* for example, the backstory showed the moment when Jed Clampett discovered oil, and his subsequent move to Beverly Hills.

Bible: a book used by writers as a blueprint for a series; it contains detailed descriptions of a show's backstory, premise, and especially its characters.

Blowup: the climax or unraveling of the plot in an episode; blowups typically occur in the penultimate scene and are resolved in the final scene.

Button: the last joke in an act, the function of which is to hold the audience during a commercial.

SCHAEFER: Right. And you always have the couple hit the same beat when they pull in and look at the place.

EELLS: Call it *Gas, Food, Lodging,* just like the highway signs.

TODD: I like this. It's a *Barney Miller* kind of comedy that really depends on the mix of new people and what they say and how you resolve the story. You could really open up the show, get it out of some damn living room, and write about today's real problems.

HITT: If you were pitching this series to the networks, how would you do it?

TODD: I'd start with the characters. Talk about the couple.

HITT: How would you describe the guy?

TODD: I see him as an idealist, a guy who won't give up. He's brought to his knees periodically but bounces back. It's not a problem. It's never a problem. He's got it licked no matter how tough it is. He's an older Tom Hanks in the

---

Cold opening: an opening scene that begins the plot immediately and relates directly to the rest of the show.

Four-camera tape: a style of producing a series, in which four cameras record a continuous performance before a live audience; during the taping the director selects the various camera angles—close-ups, two-shots, and group shots—to create the final show; see *one-camera film*.

Heat: some small conflict that motivates a character's actions in the context of a single show; often requested by the producer, as in, "Get some heat in there"; see *spin*.

K words: according to comedy lore, words that begin with a hard C or K sound are funny; thus, it's better to say, "Catch the ketchup" than "Seize the mustard."

Light the lantern: a writer's term for highlighting some special trait of a character; if a writer for *Family Ties* were to accentuate the greediness of Michael J. Fox's character, he would be "lighting Alex's lantern."

face of adversity—you can't get him down. The indomitable American.

HITT: And the woman?

S. LAPIDUSS: You could go a couple of different ways with the woman. She could be skeptical of the whole venture, but she loves her husband, and so she'll give it a year or two. Or she could be a pain in the ass, spoiled and willing to let everyone know it—à la Julia Duffy in *Newhart* or Claudette Colbert in *It Happened One Night*. Maybe her career could lend itself to traveling. She's a sociologist or journalist. She could become the Charlotte Kuralt of the '90s, reporting her experiences on the road. Whichever characterization you chose would depend on which one you thought you could write about week after week, which character you could get the most out of as the show develops.

One-camera film: a style of producing a series, employing one mobile camera; episodes are shot on location or on a variety of sets; see *four-camera tape*.

Open up: to expand the possibilities of a series by introducing new characters or changing set locations.

Pipe: exposition used to set up punch lines; according to Hollywood lore, when Ron Howard complained to *Happy Days* producer Garry Marshall that Henry "the Fonz" Winkler was getting too many jokes, and that Howard had to supply too much exposition, Marshall replied, "Ron, even Olivier had to lay pipe."

Spin: what usually follows heat; if a writer applies heat to a character by making him lie, the spin would be having the character get caught lying.

Tag: the last thirty or sixty seconds of an episode, usually self-contained, with one or two jokes.

Teaser: the opening of an episode, usually self-contained, with one or two jokes; the opening vignette of *Cheers* is a teaser.

TODD: That's how I'd pitch it. I'd want to create characters that the networks could envision on the air. If I go to the networks and say I have an idea about people traveling around the country, I'm dead. I have to start with the characters. That's what the networks are interested in, frankly, because that's what the audience is interested in.

Two 'Hell's and a 'Damn'

HITT: What about standards and practices with this kind of show? For example, one episode of St. Elsewhere opened with Howie Mandel in his underwear and his wife in a teddy. She takes a bowl of whipped cream and rubs it on his face. Then she kisses him, and with cream oozing from her lips, she ties him to the bed. There's a knock at the door: it's his mother. Then the credits roll. I was stunned, I—

SCHAEFER: —had to take a shower?

TODD: Maybe we should talk about you for a minute.

HITT: Is there anything left to do on TV? If the networks came to you and said, "We want Gas, Food, Lodging to be controversial—"

M. LAPIDUSS: —but the "gas" has to go.

SCHAEFER: It depends on the hour.

HITT: What's the difference?

SCHAEFER: At 8 P.M. you can get away with very little. An 8 o'clock show is a kind of show. It has its own tone. And there are story lines you can't do at 8 P.M. that you can do at 9 P.M.

TODD: There's even a difference between 10 and 10:30 P.M. There are things you can do in the second half-hour of L.A. Law that you can't do in the first half.

HITT: For example?

TODD: Remember when they mentioned the sexual technique the "Venus Butterfly" on L.A. Law? You could never do that at 9 o'clock.

M. LAPIDUSS: Once on *L.A. Law*, a woman appeared wearing a tight leather dress. There was some line about "bush." At that same moment she stood up and walked—with her crotch in center frame—right at the camera. The whole time you saw Becker eyeing her up and down. When I saw that, my mouth just hung open.

EELLS: What you can do depends on the show, too. For example, *Hill Street Blues, St. Elsewhere,* and *L.A. Law* can get away with more because the networks trust the taste of the producer—

TODD: —and the audience.

SCHAEFER: But you push because you know you will have to go into a meeting and argue for these things.

HITT: Do you go in and say, "Look, I really want this scene. The character's going to say 'bush,' and I want this particular camera shot"?

TODD: No, you don't do it like that. You put the scene in, and you wait for them to catch it. If they catch it, you make *them* tell you what's wrong with it. Make *them* put it into words, and they don't know many words.

S. LAPIDUSS: You hear stories about writers who really want to get in one controversial bit of dialogue, so they put in five bits that they don't mind losing.

HITT: Can you imagine a controversial scene in *Gas, Food, Lodging*?

M. LAPIDUSS: Maybe a trailer park where there are fifteen trailers and all the lights go out. It's a long crane shot and you see all the trailers rocking at the same time. You realize that everyone is making love in the trailers simultaneously. But how would you argue in favor of that?

EELLS: I'd say, "What are you talking about? It's an earthquake."

M. LAPIDUSS: But remember how much grief we got for a stupid word like "slime"? We tried it in an after-school special. The line was something like "Gee, that guy is a real slime." And they wouldn't let us use it.

EELLS: The funny thing is, of all words that an adolescent would really use—scumball, jerk-off—we toned it down to "slime," and they said no.

SCHAEFER: See, that's a 3 o'clock show. I'm not being facetious. Every hour makes a difference.

HITT: Someone told me that one of the networks ran a movie recently and deliberately included the word "shit" to see how much mail they would get.

SCHAEFER: PBS does it all the time.

HITT: Isn't that one of the reasons the networks seem willing to go further—precisely, because cable and public television are putting them to the test?

TODD: Definitely.

SCHAEFER: Standards are loosening. The networks have cut back—in some cases eliminated—departments of broadcast standards and practices.

M. LAPIDUSS: There's also a certain momentum with some words. I remember the first time I heard the word "bitch" on TV. John Belushi said it on *Saturday Night Live*. I was floored, but then, suddenly, at 10:30 every night, someone on some channel would say "bitch."

SCHAEFER: Yeah, there are boomlets for certain words.

HITT: What's booming now?

SCHAEFER: Well, "butt" is really big now.

M. LAPIDUSS: Butt is *big*?

TODD: As a writer you write whatever you want, and then your worry later if they catch it. Generally, you get a call from somebody in the network's department of standards who will give you specific notes.

HITT: Like?

TODD: Sometimes they are less worried about the word itself than the frequency. Once on *Misfits of Science*, I got notes such as "Take out three 'hell's and two 'damn's." I'd negotiate by saying: "I'll take out two 'hell's and one 'damn.' "

M. LAPIDUSS: I'll give you one "damn" but not a "hell."

SCHAEFER: I'll raise you a "butt."

TODD: That's exactly how the conversation goes. You have to negotiate. Be flexible.

HITT: What's the next word we can sneak on the air?

M. LAPIDUSS: Euphemisms are in these days. *Moonlighting* might have started it. "Boinking" was one of theirs.

TODD: Didn't you try to put the word "vagina" in a script?

EELLS: Yes, we had a vagina joke.

M. LAPIDUSS: We knew it was a great laugh, and we tried to get it in.

HITT: Excuse me?

M. LAPIDUSS: It was a takeoff on the *Reader's Digest* series that had articles like "I Am Joe's Spleen."

EELLS: One of our characters said, "I've just written an article for *Reader's Digest* entitled 'I Am Jane's Vagina: If These Walls Could Talk.' "

TODD: But you knew it wouldn't go any further than the script.

HITT: Why? Is it too clinical?

TODD: It depends on the circumstances.

S. LAPIDUSS: You could probably get it on *St. Elsewhere.*

HITT: In a hospital context.

TODD: You've got to justify it. If the *word* is the punch line, and you expect to get a laugh just using the word, forget it. You're calling too much attention to the word itself. They won't like it. For example, you couldn't use the word "poontang."

HITT: Not at my dinner table you couldn't.

M. LAPIDUSS: But you can say "bush" at 10 o'clock and show shots?

SCHAEFER: Could you say "tang"?

M. LAPIDUSS: How about "poon"?

SCHAEFER: Could you say "punjab"?

S. LAPIDUSS: You couldn't describe a "punjab."

SCHAEFER: Or how much a "punjab" costs.

HITT: This is getting really Sikh.

TODD: Is the point of writing television sitcoms just to see how far you can go?

SCHAEFER: Sure.

TODD: A lot of people just want to do that—

SCHAEFER: It's breaking new ground.

TODD: If the word comes up when you're writing, yes. But do you really sit down and figure out what will push the boundary this week?

SCHAEFER: I don't know. I think it's in my nature.

TODD: Shouldn't it be an extension of the story?

SCHAEFER: I wouldn't do it just for the sake—

TODD: *St. Elsewhere* did it all the time. I heard a character say "doo-doo." Does anyone ever *need* to say doo-doo? I mean, why doo-doo?

SCHAEFER: Well, I think you're delving into one of the great profundities of TV. Why doo-doo? I mean, is there a purpose to all this, or do we say doo-doo for doo-doo's sake?

Getting to Pilot

HITT: Now let's return to the rest of our show, *Gas, Food, Lodging*. What would be the opening scene?

M. LAPIDUSS: The guy is applying for a job that he's totally overqualified for, and he—

SCHAEFER: —has to have that job.

TODD: This is a good pilot episode. Maybe the guy gets turned down for a job because he's overqualified. Now he has to convince the personnel director that—

SCHAEFER: —he's dumb enough—

TODD: —to do the job.

EELLS: The nightmare is that he *does* convince them that he can do the job, but when he's given the chance, he can't. Which is what happened at my first job. I said that I could type, and I couldn't.

TODD: A good opening scene. You don't have to set up what happened. You can open with a scene in the personnel office and the main character comes in. By the end of the scene, we find out how desperate he is. If he gets turned down for the job, you have the problem of the pilot.

HITT: Wait a minute. Are you talking about the opening few minutes of the pilot?

M. LAPIDUSS: The first minute of the show would be the credits. And in the credits you could backstory the family history.

HITT: "Backstory"? Is that a verb?

M. LAPIDUSS: Yeah. Remember the opening of *The Beverly Hillbillies*? It cut back and forth between the mansion and the shack where they used to live.

SCHAEFER: *Come and listen to a story 'bout a man named Jed.*

M. LAPIDUSS: That's the backstory. You can convey a lot of information in thirty seconds.

HITT: So the credits are superimposed on the backstory. Then what? Do you go to—

TODD: —a commercial. The other alternative is the teaser format: you open with a little bit of show, then credits, commercial, and back to the show.

HITT: Like *Cheers*? It opens with a minute of jokes, then a commercial, and then the show.

TODD: Right. Teaser, commercial, act one.

EELLS: The teaser usually ends with a drawing or title logo, as in *Cheers*. You see the main titles and hear the theme music. But that format is used less and less these days.

HITT: Would you want a teaser with this show?

TODD: It's all personal. But I don't like them.

HITT: Why?

TODD: It locks you into creating another beginning for the show after the commercial. I prefer credits, commercial, and then straight up on act one.

HITT: How long is each act?

M. LAPIDUSS: About eleven minutes. At least eight minutes of each half-hour show are commercials and credits.

S. LAPIDUSS: Sitcoms are very formulaic. The general structure is two acts with three or four scenes per act. Some even have a requisite number of jokes per page.

HITT: Don't you even have specific terms for kinds of jokes? Isn't the "button" the joke you hear just before a commercial, and don't comedy writers emphasize "K words"— words that begin with a hard C or K sound—because they are thought to be funnier to the human ear?

S. LAPIDUSS: Yeah, but those terms are more a part of comedy folklore than comedy writing. Far more pertinent to the writing is the kind of show it is. If it's one-camera film, such as *M*A*S*H* or *Molly Dodd*, you can play around more, visually—open it up—because it's like writing and shooting a mini-film. But most shows use four-camera tape, like *All in the Family*. They are shot before a live audience. You have two or three regular sets with an occasional swing set—that is, a set that's probably used just once. If you think of one-camera film as a mini-movie, then the four-camera tape is more like a mini-play.

HITT: Is each act self-contained, a playlet?

TODD: Yes. I prefer that format because you only have to begin and end twice in a show.

EELLS: The other bad thing about teasers is that they had better be good because if they're not, you lose your audience at the commercial. The whole idea is to grab them.

TODD: While we're on it, no tags on this show either.

HITT: Tags?

SCHAEFER: That's the last joke after the last commercial.

HITT: You mean those last thirty seconds of *Star Trek* when Dr. McCoy sneeringly tells Spock he's a dispassionate automaton? And Spock says something wry about human nature, and then up comes the wanky, upbeat music?

TODD: Precisely. Now you know why I don't like them.

M. LAPIDUSS: Some formats use them well. *Kate and Allie* began and ended with the two of them talking. It works nicely, bookending the show.

HITT: So where are we? No teaser, no tags. *Gas, Food, Lodging* will open on a backstory with credits, then commercial, and then act one. Can the backstory have dialogue?

TODD: Primarily it's images and a catchy tune.

SCHAEFER: If you're cursed, it's a banjo.

EELLS: With lyrics that sum up the backstory: *I used to be rich; now life's a bitch. La-dee-da.*

M. LAPIDUSS: The backstory might show our couple getting fired. And you might throw in a few shots of what their life was like before. So you know they're at the end of their rope. Then they head out to start something new.

TODD: And they throw their hat in the air.

S. LAPIDUSS: *They're gonna make it after all.*

EELLS: They throw the trailer.

S. LAPIDUSS: They throw the steering wheel.

M. LAPIDUSS: They throw up.

SCHAEFER: Can you throw up in prime time?

TODD: After 8:30 P.M. you can throw up, I think.

S. LAPIDUSS: All right. The backstory could show the husband being fired and then show the woman trading in their BMW for a used Chevy. Then commercial and act one.

HITT: How would you open the first show?

TODD: The first scene of an act is called the A scene, the second the B scene, etc. Don't ask why. Anyway, our A scene could start with the decision to hit the road. And in the B scene they get the trailer. Or you could actually stretch the whole first act out with the decision to discover America.

EELLS: Is that Albert Brooks's lawyer on the telephone?

SCHAEFER: And have them, at the end of the first act, deciding to leave.

TODD: Maybe the A scene is the crisis, losing the job; and the B scene could end with the decision to head out on the road.

M. LAPIDUSS: Wait. The A scene could open the show with a garage sale, and for whatever reason the wife or the husband can't bear to part with anything. So, suddenly, in the next scene you cut to them in their trailer and it's packed with all the stuff. You want to think in terms of sight gags for the A scene.

SCHAEFER: Well, decide what it is they're selling and pick items that represent some personal history, some funny props that trigger some revealing fact.

TODD: Or it might be something ordinary. The husband says, "You're not going to sell that," and then you tell a story. The more ordinary the better, because then you don't have to rely entirely on sight gags for the A scene.

What if your B scene is the man trying to get a job? They sell all their stuff or try to, and then we backstory their problem, and then he says, "Okay, I can get a job." But he can't, and so they hit the road.

SCHAEFER: Move them to different places and have them getting work as long as they can.

M. LAPIDUSS: *Then Came Bronson—*

EELLS: —only in a trailer.

TODD: But ultimately the writers have to have a reverence and an eye for what makes people get through their day. That's what this couple start to discover. All of us are driven toward some goal, but what if that goal is taken away? What drives us? What drives most people?

S. LAPIDUSS: Maybe he keeps a diary.

SCHAEFER: You could get in a lot of Americana with that.

TODD: You could format it as a voice-over at the top of the A scene. A diary entry. Not to be too silly, but "Star Date 3576," or whatever.

M. LAPIDUSS: With a slow close-up shot of a map.

SCHAEFER: A klingon just cut me off—

M. LAPIDUSS: —on I-90.

TODD: Seriously. "Yuma, Arizona, September 19." Then straight up on your story.

S. LAPIDUSS: Rod Serling comes out of the mist.

M. LAPIDUSS: Submitted for your consideration: "Where are we?" "What are we going to do?"

TODD: This show is about the basic need to survive. It's a series about getting through, playing off the humor inherent in people trying to adjust to their new, more humble life even as they try to recapture the grandeur of their old one.

S. LAPIDUSS: Exactly. Check, please . . .

Plotting the
Perfect Murder

Perhaps it is because the crime has become too cheap or too easy or commonplace. Or maybe it is because the streets have become too dangerous—the statistics on random violence rise as steadily as the price of crack declines. Whatever the reason, hardly anybody takes pleasure anymore in the well-told tale of a well-performed murder. All discussion of elegant homicide—the first love of Sherlock Holmes—has been abandoned to the whispers of street-gang chieftains and Mafia underlings. Even the practice of murder has been reduced to generic killing: in the city, people simply get tossed in front of subway cars, and in the country, they're shot between the eyes.

Imaginative murder needs to reclaim its proper place. As Alfred Hitchcock said, upon moving his art to the small screen of television, "Murder should be put back in the home—where it belongs." To facilitate murder's renascence in America's more refined conversations, *Harper's Magazine* recently asked five mystery writers to conjure up the details of a domestic killing both beautiful and baroque—that philosophers' stone of crime: the perfect murder.

---◆---

*T*he following forum is based on a discussion held at the Union Club, in New York City. Jack Hitt served as moderator.

JACK HITT
is a senior editor at Harper's Magazine.

SARAH CAUDWELL
read law at Oxford. She is the author of Thus Was Adonis Murdered, The Shortest Way to Hades, *and* The Sirens Sang of Murder.

TONY HILLERMAN
is a former police reporter and the author of more than ten mystery novels, all of which concern the Navajo Tribal Police.

PETER LOVESEY
created Sergeant Cribb, the Victorian policeman who is featured in the Mystery! *television series. He is the author of* Bertie and the Tinman *which casts King Edward VII as a detective.*

NANCY PICKARD
has won the Anthony and Macavity awards. Her fifth novel is Dead Crazy.

DONALD E. WESTLAKE
has written more than fifty mystery novels.

48

JACK HITT: Let us suppose that my name is Carl. I have been married to Linda for five years. Linda is a wealthy woman and has made me the sole beneficiary of her will. I recently discovered that she is having an affair with my best friend, Blazes Boylan. I have also learned that Linda has a meeting scheduled with her attorney in two weeks in which she intends to file for divorce and rewrite her will—taking me out of it. Instead of letting that happen, I have decided to kill her, take the inheritance, and cleverly set up the murder so that the blame falls to my erstwhile friend, Blazes. Like any man of breeding, I wish to kill her with élan, and therefore I need a retinue of advisers, consultants, and stage managers. That is why I have called you here today.

SARAH CAUDWELL: It would be a pity to rush into murder in just two weeks if you didn't have to, and I don't think a great murderer would want to. Let Linda make her will, and presumably she'll make it in favor of the wicked Blazes so he gets the money. But if we can arrange a foolproof way of getting Blazes convicted for her murder, no court of law will let him profit by it. So the will in his favor fails, Linda dies intestate, and you get the loot. Best of all, it looks far more suspicious for Blazes if she dies after she's changed the will, and less suspicious for you.

TONY HILLERMAN: The time limit doesn't pose a problem for me. Having occasionally worked with lawyers, I know that when a lawyer tells you he'll have the will ready in two weeks, he never does. I'd say you have plenty of time.

But let's consider Carl's peculiar problem. He is obviously the person who killed his wife. He has the motive. The police will suspect him instantly. Therefore, make it even more obvious that he killed Linda.

Take your time and build a frame, so that when the police look for what they call the "theory of the crime,"

49

they see a murder so suicidally obvious that they begin to wonder. Make the police do the work for you, and have them conclude that Blazes was indeed framing Carl with murder.

CAUDWELL: You might prepare the ground a little bit by saying to a neighbor, "Oh, dear, I'll let Linda go if that's what she wants. But I wish I didn't know the things I know about Blazes and how he treats women. I'm really worried about what might happen to Linda."

HILLERMAN: Tell Blazes that you bought a pistol at the gun shop and get him to pick it up. Then the gun-shop owner remembers him. This is how you build the frame that the police will run into. We set up Blazes to look as if he is framing you, but actually you are framing Blazes.

HITT: Isn't using a gun an easy way of getting caught?

HILLERMAN: But we don't even use the gun, see? I'm assuming this is a murder that strives for the effects of a novel, not a short story. The gun is part of the frame. For the actual murder, I'd like to use some mushrooms I recently heard about. They are not only lethal but untraceable. So while Blazes is getting the gun and the gunsmith is forming his own suspicions, you kill Linda with the mushrooms. You hate to waste anything this good, right?

DONALD WESTLAKE: I do know of an actual book—one of those large picture books—of mushrooms, beautiful color photographs of mushrooms. It's in English but it was done in Japan. There's an errata sheet; apparently about twelve of the mushrooms have been misidentified. Of course the errata sheet is unattached to the book, just sort of slipped in at the back. And it says things like, "The mushroom described as edible on page 20 is actually poisonous . . ." I have the book at home! I don't plan my menus from it. But I think for our purposes we could have the errata sheet found in Blazes's pocket. If you're going to kill with mushrooms, there's nothing better than a false authoritative source.

HILLERMAN: I agree. But I was going beyond a single killing. Now these mushrooms take from thirty-six hours to three days to take effect. The victim falls into an irreversible coma—there's no antidote. So here's my idea: get a bunch of these 'shrooms and dump them into the Safeway mushroom bin.

WESTLAKE: I like it.

HILLERMAN: So you put them in the mushroom bin and you have a mass murder. Then you make certain that Linda has a few of these mushrooms in her soup before the dying starts. She is among the first to go. Later the whole neighborhood is also wiped out!

CAUDWELL: I love that.

NANCY PICKARD: Intriguing.

HITT: How do we pin that on Blazes? Do we set him up as a mushroom collector?

HILLERMAN: Wait, so now you've got a dead wife.

HITT: And no neighborhood.

WESTLAKE: And the property value of Linda's estate is shot.

HILLERMAN: You can see why I never outline my books.

PETER LOVESEY: I like Tony's idea. It's good because it's done on the grand scale. That's what we're looking for. Something that Carl can write about in his memoirs years later. Something really memorable. I think that a mass killing might do it.

CAUDWELL: I don't think that a mass murder offers much pleasure in the way of revenge. I think you want to set up a situation where it is Blazes who actually kills Linda. He is the man with the weapon. I know it's difficult to set up, but it is more satisfying than poison. Say, a knife or a gun or a bludgeon. Maybe Blazes knifes something he thinks is a dead animal, or he's cutting it up, or he thinks it's a cushion. Maybe he fires at a target in target practice and she is hidden behind it. Those are not very good ideas in themselves but you want to create that situation—where Blazes strikes the blow himself.

WESTLAKE: I think this connects with one of my ideas. If you go to Blazes and say, "You've been my best friend since we were two and a half years old. And you know that I am unhappily married. Well, old friend, I know that Linda is seeing someone else. Isn't that awful? But I don't know who it is. And since Linda has all the money, I can't leave her. So I want to avenge myself. I'm going to kill her and I want you to help me." Now Blazes is in the position of not being able to tell the truth about anything. Since he is the lover, his tendency is to say, "Oh, sure, tell me more." Because if he doesn't help, perhaps you will get someone else. So he will go to Linda and say, "Believe it or not, he's intending to do away with you." Now Blazes has to kill you. Then you tell him, "You'll be here and I'll be there and Linda will be there. And we'll do it." Ultimately, when he thinks he's killing you, he's actually killing her.

HILLERMAN: First, you motivate him, as my editors are always telling me. In addition, Carl tells Blazes, "I'm either going to kill Linda or I am going to fight this divorce all the way."

WESTLAKE: Or, "I'm going to get a private detective to find out who the guy is."

HILLERMAN: So Blazes is motivated to take advantage of this opportunity.

PICKARD: What about inveigling Blazes to be, in essence, the private investigator to find the man that the wife is having the affair with? You tell him, "My wife is having an affair. I need you to follow her around and tell me who this guy is." Then he's got to come up with something. This way you draw Blazes into your frame. Although, as everyone knows, you can always get a wife, but you can't always get a best friend.

CAUDWELL: You Americans assume that you can easily persuade people to kill one another. Not in England. You assume that as Blazes finds out you're going to try to kill her, he will immediately react by being willing to kill you. I think he might just get the police, which would spoil everything.

WESTLAKE: Hmmm.

HILLERMAN: Good point.

HITT: Say I wanted to get rid of both of them. Can you arrange a murder-suicide for me, one in which Blazes appears to have killed my wife and then takes his own life?

WESTLAKE: Why would Blazes feel that it was best to leave and take her with him? If he's on the verge of taking her away from you and getting her and all the money, it seems as though he's doing pretty well.

CAUDWELL: Suicide-murders are fairly easy to set up actually. But your real problem, Carl, is that you are vain. You want to have a cunning story of murder for your memoirs. If you were a simple, economical man and you did not want to have a nice story, you could easily kill them both. It's much easier to kill if Blazes doesn't survive. Let's face it. If Blazes survives, he at least is there to say, but I didn't do it. If they're both dead, it's entirely too easy.

Although there was a real case of this in England, a perfectly executed suicide-murder, except for one silly mistake. The murderer's adopted sister was supposed to have shot their two wealthy parents and her own children and then shot herself. The ground was laid perfectly by circumstances. The parents had always told the neighbors that they had "one good son and one bad daughter, who is wicked and unstable." So one day, when the son ran off to the neighbors crying, "Something dreadful has happened at home, and my sister has completely lost all reason. Please, can somebody come around?" they were prepared for this dreadful scene. And of course they said, "Oh yes, she shot the whole family." The police almost didn't investigate. Weeks later, someone noticed that the daughter, who had committed "suicide," had shot herself three times in the heart.

HITT: Is there some way to set up Blazes so that when I kill both him and Linda, I will appear innocent?

WESTLAKE: You could begin by creating doubt in Blazes's mind. Say to Blazes, "I think Linda is seeing somebody, but I don't know who. I've never seen him." Then describe an incident when you know Blazes was not with Linda. So he thinks, "My God, if she fools around with me, maybe she'll fool around with somebody else as well." Drive a wedge between them.

PICKARD: Now he's got a real motive.

HILLERMAN: And if we give him opportunities, he might do it. If you, Carl, keep saying, "I'm on the brink of killing her," and feeding Blazes different murder methods, you plant the idea. Say, "I was thinking I would knife her. I was thinking I would shoot her. I was thinking I would poison her." At the same time you're driving that wedge deeper with small details. Tell him that you followed her around—it's a guy in a Cadillac. Give him little details.

WESTLAKE: Make it easy for him to pin it on you. Let him know where your gun is.

CAUDWELL: I would stress also that you must build on firmer ground, just in case Blazes doesn't murder her and you have to. Carl and Blazes must have friends in common. Go back to them, go back to your old schoolmasters, and say, "You remember how violent and unstable Blazes was at school." He probably wasn't, but you can remind people of almost anything and they will remember it.

WESTLAKE: There is a wonderful short story by Stephen Crane. A farmer comes into the house at dinnertime and murders his wife with an ax in front of the children. He leaves and comes back half an hour later and says, "My God, what happened to Mother?" And they say, "Daddy, you came and killed her." And he says, "A man who looked like me?" He keeps talking to them: "Was he as tall as I am? Shorter? Was his hair a little more red than mine?" Gradually they question their own convictions and they give a completely different description of the killer. It's no longer Daddy who did it. But the ending of the story is that the jury—composed entirely of adults—convicts him and he is hanged. That's a lovely story.

PICKARD: Sometimes Linda has to spend time with her husband, right? So one day after she's told Blazes that she's been with her husband, Carl says, "No, Blazes, I wasn't with Linda then."

WESTLAKE: There you go.

CAUDWELL: You can plant physical evidence as well. Blazes might open her handbag and find a pouch of tobacco, knowing that neither she nor Carl smokes.

LOVESEY: What about the attorney? Can we bring him in? He's an amorous type. Could we make Blazes jealous of him?

WESTLAKE: An amorous attorney? The problem with fiction is it must be credible, able to stand the test of verisimilitude.

HILLERMAN: Besides, everyone suspects his own attorney. For good reason.

PICKARD: I think we should keep this simple. Carl plants the idea; he denies being with Linda when she says she's with him. We shouldn't introduce any other real suspect.

CAUDWELL: I think that's right because then there is nothing that she can disprove. When Blazes accuses her and says, "You have been having an affair, you slut, you whore," she says, "No, no!" He says, "Yes, I know you weren't in your office last Tuesday." She says, "Really, ask my secretary. I was away on business." But if Blazes doesn't know exact details, he can't make specific accusations, so she can never rebut a specific accusation. That will make it far more difficult for her to dissuade him.

PICKARD: And she'll be trying harder and harder to prove she loves him, and be more willing to speed up the signing of the will. We can get this murder over within a week.

LOVESEY: Very tidy.

PICKARD: But wait, doesn't somebody else have to know of this affair? Otherwise, Blazes's suspicions would rest exclusively on the husband's word.

HILLERMAN: Let the copy editor work that out.

WESTLAKE: Since Blazes is a businessman, he must have a personal secretary who is privy to most of his business. So make certain that she is aware of most of the information you are giving to Blazes. She's in the room when you speak. Or you call his office when you know that Blazes and Linda are out separately, and say, "When Blazes comes in, would you tell him I am worried about Linda. She didn't come home last night." The secretary has a double purpose for Carl: She thinks that Linda is having an affair and that Carl is completely innocent.

LOVESEY: This is nice but it's not baroque. I thought Carl wanted to stun the world with his cleverness. The letter inviting us here today charged us: "This cannot be just any old perfect murder. It must aspire to greatness. It must reach for homicidal grandeur. It must be baroque, rococo in detail."

CAUDWELL: Well, I had a notion about these two old friends. Carl would obviously know all Blazes's terrors and phobias. I thought perhaps Blazes might have a phobia about snakes, which would make him react violently when there was a snake in the room. You might perhaps give Linda a beautiful negligee for her birthday, which you have had specially woven. It would be one of those gowns that have woven into it luminous threads, which you can't see by daylight, but you can see with a little moonlight. The image would be a huge cobra winding down the back of her negligee. You then set up a scene where you are all staying in the same country house, and you have time alone with her. She's being respectable; she's staying in the matrimonial suite. But you have a row with her late at night, and she sweeps out of the bedroom and goes to Blazes's suite, as you know perfectly well she will. She lies down on Blazes's bed, and—as you've arranged—he is out late. She falls asleep (Linda always sleeps on her stomach) before he gets back. When he returns to his dimly lit bedroom, there, crawling on his bed, is this gleaming and horrible snake. And he strikes out at it wildly, bludgeoning and bludgeoning until by the time he's finished, there isn't much left of Linda. Then the screams are heard, and the whole household comes upon it.

HILLERMAN: So all Blazes sees is the snake.

CAUDWELL: Yes, and I don't think even competent police, when they see this bludgeoned woman, will test the fabric of her nightdress to see whether it has luminous threads.

HILLERMAN: You could even make the luminosity temporary.

CAUDWELL: Absolutely.

PICKARD: Diabolical.

LOVESEY: I like it.

HILLERMAN: Very nice. Does Carl know any weavers?

LOVESEY: I think Tony's idea of mass murder still has a certain grandeur about it.

HILLERMAN: It's good if Carl wants to start his memoirs, "Remember the week we depopulated Newport with mushroom poisoning, 72,000 simultaneous funerals . . ."

HITT: But mass murder is kind of a blunt instrument, isn't it? Just to rid myself of one wife.

CAUDWELL: Well, you could render her unconscious and have her placed in one of those marvelous ice confections. A huge centerpiece at a banquet. And you are wondering, where is Linda? But in the end you don't delay your guests and you invite your guest of honor, who is your best friend, Blazes, to cut the first slice of this confection. And he plunges in the knife and it goes straight through her heart.

HILLERMAN: What happens if Blazes stabs her instep or something?

CAUDWELL: Well, this superb confection has a special place at the center where the knife must go in. It is clearly marked. It is just above Linda's heart.

HILLERMAN: This is some confection.

CAUDWELL: A confection of considerable scope. It may even be in the shape of Linda, like a waxwork.

LOVESEY: But this sort of thing has been done before. Cora Pearl, the famous Parisian courtesan of, well, many distinctions, was served to King Edward VII on a covered platter. When the lid was taken off, she was naked.

HILLERMAN: Could Linda be alive under this confection? I mean, I assume it's mainly ice cream.

CAUDWELL: She'd have to be drugged. But alive.

LOVESEY: Maybe Linda has been persuaded that she can make a good impression by doing this.

CAUDWELL: She is trying to advance her career as an actress. And she is going to have a fantastic moment at which she arises naked from the confection. You feed the idea to Linda so that she tells others who think it is her idea. Of course, Blazes can't know, otherwise he wouldn't plunge the knife into her. It must be Linda, who thinks it will all be a great erotic scene.

LOVESEY: These ideas are okay but it seems to me that they're not on the grand scale. I think Tony was going along the right lines when he talked about a mass murder. My inclination would be to murder Linda on the stage of the Metropolitan Opera in front of 4,000 people during a performance of *Aida*. Here's how you could do it:

I know of a nerve gas that is quite undetectable. Very dangerous, I wouldn't like anyone else in this group to know about it. It is called DMWTS, but that's just the name toxicologists give it. It's a secret chemical formula. Don't mess with this stuff.

Suppose Linda is an opera singer of some note but not the star of the Met. We will create a situation whereby she, the understudy, plays Aida on the big night. She will wear a necklace with a pendant in the form of a scarab that will contain a small gelatine capsule of this nerve gas. It is the last act, when the couple is being entombed in the crypt and the stones are coming down. As the scene demands, Aida rushes into the arms of the great tenor, Enrico Enormoso. The heat from the pressure of their embrace melts the gelatine capsule and releases the nerve gas, and they both die to the thunderous applause of the audience.

PICKARD: Quite good.

HILLERMAN: I like it. But maybe it's a trendy new version of *Otello*, directed by Peter Sellars. Otello is a mugger in this hip interpretation. The woman who must die is not the prima donna but a supernumerary, played by Linda. Early on in the opera, our mugger sees a gold chain around Linda's neck. It's a breakaway chain, except we've woven a piece of piano wire into it, see. Blazes Boylan is the talented tenor, who, in this case, is playing Otello. He grabs this breakaway chain, only it doesn't seem to be immediately breaking away. But he's determined; he's not going to blow this part. So he rips the chain off! It's not only dramatic, but it's a public decapitation. We haven't seen one of those in years.

WESTLAKE: Very nice.

PICKARD: But it's not mass murder.

WESTLAKE: No, but it has the virtue of mass revulsion.

HITT: A New York audience would love it.

HILLERMAN: And even if Blazes is not dead, and even if he's not charged with murder, at least his reputation is besmirched.

CAUDWELL: I'm not sure. There was a story of one Otello in England who strangled three Desdemonas and it didn't ruin his career at all. But I'm worried because if someone is killed on the public stage, you don't suspect the obvious murderer. The fact is that when you know something has gone wrong in a stage performance, you then say of the chap who did it, "Of course, he's not the man who really did it. Poor chap. Terrible accident." I don't think that satisfies your desire for revenge.

HITT: Maybe the thing to do is cast myself as Otello and I pull the chain. According to your logic, then it would be obvious that I was not the killer.

HILLERMAN: There you go. You're catching on.

LOVESEY: I can't see Blazes as a tenor. I see him as a stage-hand in *Aida* who has been responsible for these great stones which come down and entomb the couple. You know Blazes is responsible for the stones, and you, Carl, cut the rope short by about a foot. Then when they're singing the beautiful duet at the end, the thing comes down with a thump or too soon and ruins the tenor's part. He insists that Blazes be dismissed. Now Blazes has a big grudge against the tenor.

HILLERMAN: So this sets up Blazes to kill my wife?

LOVESEY: No. Blazes is now motivated to kill the tenor. In the meantime, Linda, who is the understudy for the lead, has never gone on the stage herself. You can play off that frustration by convincing her that the only way she will ever sing is if the lead gets ill. So you suggest to Linda that she put some cascara in the soprano's cappuccino. Now where did she get the cascara from? She gets Blazes to get it for her. "What do you want with that?" Blazes might ask. And she might even tell him. But later on when he starts buying cascara tablets, then he looks like a really guilty character, doesn't he?

HITT: What is cascara?

LOVESEY: In opera, you say a show will have a long run. Well, cascara makes you have a lot of short runs, you see?

HITT: Ah!

LOVESEY: Cascara makes it impossible for the lead to go on.

HILLERMAN: I think you've hit upon the way we can really make this work. I really like this idea much better than mushrooms.

LOVESEY: And are you prepared to go along with my nerve gas? I do so like the idea of something being squeezed between them when they sort of press up to each other in the final scene, and they die appropriately in the tomb. There is a pleasant unity about it all.

HILLERMAN: This is good because you don't want Carl to look like the mastermind. You want it to look like a clumsy attempt to kill the tenor that accidentally kills both the tenor and the stand-in because the prima donna is indisposed.

HITT: What about an alibi?

LOVESEY: You can be away. You needn't even be there. You are spending time with your friend, the chief of police. Spending the evening playing cards.

PICKARD: I think Carl would want to be there in the audience.

HILLERMAN: Oh, yes. Naturally. Alibis are overrated. He would want to be there, enjoying his work. Pondering the clever phrasings of his memoirs.

CAUDWELL: Absolutely. Who wouldn't want to be there? Besides, I have it on the authority of a New York criminal attorney of considerable experience: the farther away the spouse is at the time of death, the more certain that it's murder.

II

Improvising on a Theme

In his dictionary, Samuel Johnson defined the essay as a "loose sally of the mind"—a piece of writing lacking "regular and orderly composition." Then, of course, the British gave their one official form of whimsy a regular and orderly shape, and have spent the three centuries since Johnson in bitter and protracted argument about what properly constitutes an essay and what does not. In America, the essay never achieved the central importance it did in British culture. Perhaps the reason is that Americans come to improvisation more comfortably and have found a number of different outlets for it. We exercise the more harebrained side of ourselves, the side that says "wing it" and "make it up" in so many ways.

Harper's Magazine occasionally asks different writers to satisfy their natural caprice in novel ways—say, writing up a guide to paradise, or composing letters to extraterrestrials. Or, at other

63

times, we set out to find those exercising their whimsy with no prompting from us. During the Reagan era, we found avant-garde talkers—monologuists—who in the 1980s began to take the stages of Bohemia, sit on a stool, and extemporaneously tell a wild tale.

Stranger Than Fiction!

The triumph of style over substance, the hallmark of the Reagan era, is also this decade's legacy to the arts. What literary archaeologists might call the "story" lies buried beneath a profusion of spectacle: the multimillion-dollar computerized effects of cinema, the lurid video novels of writers barely old enough to vote, the garish *son et lumière* of Broadway extravaganzas.

Against this bias for aesthetic splendor, the simple unadorned tale is making a comeback—from storytelling festivals in the South, to stand-up routines on cable television, to performance-art monologues. The monologuists owe their popularity in part to President Reagan himself. After the scaffolding of government support was dismantled in the early 1980s, many of the avant-garde troupes withered. In their place came streamlined, no-frills theater: one-man and one-woman shows.

The curious voices that emerged—often autobiographical, sometimes glib, usually weird—have become a staple of the underfunded arts parlors of the big cities. *Harper's Magazine* recently visited Bohemia to gather an anthology of this work. The following monologues were performed at LaMama theater in New York City on March 15, 1988.

---◆---

KIMBERLY FLYNN
BETH BROWDE
MIKE FEDER
DEBORAH MARGOLIN
JEFFREY ESSMANN

♦

KIMBERLY FLYNN *has performed her one-woman shows at several New York City theaters, including Dixon Place, La Mama, and WOW. She recently played the leading roles in two feature films,* Revolution *and* Requiem.

Beauty-School Blues

Check it out. It's just a few months ago I decided to go back to school. So I chose beauty school. I thought, I'll get in, no problem. I'm beautiful. But really, there is a lot to learn, and I think it's fascinating. Sideburns, they have a whole history, they may seem out of it, but you can work 'em. Take bangs for instance, some people don't want bangs but need 'em. Last week alone, I went down four seconds on a pin curl and three on a dry set. But that ain't nothin.' 'Cause my cousin Rosie does a Dippity-Do beehive in under three minutes. And that's with the pink tape. Yes, I must admit, some things is hard though. Like, I was never good at math. Especially geometry. So learning face shapes is really hard for me. Like, if you're a square or a triangle, your hair should not be pointed, I think. Like, I had this test cut. She was a square. I set and cut her for a triangle. Big deal. She didn't know the difference. My beauty-training technician throws a conniption and tells her, loud, in front of everyone. But other things is a cinch. Like now we're doing eyebrows. This decade has been one of upheaval and revolution for the eyebrow. So at this point, anything goes. Which especially means, I gotta learn them all. I made eyebrow flashcards. There are seventy-two. And I stayed up all night studying them. And I missed *Miami Vice.* You see, I really need the A in eyebrows 'cause I'm takin' a C in face shapes. Otherwise, I love school. I'm learning things, I love the teachers, everything's great. I got ideas all the time. There's so much to talk about. And meanwhile, Frankie, he's my boyfriend, what's he say? "Charlene, you ain't no fun no more." Frankie, lay off. I mean, he is so pissed off these days. He's not takin' care of himself. I said, Frankie, come on, let me help you. He says, he likes his eyebrow the way it is. I mean, you don't think that if a guy plucks his eyebrows he's a fairy, do you? That's what Frankie thinks. You know what my mother says? He's jealous. Yeah, I think he is jealous. 'Cause I am gonna be a professional. My cousin Rosie started out in Yonkers doing $10 cuts. And now she's in California cuttin' hair for *Star Search*. Check that out. Now, with Frankie, okay, things are not the way they used to be. I mean Frankie used to be all over me all the time; it was great! But now, no way. And I'm tryin', I mean, he's the one. So, I decided to put a little romance back into this relationship. I get all dressed up; I plan this big day. I don't know why, but he blows up at me. "Charlene, if you don't stop talkin' permanents and tint jobs, I'm gonna crack your head with this bowling ball." My game is totally off. I could not keep the ball in the lane. "Just can't stay out of the gutter, can you, Charlene?" I am not playing no more. I'll keep score. I mean, I got choices. Now, I never keep score. Like I said, math ain't my thing. Hair is. Now, all around them score sheets they got advertisements, and there is one for the Lucky Star Motor Inn. It's right off the turnpike. You gotta watch when you come out of the tunnel or you're gonna miss it. Check this out. "We specialize in the sophisticated fantasy. Luxury waterbeds. Designer elegance. Couples welcome." And the really good thing about it is, you don't gotta pay for the whole night. Just for four hours. So, I make these little plans, and then I say, "Hey Frankie, I gotta surprise for you." And he says, "Let me guess. Last week it was Disney Doo Orange. The one before, Color Me Plum. As of yesterday, I think you got a special on Frost & Tip." Frankie, you ain't got no imagination. Besides, it's something else. "Good. 'Cause listen, Charlene. I had it up to here with this beauty school. You better start making choices." Check this out. "It goes, or you go." Okay, okay, okay. I don't let this get me down. I go around, I make my plans. I get everything going. Now, I don't give him the name of the place, you see. I just tell him the time, the address. I give him the directions. And I tell him, Frankie, you better be there, because this is very important. Now I get to this Lucky Star Motor Inn, and I am telling you, these people got class. They give me a box of Fanny Farmer. And a six of Calvin Cooler. Raspberry. I get into this elevator. Even the floor is mirrors. I open the door to my room, and the music starts just like that. Now, I was going crazy with all them room choices: Arabian Nights, Bubble Boudoir, King Tut's WaWa Hut, Alcatraz, Lemon Lounge, Tropical Cabana, and Heaven's Hideaway. What's Frankie gonna like best? I picked the Fun Room. This room, I could not find the bed. And then I realize, it's done up like a pool table. I pull back the covers. There are domino sateen sheets, astroturf for carpeting, stadium lights, a volleyball net over the bathtub, exercise bikes, and a hot-dog cart. And do you know what's in it? Hot dogs. All beef. Now, I figure, okay, Frankie, he's gonna be fifteen minutes late. This gives me time for a hot-oil treatment and a no-set quick curl. When I am done, even my hair is voluptuous. Guess what I wore? Golf shoes. Just golf shoes. With the tassles, the spikes, the works. So I take this sexy little pose on the pool-table bed. I take a cue stick. A couple of bowling balls. Now I'm lying there. Fifteen more minutes pass. Piss me off, why don't he. I left my blow-drying seminar twenty minutes early to be on time. Fifteen more minutes pass. My foot is falling asleep. Twenty more minutes. One hour passes. Now it's two hours later. Excuse me. What am I doing all alone at the Lucky Star Motor Inn? I mean, I got choices, don't I? I mean, am I a modern woman or not? I am tired of waitin' on this guy. From now on, I will do whatever I want. And so I had me some fun in that Fun Room. And I don't just mean I took a bubble bath. Big deal. I went into the Lucky Star alone. Big deal. I left the Lucky Star alone. Doesn't bother me. I got pride. Go home, act like I had not been stood up, and started studying for my rods-and-rollers exam. This morning, I wake up, I go downstairs. Who is sitting out front in his car? Frankie. Well, I walk over to him real cool and say, Hey, Frankie, where were you last night? "Charlene, I was there." Check it out. "Lemon Lounge. We had a great time. Get in. Want a ride?" Okay, okay, okay. I look at this lowlife, and I say to him, No thanks, I'll walk. So I walked, and I was thinkin', okay, when Frankie comes to me on his grubby little hands and knees and says, "Charlene, I'm sorry, let's make up, huh?" I won't! And when he says, "Give your Frankie a kissie, kissie, kissie," I won't. And when he says, "Tell your Frankie who's the best-lookin' guy you know? Tell me, tell me, tell me," I won't. Check this out. I will do whatever I want. Because one day, I'll be in Hollywood, cuttin' hair for *Star Search*.

BETH BROWDE *is a playwright and an actress. This monologue has become part of a novel in progress entitled* Snow White Walks on the Yellow Line.

Temporary Shelter

My mom tried to drive me off a bridge once. I'm not kidding. The Triborough Bridge. She was in a really bad mood—really bad. She was taking me to the airport so I could visit my dad in Paris. The whole thing was her idea—I didn't want to go to Paris anyway, and I would've been happy to take the bus to the airport.

Now the truth is, I think she'd been mad at me for a while—basically since I was born. But some days we got along fine. Anyway, she's driving me to the airport and Grandpa is in the front seat. Now Grandpa was the best person I ever knew. He was nice to everyone no matter what. So she stops the car and says to him, Get out of the car. I'm going to kill her and I don't want you to get hurt. He doesn't really believe her. You don't mean that, dear, he says. But she insists she does mean it. She is going to kill me. And he gets out. One hundred twenty-fifth and Broadway.

Now, I don't think I thought she meant it, 'cause I just stayed there in the backseat and didn't say a word. At the time I thought silence was the most sophisticated approach—I mean, I was only eighteen. But whenever she started screaming at me, I would just shut up and look out the window. She hated that. I don't remember what she was saying. She always liked to discuss her impending divorce in the car.

One time on Interstate 81, in the middle of Pennsylvania, she's yelling at me and my brother and she just stops the car—right in the middle lane. She says to my brother, I'm not going any further until you tell me who you would rather see dead—me or your father. Cars are whizzing by us, honking and pointing. My brother thinks the whole thing is pretty funny, and he says, If I promise to answer the question, will you drive? So she says Yes and starts driving and he says, You. I'd rather see you dead.

The next day she tried to run him over.

That's the main reason to keep my mouth shut.

That's what I did the whole time I was growing up—kept my mouth shut. There's a good and a bad side to it. The bad side is it can take you half an hour to find the bathroom in a strange place. But the good side is you don't say anything stupid, even if you are thinking it. If you keep your mouth shut long enough, someone's bound to give you a hint.

But sometimes I can't help talking. Probably I said something wrong. Anyway, there we were driving along 125th Street. She's telling me about how I'm gonna get up in court and tell the truth about what a bastard my father is. Then I make a mistake. We're just about at Lenox Avenue and I say, Look Mom, I don't understand. What's the point of being married to someone who doesn't want to be married to you? She starts screaming, floors it, and tries to drive the car right into the wall of this Kentucky Fried Chicken—she turned into two lanes of oncoming traffic. So I dive headfirst from the backseat into the brake. Her legs are jerking and she's spazzing out. Somehow we stop and I grab the keys, screaming my head off for help. The only thing is, we're there in this giant Oldsmobile Ninety-Eight blocking an entire intersection in the middle of Harlem. She's wearing her mink coat and all this jewelry. All these black people are crowding around the car. We look like two rich crazy ladies, and I think: I'm a liberal, but how are they going to know? And I'm afraid to open the door. I'm totally panicked. And all of a sudden my mom is completely calm. She says, Janice, give me the keys and I will drive you to the airport. That's it. Not please, not I'm sorry, just give me the keys. And you know what? I gave her the keys.

So she starts up again and I'm in the front seat this time. We don't talk. I just look out the window. I don't even remember thinking—just blank. Soon she's saying I should have a good time in Paris, because she'll be dead when I get back. And I say something really stupid, So, who's supposed to feed the dog while you're dead? I mean, I know it was a really stupid thing to say, but I was thinking of the time before when she took fifty Seconals and left a note in the kitchen that said, While I'm dead, feed the dog.

By now we're on the bridge. She starts screaming that she is really going to kill me, and she turns sharp to the right across two lanes. I grab the wheel and try to jam on the brake, and we sort of bounce off this cement embankment. And I grab the keys again.

And the same thing happens again. I'm crying and screaming, and she's yelling and spazzing out. Two lanes of traffic on the bridge are stopped and honking at us. Then all of a sudden she's fine, like nothing happened. She tells me to give her back the keys, she promises not to kill me, and so I do.

That seems really weird, doesn't it—me just giving her back the keys like that.

So it was about four years later that I went and found this shrink, Phyllis. She was nice. By then my mom had died. It was like, while she was alive, I didn't really want to talk about it too much. I mean, I guess I'm lucky she died so I could stop thinking I was the one who was crazy.

But one day I'm in there telling this shrink, Phyllis, about being driven off the bridge, and the time she tried to run my brother over and the Seconals—all those stories. And Phyllis is listening real intently. And suddenly I think, oh my God. How is she gonna know I'm not just making this up? What if my mom was just this nice lady who baked cookies and sent me presents? How would she know? Everything she knows about me is what I say. What if I'm lying and don't even know it, and I'm just deluded, and none of the stuff I remember actually happened?

So, anyway, here's what happened with my mom. She finally gets me to the airport. Nobody was dead, but I have to say I was probably the least excited person with a ticket to Paris at Kennedy Airport. I don't have the slightest idea what I said to her when I got there, but she stormed out, saying, Have a good time. I'll be dead when you get back. At that point I wouldn't have minded if she was dead, but I still wasn't in the mood to go to Paris. I find out that there's a place in the basement of the airport where you can make an emergency transatlantic call. So I go down there and I find this Air France office, and I tell the guy it's an emergency, I have to call my father in Paris. Now, you would think, just by the way I looked—I was crying so hard I could hardly talk—you would think someone would just make the call. But this guy says he has to know why or he can't do it. So I tell him basically my mother just tried to kill me on the way to the airport and just left saying she was going to kill herself. He gets the number of my dad's hotel and calls. But there's no answer.

So he says to me in his most sympathetic voice, I'm a businessman, just like your father. And the most efficient way to handle this is for you to get on the plane, meet with him in Paris, and then, if you want to, take the next flight back. That was the most absurd thing I had ever heard.

I started to argue with him, when in walks my mother like she's on her way to a garden party, smiling and completely together. She says, I thought you'd be here. Come on, dear, we don't want you to miss your plane.

Well, that guy just looked at me like I was out of my mind. So this must be your mother, he says. Your daughter and I were just having a little chat. He smiled at me.

MIKE FEDER is the author of New York Son, a collection of autobiographical stories, some of which have been performed on National Public Radio and the British Broadcasting Company. His radio show, Hardwork, airs Sundays on WBAI-FM in New York City, and his column appeared regularly in Wigwag.

Here's Herbie

When I was about fifteen, I was possessed of a great many psychosomatic complaints. A lot of this had to do with just trying to compete, although fruitlessly, with my mother, who was always sick on a very grand scale—mentally and physically. Nevertheless, as a loving son, I had inherited a great deal of her complaints and ailments, although I believe I was probably much healthier than I thought I was.

I was very allergic in those days to cats, grass, and trees, and I had a great many other allergies that I think a lot of Jewish boys are familiar with. There was an allergist I had to go to. He lived in Manhattan, which for a wimp boy like myself was a long, adventurous trip. It held a lot of terrors for me, one of which was the subway. I lived way out in Queens, on the edge of the city near Nassau County. I had to take a bus to the train, then catch the F train into Manhattan, get off, go to the allergist, and come back.

One morning I'm leaving my house, and I'm in my constant state of teenage depression because in those days my mother was often ill, and she was sitting in her room moaning or calling her mother to complain that she wished she never had children. Sort of a cheery way to start my day.

Back then there wasn't all that much subway violence. There weren't that many teenagers wandering around eating people and throwing them on the tracks. What bothered me was that there were so many machines down there of such a powerful nature, and it was so dark and so far under the ground that I always felt that the tunnel was going to fall in on me, that the train would smash into a wall and kill us all. I should have brought a book. I would have been better off.

I get on the front car. I always got on the front car of a train, and to this day I still like to get on the front car. I think it has something to do with some sort of identification with the surge of power that's involved in being in the front of a train. When you're a teenager in the city, one of the most powerful things that you can have any personal connection with, since horses and bulls are not around, is a train. When that train comes rumbling and roaring into the station and you're a teenager, it just fills your blood with a kind of crazy excitement. So I always used to get on the first car of the train and sit down. Also, without realizing it, I always sat somewhere near the front of the front car and looked a little bit out the window with the reinforced glass in the front of the car. I would sit there, but one thing I never seemed to have the nerve to do, although I wanted to, was to go up and look out the window.

First of all, I felt that it would be extremely uncool to stand there like some jerk-off and just stare out the window. When I was fifteen, I didn't want to seem like I was six. I wanted to look out the front of the train but I never would, so a terrible tug-of-war took place in my mind. The best I could do was sit close to the window and look from the corner of my eye out the window.

We're rumbling along, and we go about three or four stops, the doors open and they close and just before they close absolutely a big fat hand gets thrust through the doors. So then the doors open again 'cause this hand wouldn't move, and in comes what we used to call, when I was a teenager, a retard. This guy, who could have been anywhere from fifteen to thirty-five, retarded, comes onto the train with a nutty look on his face. Now, on this car that I was sitting in there were about four or five people—two businessmen, a few ladies going shopping—and they're all looking at books or Bibles or reading the *New York Times*, or something like that. And I wasn't doing anything except sitting there, worried—the Jewish Hamlet from Queens wondering about whether to be or not to be on the F train.

I'm sitting there, and this guy comes in and says, "Herbie's here. Herbie is here!" with this loud voice and the stupidest grin. He was slump-shouldered with a potbelly, had flat black shoes on, and a loose jacket that looked real big in front, like he was pregnant. He had dim eyes, a big thick jaw, and big hairy ears. And he says to nobody in particular, but in a loud and happy voice, "Here's Herbie. Herbie is here!"

I'm thinking to myself, oh God, don't let this retard sit down next to me. I want a little privacy in my misery. Everybody else in the train just kept staring at their newspapers. But I couldn't help watching this guy Herbie with that terrible sick knowledge that people who are a little freakish or lonely or who live in a very strange family like I did, unfortunately, have in common with other people who have problems. So I was watching him with a combined feeling of disgust and terrible unwanted identity. He's yelling, "Here's Herbie, here's Herbie," looks around, sees that nobody really cares, and then without further ado, he unzips his jacket and pulls out, of all things, a steering wheel—the kind you give kids, with a suction cup to stick on the dashboard—and he goes over to this window that I had sort of been looking out of but didn't have the nerve to go to. He moistens the suction cup with some spit—disgusting—and sticks it right on the window. So this retard is now steering the train. And he has absolutely no doubts—he's like Albert Schweitzer and Jonas Salk, this guy. From the day he is born he knows he's gonna conquer the Zambezi or be the greatest ice-cream salesman—one of those kinds of guys. Whereas me, a total halfwit, I had no idea what I wanted to do, if I even wanted to do anything, or if I even wanted to be.

So the train is rumbling along and Herbie is standing there with his red plastic steering wheel steering the train. The train pulls into Hillside Avenue, and then pulls out, and it's rumbling along, clackety, clackety, clack. On a hard curve, he just sort of leans into it, like when you're driving a car. He's having the time of his life. The other passengers, since he wasn't looking around, were looking at him with this amused, tolerant, pitying look on their faces.

I was thinking to myself, Jesus Christ, here's this guy, a retard, a jerk, and I am so brilliant, I do well in school, I'm a handsome little devil, my mother loves me, I'm athletic, do baseball cards better, and here's this guy nobody could possibly care about, who looks like a pile of hay, comes on and does the one thing that I had sort of always wanted to do on the train. He just went right up there and he's driving the train.

The train's running along and I see the conductor pushing the levers and looking out. He might as well have been reading a magazine. Next to him, about a foot away, although he can't see him, is Herbie riding for his life, driving what might as well have been the USS *Enterprise* on its five-year mission through space.

Now we're crossing the river. We roar through the tunnel into Manhattan. More people are getting on the train, and they see Herbie, and—you know how in New York you create a vacuum between yourself and whatever nut du jour happens to be on, you just stay away from him—so people are coming on and getting off, and Herbie notices not a bit.

He's screaming, "Here's Herbie, here's Herbie," and he's driving that train wherever it has to go.

Well, all strange things come to an end. We got to my stop on the East Side. As I leave, Herbie is still there, drumming his foot, waiting impatiently to drive his train.

I get to the allergist, and this schmegege says, "How are we doin', Mike?" This guy's World War II vintage. He's about fifty, bald, a gigantic guy, tough, bluff, and hearty, who makes his living by sticking needles in young people. Whether it did any good is beyond me. I continued to sneeze my head off until I was thirty-four years old anyhow. He sticks a couple of needles in my arm and I get out fast.

So I get back on the train and I'm headed toward Queens. The train gathers speed, it's about three in the afternoon, and I'm very depressed now. First of all, this experience with Herbie driving the train and me not being able to do it really got on my nerves. And I know I'm going to go home and my mother's gonna be in her room, and she's gonna be upset, and the rabbi is gonna be there, probably. And I'm smarting from these injections in my arm, thinking about Herbie.

Without thinking, I'd gotten on the first car again. I look sideways at the front window, and this feeling comes over me of what-the-hell. My life is a total cesspool anyhow, and here I am—life is passing me by, there are millions of things I want to do, and I never do them. I'm just gonna do it.

I walk over, and I put my face right up against the window of the train, and I look out. I started losing my feeling of self-consciousness that anybody was looking at me. It was as beautiful as I ever imagined it to be. Here I am in the front of this great train which has no thought for anybody else at all. This train represents pure power. It just surges through this tunnel. It's gotta be the feeling that the first sperm has when those millions and billions of sperms just get out there and a gun goes off and they start to race for that egg. The first, strongest, biggest sperm goes whammo—he knows just where he's going. Well, that's what the train was doing. It was charging through that tunnel, passing people by like they were ants. It represented everything that I wasn't. Here I am, this little weak wimp boy getting ready to go home to my mommy in Queens, and this train is zooming along.

I stick my nose and my face against the window and I look down the track. Have you ever had the childlikeness or even just the guts to get up there and look out the front of a train? It's fantastic. It's a great sight. You have this beautiful, dark, long, cool tunnel, and the train charges through it because even though it's only going maybe thirty or thirty-five miles per hour, if that fast, with the walls only a half a foot away it seems like it's charging at a hundred miles an hour. At the far end you can see the lights of another station, but in between, when it's really dark, you can see all kinds of red and green traffic and signal lights. They look like beautiful stars or jewels off in the distance.

All of a sudden everything disappears, and it's just me and this train. And all of a sudden, I'm driving this train. I feel my fingers kind of twitching and I wish I had the same kind of steering wheel Herbie has. About halfway along, in Astoria, I'm really into it. I'm driving this train and these beautiful lights are ahead of me in this dark tunnel.

Then all of a sudden I pass one of those spots—you know, where you can see a train coming in the other direction because there's not a wall in between—and the train slows down a little bit, and I see another train coming in the distance. I look in the front window and who do I see but Herbie driving the train the other way! I couldn't believe it. There he is, he's getting closer and closer, and then I know he sees me. I see him with his steering wheel, he's driving the train, he sees me, I'm driving this train, and it was a moment of identification I cannot describe to you. The kind of moment known to only a great starfleet commander, Captain Kirk, or the leader of a great squad of airplanes, Colonel Doolittle. It's a moment that only a few people have in common. We're both driving these powerful machines, many lives depend on us, the destiny perhaps of the universe, and we're coming closer and closer, and he lifts his hand, smiles, and waves at me, and I forget everything. I forget my self-consciousness. I forget I'm not a retard. I forget he is a retard. I forget I'm a wimp, I raise my hand, and we give each other a salute, kind of a grim but professional understanding that two great men, responsible for the destinies of millions of people, are at the helm.

JEFFREY ESSMANN *has written and performed his own material since the late 1970s. He is also the author of several plays, among them the cult hit,* Triplets in Uniform, *and is currently working on two sitcom projects for the cable networks HA! and Nick-at-Nite.*

Heaven and Mr. Taylor

My brother wore a bracelet. A little silver one with his name, address, and birth date on it. My sister had one, too, and every time she'd show it to me she'd jerk her hair behind her ear except for a few strands that always got stuck on the corner of her mouth. I'd say she looked like a spaz. She'd say she wanted that to happen.

So they both had these bracelets. Death bracelets. If anything ever happened to them, like if they ever hid in a pile of leaves by the curb and a car parked on them, these bracelets would identify what was left. My parents didn't get me a bracelet. I wasn't the kind of kid who figured they'd realize how much they loved me if I were dead. I was the kind of kid who figured they'd realize how much they loved me if my brother and sister were dead. But I don't think I wanted them dead. I don't think so. I just wanted them gone, and besides, something about kidnapping had always appealed to me. Lying in the lower bunk at night, sucking my thumb, I'd pictured it a million times: the car pulling over, the door opening, the smell of chocolate and stale Old Spice, tobacco-stained teeth—"Your mother sent me to pick you up from school."

I'd know I was supposed to scratch the license number in the dirt, but just as I reached for the stick a hand would grab my wrist. Timex watch. He'd smile at me—and I think I'd smile back. I'd wake up with teeth prints in my thumb.

It was hot the afternoon I met Mr. Taylor. I'd been playing with my doctor kit, I'd eaten all my pills and I was bored. Then I heard bells. I thought it was just the pills. But it wasn't; it was Good Humor. The truck was halfway down the block. I jumped the porch railing and ran across the lawn. Just as I reached the edge, my foot caught the handle of my wagon, and I came down hard on the sidewalk. There was blood. The truck pulled over and Taylor jumped out.

"You okay, kid?"

But I couldn't hear him through the bells and the blood pounding in my head. I just keep watching the red leak out of my knee and hoping that a whole bunch of ants wouldn't come out of the lawn and eat me. Taylor ran to the truck and came back with a handful of ice shavings and a grape popsicle. When the ice touched my knee, I wanted to cry, but I wouldn't. Not in front of him.

"Anything else I can do for you, kid?"

"Yeah, you can turn off those goddamn bells."

I'd listened to my father watch football on TV.

Taylor was an all-right guy, like any chump in the ice-cream racket. He couldn't have been more than sixteen. He wore a spiffy white suit and had a goofy sneer of a smile that showed off a chipped front tooth. I liked that. But then I liked anyone with teeth problems since I had lost most of mine that year.

I was still wearing my little stethoscope. He flipped it and said, "So you're a doctor, huh?" My lips were turning purple. There were heat bugs. I said, "Yeah, lemme check your heart." I put the stethoscope right over a chocolate stain on his front pocket and—cross my heart—I could hear it beating. Then my stupid brother came out in his Zorro outfit. My sister was right behind him in a hula shirt and handcuffs.

"Mom says you're supposed to pick up all this stuff and come in the house."

Something about the way he was waving his arm made his bracelet catch the sun and it was shining right in my eyes. I don't know, I guess I went crazy for a second. I shoved the bloody ice right in his face and said, "Look, real blood!"

My sister screamed, my brother said he was telling, and both of them ran in the house.

"I guess I better go in. Thanks for saving my knee and stuff."

I turned to go in the house. The heat bugs were screaming. Taylor said, "If I had a brother like that, I'd kill him."

"You would? You, uh, you gotta push popsicles all afternoon or you get some time off?"

"I get off later this afternoon."

"Yeah? Why 'oncha meet me at Parker's drugstore when

the big hand is on the twelve and the little hand is on the four."

Parker's. Nobody went to Parker's anymore, not since they opened the mall. Nobody except Billy Thompson. Poor kid. Flunked second grade, and, well, you know the rest. That soda after school became three or four. At school you'd always notice he had a few Hershey's Kisses in his pocket. "I can stop whenever I want to," he said.

Then the money ran out. He sold his baseball card collection, his bike—even rented his little brother to the girls to play house. Now he hung out at Parker's. If he got lucky, Mrs. Parker would turn her back and he could swipe a Chunky. Today he wasn't so lucky. He was eating pure sugar out of little envelopes with pictures of the presidents on them. He was missing James Polk.

I flipped through a coloring book while I waited for Taylor. Billy fingered me for a nickel.

"Here's a dime. Now beat it, has-been."

Taylor showed in his civvies: faded jeans ripped at the knee and a madras shirt with a bad case of hemophilia. We ordered a couple root beers. Taylor pulled out a cigarette like it was a concealed weapon and lit a kitchen match with his thumb. He was that cool.

"So what's up, kid?"

"You like stories, Taylor? Bedtime stories? I do. Lemme tell you one of my favorites: Once upon a time a little boy and girl were coming home late from school. A nice stranger offered them a ride and they were never seen again. And their little brother lived happily ever after."

"And the nice stranger?"

"He sent a ransom note and got very rich."

"Ransom note? So he brings the kids back?"

"No, he doesn't bring them back."

"Well, what—"

"I don't know what happens to them. I don't want to know what happens to them. Parker, two more root beers. Please!"

Taylor squinted at me through the smoke and started to smile that sneer of his. I wanted to spin around on my stool, but I wouldn't give him that satisfaction. I stared at the counter. There was a fortune-teller napkin holder on it. It had a little gypsy's face on it and eight or nine little question marks floating around her head.

"So, Taylor, are you in or aren't you?"

He took a penny from his loafer and put it in the fortune-teller napkin holder. He handed me the fortune. I wished I could read.

The day of the job my brother had a Boy Scout meeting after school and my sister stayed after to hang molecules for the science fair. They were about halfway home before they noticed they were being tailed by a Good Humor truck. They fell for it—almost. They got suspicious when Taylor said he was out of Dream Pops but if they got in the truck he'd take them back to the factory for more. They'd started to back away when I came out from behind a tree with my miniature Indian scalping knife I'd gotten up at the lake that summer.

"All right, get into the truck nice and quiet."

Of course my stupid brother had to show off. He hit me in the chest really hard and the knife flew up and cut my cheek. More blood. When I got home, my parents asked how I'd hurt myself. I told them I'd gotten on the wrong side of a hula hoop.

It was a clean job: no tape recordings, no phone calls, no body parts in the mail. Just the ransom note. And the bracelets. Easy street, right? But when the money was paid and no kids showed, it got tense around the house. It started to get to me. I got into strange trips. Like bed-wetting.

The double cross hit a couple days later. Coming out of my nap one afternoon, I thought I heard voices, little kids' voices, accusing, telling on me. When I came downstairs, the old man was just shutting the front door and my mother was putting something in the ashtray.

"Who was here?"

"No one, honey. You must have been dreaming."

But they were acting funny, too quiet, guilty. Like the time I came in their room without knocking and they said they were just taking mommy's temperature. When they left the living room, I unfolded the thing she'd put in the ashtray. It was a little white envelope with a few grains of sugar still in it. It was James Polk.

They dropped the net at the memorial service. Coming out of the chapel, my cousin Frank said to me, "My mom says you're going to have to go live with Aunt Gladys." Aunt Gladys. She always smelled of lavender water and her teeth clicked when she ate. Everything started spinning, and for a second there I thought I was gonna blow my Maypo. I had a vision of Billy Thompson swinging very high on a swing—by his neck. But it was interrupted by a car pulling up to the curb, the door opening, the Timex watch—and Taylor. He pulled me into the front seat and we gunned it.

The siblings were stashed at his parents' cabin upstate. We were gonna pick them up and head for Africa and they were gonna have to do whatever we said for the rest of their lives. What a setup.

Getting hit by a Mack truck is everything it's cracked up to be. Taylor and I never saw him; he never saw us. I remembered hearing once that if you died before you were seven, you got to be an angel. I figured if you were that young, you didn't get to be a powerful one like an archangel or even a guardian angel. You probably had to be one of the little ones hovering around the Blessed Virgin Mary's feet. They were always too fat and had their peepees showing. Or else they had no bodies at all, just little wings. I didn't want that.

My body wasn't identified for about a week. You see, I didn't have a bracelet.

DEBORAH MARGOLIN *has performed her one-woman shows at Dixon Place, P.S. 122, Westbeth Theatre Center, and WOW in New York City. She is a founding member of The Split Britches Theater Company and was artist-in-residence at Hampshire College in 1989.*

N

Pleased to meet you . . . I'm silent N . . . I'm the letter N in the word CONDEMN . . . NNNNN . . . Jesus! A man said me the other day . . . it was strange . . . First I was floating on the lips of a French woman who was using a lot of plural verbs . . . PLEUR . . . *Elles pleur* . . . ENT . . . I was stuck all day between E and T, and wishing they would just phone home . . . when a strange man said me . . . he said me so

beautifully . . . he tongued me . . . He said, This painting of
a woman looks like it's all one stroke . . . just one line . . . I
feel that I could pick the line up off the canvas at her finger-
tips and pull 'til she's completely dislimNed. He was a handsome and sexy man . . . I turned to smoke on his soft palate,
perched on the tip of his tongue, and I floated out his nostrils
and around to where his hair touched his collar. I love that
area of a person . . . the Nape of the Neck . . . I spend a lot
of time in people's nostrils . . . you know, people with colds,
that kind of thing . . . I figure prominently in the sneeze . . .
I come roaring out like one of Bob Fosse's dancers split right
down the middle in a crash of jazz . . .

But this man . . . mmmmmmNNNNNNNN . . . I wanted
to get him mad enough to curse because I wanted him to say
me really sweet . . . so I went through his nostrils into his
sinus cavity and created a rite-of-spring sort of disturbance
. . . the kind bees make in honeysuckle . . . He was flirting
with someone at the museum. And he made this pretentious
remark about the nude painting being so DISLIMNABLE . . . I
think he was about to kiss her . . .

Yeah . . . so he was about to kiss her when I altered his
senses completely . . . his eyes filled with water and he said it,
O, he said it, O, he said, GODDAMNNNNNNNNNNNNNNNN!

I flew back to his uvula and shook with the air . . . and the
woman left . . . she was too good for him anyway . . . she
didn't buy that bullshit . . . it saved her slapping his face . . .

When I'm silent, I'm undressed, y'know . . . but when I
get voiced, I get dressed . . . when the going gets tough, the
tough get going . . . SOLEMN becomes SOLEMNNNITY . . .
And I go from nude to dressed in a moment . . . like that
woman in the painting . . . I bet she wanted to grab a
bathrobe real fast in front of a lech like that . . .

You know, when letters meet in words, it's not a simple
thing . . . a word is a whole show made up of active letters
. . . and the energy between letters is . . . physical, you
know . . . like actors on the stage. When you say a word,
you see it, don't you? . . . you lick it . . . and when you write
a word down, you paint portraits of these actors . . . for
example, the word MISOGYNIST is like a Chekhov play because all the letters just stand around wondering how to

relate to each other, the Greek roots stick out all over the place, and when it's said and done, the meaning is very sad . . .

So. I was in a relationship . . . that didn't work out. You see me at a depressed and unfocused moment in my life, rushing around people's mouths and nostrils . . . I didn't used to do that so much . . . and I . . . I had everything I ever wanted but I didn't know it . . . you may already have heard . . . I was living with silent G. When he's lower case, he is so well HuNGNG, down below the baseline, the floor of the letter, and when he's upper case, his form is so beautiful, curving around and back in toward himself like self-recrimination . . . like remorse . . . like GUILT!

I first met him when we were both in the word IMPuGN, and then we started hanging around together in formal words like CONDiGN . . . or in words where I was voiced, and cuddled myself on either side of him while he stayed silent . . . women do that shit for men all the time . . .

Then we moved toward a more mutual relationship . . . we were INDiGNANT! both voiced and full of bristle . . . and I was . . . in love, I think . . . and I found I was PREGNANT . . . my body was changing . . . then things deepened . . . we became POIGNANT . . .

I had baby YYY and he went silent again . . . I don't know . . . he took a traveling job . . . he's a lug nut on the wheel of a truck that's moving, moving, moving all night . . . the way he used to move me . . . I feel it when he gets knocked out of ALiGNMENT . . . one of the places where we lived together for so long . . . so long . . .

So what's left for me? The ballet of my upper case, the yoga of my lower case, my little place in the dictionary upstate. Come visit me there, if you want, unvoiced, on the tip of some word. Whoever you are, we'll find a way to be together, or at least on either side of a vowel.

Or, if you want, just write me a letter . . .

Notes in an Interplanetary Bottle

On August 20, 1977, NASA launched Voyager 2, a spacecraft which sent back photos of Jupiter and Saturn before leaving the solar system. Voyager 2 carried a message for any extraterrestrials who might someday salvage it: a gold-plated phonograph record containing, among other things, 118 electronically encoded photographs of life on our planet and ninety minutes of music ranging from a Brandenburg Concerto to "Johnny B. Goode."

The Voyager Interstellar Record, according to Carl Sagan, its executive producer, was designed to convey "a hopeful rather than a despairing view of humanity and its possible future." It therefore contains no baleful images of death and destruction. But what if some hostile alien, having received so benign and welcoming a message, subsequently decides to pay us an unfriendly call? *Harper's Magazine* invited a diverse group of cultural observers to help frame a new message aimed at forestalling any extraterrestrial attempt at conquest or tourism: one suggesting that the earth, for all its manifold beauties, is nonetheless a terrible place to visit.

CARL SAGAN
VASSILY AKSYONOV
GREGORY BENFORD
WILLIAM BURROUGHS
EDWARD I. KOCH
ROBERT NISBET
JOHN SIMON
AUBERON WAUGH
DAVID BYRNE
LEWIS H. LAPHAM

CARL SAGAN *is the David Duncan Professor of Astronomy and Space Sciences and director of the Laboratory for Planetary Studies at Cornell University. His books include* Broca's Brain, The Dragons of Eden, Cosmos, Contact, *and* The Path Where No Man Thought, *with Richard Turco. He was chairman of the NASA Voyager Record Committee and executive producer of the Voyager Interstellar Record.*

The best strategy to keep such extraterrestrials away, if they exist, is to broadcast credible signs of sanity and stability. Unfortunately, the entire corpus of American commercial and Soviet state television broadcasting is expanding in spherical waves away from Earth at the speed of light, and will have arrived at every other planetary system in the galaxy before any new message could be received. I suppose we might consider broadcasting a signal that reads "Disregard previous messages."

VASSILY AKSYONOV *is the author of numerous stories, plays, and novels. He was exiled from the Soviet Union in 1980 following the publication in the West of his novel* The Burn.

How can we know what aliens will dislike? Suppose we send them a skunk and they find it the most fragrant creature ever born? Suppose we send them an episode of *The Love Boat*, complete with commercials, and they find it more mesmerizing than, say, *Much Ado About Nothing*? Nevertheless, let us assume that they are by and large like us: that is, gifted with a similar sense of squeamishness and perception of logic, but with a proclivity for the brutal colonization of other planets. We have countless things to disgust such creatures. Send them a picture of Beirut (a place to dwell) or a sample of soil from Chernobyl (a place to sow). To bewilder their strategists we can put in our capsule a grab bag containing such mysterious earthly objects as Michael Jackson's missing glove, Raisa Gorbachev's American Express card, and a toothbrush of the Ethiopian colonel Mengistu. Not to mention a videotape of the 1986 May Day parade in Moscow, showing the gleeful faces of the marchers, paternal smiles from atop Lenin's tomb—and, of course, a cloud of home-made fallout hovering in the background. But if none of these measures work, I, as something of an alien myself, have a last resort to propose: show them the lines at the offices of the Immigration and Naturalization Service.

GREGORY BENFORD *is a science fiction novelist and a professor of physics at the University of California at Irvine. His books include* Artifact, Against Infinity, *and* If the Stars Are Gods. *His 1980 novel* Timescape *won the Nebula Award and the British Science Fiction Award.*

The Gospel of Interstellar Goodness holds that only peaceful aliens ever travel or communicate across space, because the nasty, aggressive ones will have nuked themselves into oblivion. Don't bet on it. We can't expect aliens either to confirm or to deny humanistic hosannas about peace and brotherhood—which, after all, don't even work on us. And even if they were intergalactic librarians, intent only on gathering philosophical enlightenment, they could quickly drain us and then cast us aside like sucked oranges. Nor can we assume that only Socially Darwinian aliens reign. Aliens are *alien*. We can't anticipate their morals or strategies. We shouldn't even want to. (Who would relish aliens who always come on like Hubert Humphrey?)

Best, then, to send a motley collection of oddments we find off-putting, hoping that some might click. A preliminary list:

One pair of *Latrodectus mactans*: black widow spiders. After mating, the female often devours the male. To show how affairs work a bit farther up the food chain, accompany the spiders with typical alimony-settlement documents.

One Hollywood agent, dressed for success.

A compendium of holier-than-thou calls for world peace, spattered with dried bloodstains.

An entire Shriners' convention, seized from a hotel at 1 A.M.

A Godzilla movie in which Godzilla clearly wins, but blows it in the cease-fire negotiations.

Portraits of any three presidents-for-life from Third World people's states.

Two Jerry Lewis movies, including *The Nutty Professor*. (If the aliens speak French, substitute two John Waynes.)

An ingredient label from any package of frozen food.

A mint copy of *The Thing*. The equations behind this movie should be language-independent and intelligible to all: Scientists = Liberals; Alien Thing = Communism; U.S. Air Force = U.S. Air Force. Optional extra, space allowing: *Aliens* (the Marines go to Alpha Centauri and kick ass).

The citation for the Nobel Prize in Physics given for the discovery of pulsars. The actual discoverer, Jocelyn Bell, was not cited.

Sylvester Stallone.

A doctoral thesis in literary criticism. One based on any current French fad theory will do nicely.

A collection of time-travel stories. These show that even our more rational and idealistic groups (i.e., scientists) will, for purposes of philosophical hairsplitting, immediately use a time machine in order to go back in time and kill their grandfathers.

Minutes of a University of California Academic Senate meeting. This will prove to any aliens that a horrible demise awaits them if they meet the intelligentsia: death by boredom.

Chicken McNuggets.

This issue of *Harper's*, with no excuses.

WILLIAM BURROUGHS *is the author of eleven novels, including* Naked Lunch *and* The Soft Machine.

So we should put up a sign to warn off hostile aliens, like the signs that tramps leave for their brothers? "Good for a sandwich and coffee" . . . "Careful of the dog" . . . "Old nut with a gun" . . . But consider that *hostile* aliens means aliens who need something—energy, usually. They have run out of energy and hope to charge up here. Well, aliens, if that's what you need, this is the last place to land. Not much here but the walking dead; besides which, the whole shithouse could go up at any second. Is it food you need? The natives aren't very nutritious; many of them live on junk food, and they're rotten with nicotine and alcohol and cocaine and pills. People of such great stupidity and such barbarous manners . . . they will immediately kill any creatures different from themselves. So if you do land, you must be prepared to kill as many of them as possible. The survivors will think you are God, and you can do whatever you like with them. Unless you have the means for a demonstration of wholesale extermination, better stay away. The natives understand and respect nothing else.

EDWARD I. KOCH *was the mayor of New York City from 1978 to 1989. His books include* Mayor *and* Politics.

I love New York, but it does have its share of urban problems, as do other large cities around the world. I think sending a rat, a roach, and a photograph of the entrance to the Queens-Midtown Tunnel at rush hour would give anyone pause, even an alien. I'd also send a graffiti artist to spray paint all over the aliens' ship and a fleet of bicycle messengers with instructions to ride around inside the ship at top speed and knock the aliens down as they cross the control room.

I would also send a copy of the New York State election law and some petition forms—with instructions that all aliens must accurately complete them before landing. The frustration of having their forms repeatedly invalidated by the courts should drive the aliens to such distraction that they'd want to go home. And I would ask the editors of the *New York Post* and *Daily News* to publish editions with tough-sounding headlines to scare the aliens ("E.I.K. TO E.T.: BLAST OFF").

Other people and items I would send include: the Muammar Qaddafi, Louis Farrakhan, and Lyndon LaRouche, who all act as if they are from a different planet and should, therefore, be sent to one; copies of the Internal Revenue

Code and *Mein Kampf*; and a couple of reels of child pornography, which would, I hope, make any living creature wary of our social manners and mores, as would a movie like *The Texas Chainsaw Massacre*.

Picture and newspaper accounts of the homeless, the American farmer, children across the world suffering from malnutrition and disease, and the Chernobyl disaster would amply illustrate some of the many problems our civilization faces. Confronted by this mélange and provided with nothing to counterbalance it, I hope our brothers from another planet would take their exploration in a different direction.

One thing I definitely would *not* send: a pastrami on rye with mustard from the Carnegie Deli. People have been known to go great distances for this sandwich. After one taste, a trip through the solar system for more wouldn't surprise me in the least.

ROBERT NISBET *is an adjunct scholar at the American Enterprise Institute. His books include* Twilight of Authority, History of the Idea of Progress, The Quest for Community, *and* Conservatism: Dream and Reality.

Why not turn your space capsule into a space hearse? At one stroke, by inserting various unacceptable types into the capsule and ejecting them from the solar system, you could frighten off hostile aliens and improve the quality of life on earth. To this end, I offer the following candidates for immediate removal:

(1) The bones, at least, of the T. Boone Pickens types, who allow themselves to be set up as financial-industrial giants. Had John D. Rockefeller been the Pickens type, he would have cornered the kerosene market instead of creating the modern oil industry. And Henry Ford would have merged buggy whips, buggies, and horse manure instead of wasting time on the Model T.

(2) Woody Allen. He has transformed the once heroic schlemiel—early Chaplin, Buster Keaton, Harry Langdon—into a breathless, sniveling, shrinking wimp. I recently made two field trips to movie houses where Allen was on the

screen and discovered that most of the audience sat stone-faced, with the remainder divided between those whose strangled sounds suggested desperate money's-worth laughter and those with death's-head rictuses across their faces. While we're at it, let's throw in a movie critic or two: the kind that declares each new Woody Allen the long-awaited perfect Woody Allen, only to junk it with sneers when the next new Woody Allen comes along.

JOHN SIMON *is theater critic for* New York *magazine and film critic for* National Review. *His books include* Reverse Angle *and* Something to Declare.

The earth, dear alien contemplating to visit it, is a place whose beauty is hurtling at terrifying speed into ugliness. Ugliness, in fact, is becoming its god. Consider only the fate of what used to be our great threefold source of beauty: nature, the human form, and the arts.

The natural environment is hardly an environment any more. It no longer surrounds us, but is itself surrounded and beleaguered, dwindling away amid our industry, housing, detritus, and devastation. Fauna and flora are disappearing apace, beset by a plague of developers and exploiters worse than any locusts. In many places where greenery and animal life were plentiful, now only man proliferates: a sorry beast, bedizened with the pelts and plumes of his near-extinct victims.

As for the human form, there are still lovely women and handsome men around, and where they can be put to commercial uses—in modeling, television, advertising—they may thrive, provided they accept transmogrification to suit the latest contortions and distortions of fashion. In the theater and cinema, however, beauty has become rare, if not undesirable. The great democratic attraction is the average look, something the masses can easily emulate rather than ardently aspire to. Matters are even worse with those idols of youth, the rock musicians, who create such styles as punk, in which the ideal of ugliness is within easy reach of anyone wishing to sink to it.

This leaves art. Poetry has successfully shed rhyme, meter, and minimal lucidity, and is now, except typographically, indistinguishable from prose, which, to be sure, still produces occasional works of note. Notes in music, however, have become almost aleatorily interchangeable, electronically obsolete, or simply cacophonous, though still intermittently haunted by the ghost of some dead composer's melody. Painting, dealt a murderous blow by photography, either tries to escape from its foe into futility or disastrously attempts to outdo the enemy at his own dubious game. (There are exceptions among both composers and painters, but they are few, very few.) Sculpture is in equally parlous shape, producing three-dimensional doodles and public monuments that serve chiefly to impede pedestrian traffic. One sculptor specializes in wrapping parts of the environment, though what he should be doing is wrapping—and carting off—the works of most of his colleagues.

Most obnoxious of all is contemporary architecture, whose costly and monstrous mistakes are all but permanent, and which, under the meaningless name of postmodernism, produces an array of bad jokes. On a much larger scale, it is like the party bore who follows one around and cannot be shaken off. Once called frozen music, it is now music to freeze the blood—by Penderecki, say, or Stockhausen. In a famous poem, W.H. Auden petitioned God to "look shining at new styles of architecture." If he still cares to look, and isn't dead yet, he can die laughing at Philip Johnson or Michael Graves.

So, dear alien, unless you look like a creature from a horror film (one genre that is doing better than ever, alas), and are blind and deaf and communicate by some internalized radar, the earth is no place for you—any more than it is for us.

AUBERON WAUGH *is editor of the* Literary Review. *His most recent books are* The Diaries of Auberon Waugh: A Turbulent Decade, 1976–1985 *and* Brideshead Benighted.

The subtlest and probably most effective way to repel aliens would be to pretend to welcome them to life's feast on earth, extending a cordial invitation to join the party. Under this reasoning, I would include in my capsule a television set with an aerial capable of receiving 120 terrestrial stations, programmed ineluctably to change stations every three seconds. I would cover the warmest part of the capsule with greasy fried onions to produce the characteristic smell of junk food. The walls of the capsule would be decorated with pornographic pictures, of the sort in which the models, both heterosexual and homosexual, seem to be trying to turn themselves inside out in their anxiety to please. Strobe lights would flash and some nondescript rock music, perhaps Pink Floyd, would blare out.

But the aliens might be as degenerate as we are. Perhaps, having missed out on the sixties, they would be thrilled to bits by these exciting symbols. The real horrors of our urban civilization—the loneliness, the indifference, the cruelty—cannot be conveyed by a few objects in a capsule. Its main discomforts, however, might be illustrated, to the extent that they divide between disagreeable sensations of sound and of smell.

On this approach, I should scatter the capsule with a judicious collection of dog turds, one of the great hazards of city life. I would include a few dead rats, to give a flavor of open dustbins, and some bad fish, to re-create the smell that greets people who leave our Western civilization to find peace in Africa or Asia. As a sound track I would use the noise of a pneumatic drill interspersed with the peculiarly horrible noise of the new police and fire service sirens in Margaret Thatcher's London. Finally, I would fill the capsule with horseflies. These may not be a common nuisance in modern life, but I have always thought them even more eloquent than mankind in representing the malevolent aspect of creation.

DAVID BYRNE *is a member of the rock group* Talking Heads. *He wrote and directed the movie* True Stories.

If I were to persuade some extraterrestrial not to come here, I'd try, in a subtle way, to give him evidence that he could not physically survive: a photograph of a smoggy day in L.A., a sample of slightly polluted water, some contaminated meat, some candy, a pack of cigarettes, a leaky microwave oven, photographs of people with their pets, some newspaper articles about recent advances in disease prevention (making sure not to leave out the AIDS epidemic), some Kleenex, some decongestants, and a video game that consists of rockets shooting down invading aliens.

LEWIS H. LAPHAM *is the editor of* Harper's Magazine.

The resort to what the Secretary of Defense undoubtedly would classify as "disinformation" begs a preliminary question as to the nature of the aliens likely to come across the wandering evidence. Barbarians, certainly, and hostile, but what kind of barbarians, and in what way hostile? I can imagine sophisticated barbarians so highly evolved as to be indistinguishable from dental apparatus, but I can also imagine primitives clinging as tenaciously as Sylvester Stallone to the stuffed animals of the id.

Of the sophisticates I would expect the sort of political and cultural opinions advertised in the Sunday *New York Times.* I assume that they would prefer the anemic styles of feeling characteristic of museum curators, distrusting the clumsier genres of sexual desire, replacing the waywardness of imaginative thought with the bureaucratic sequences of a computer program, seeking whenever possible to translate the tragedy of the human predicament into the fictions of property. And if the sophisticates could be counted upon to admire the technology of Auschwitz, the primitives—polymorphous instead of asexual, astounded by fireworks and the revelations of gossip columnists, delighting in the toys and shows of violence—just as surely could be expected to applaud Hitler's speeches.

But what anthology of texts would prove equally abhorrent to both the upper and the lower houses of barbarism? The question is more difficult than it seems. Show the sophisticates the tracts of the militant feminists, or a scale model of one of Philip Johnson's buildings, or an organizational map of the federal government, and they might think the earth sufficiently advanced to be worth the effort of conquest. Allow the primitives to read the novels of Judith Krantz, watch MTV rock videos, and dote upon the photographs in *Hustler* and *Architectural Digest*, and they might think the capsule had brought them a realtor's prospectus of paradise.

As a means of dulling both the delicate and the rapacious appetite, I think it would be safe to send any text expressing the nobility of the human spirit: Shakespeare's plays or Montaigne's essays, Rembrandt's portraits or Beethoven's late quartets. The primitives would fall asleep on their couches or fur, perhaps after butchering the messengers stupid enough to have brought them such paltry relics. The sophisticates would laugh—the thin, tinkling laughter of the New York literary crowd—and make terribly clever remarks about the vulgarity of people still childish enough to assign meaning to something so small as a human life.

A Press Guide
to Paradise

As prologue to *The Dyer's Hand*, a collection of his literary criticism, W. H. Auden set himself the task of defining his standards and acknowledging his prejudices. "So long as a man writes poetry or fiction," he said, "his dream of Eden is his own business, but the moment he starts writing literary criticism, honesty demands that he describe it to his readers, so that they may be in the position to judge his judgments."

Following his own injunction, Auden filled out a questionnaire of his own making (which appears on the next page) that described Arcadia—not a biblical state of primitive innocence, but a place in which he would feel at home.

Editors occupy a position comparable to that of the literary critic—forever evaluating the passing human parade from a perspective and with a moral agenda often invisible to their readers. Bearing in mind the chronic complaints about the negative carping of the American press, *Harper's* asked a number of the nation's editors (chosen unscientifically and at random) to describe their dreams of Eden. Their sketches and blueprints provide the information that Auden said he "should like to have . . . when reading other critics."

--- ◆ ---

W. H. AUDEN
AVIATION WEEK
TIME
BOWLING
COSMOPOLITAN
GRAND STREET
SAVVY
NEW YORK NATIVE
READER'S DIGEST
FORBES
MOTHER JONES
NATIONAL LAMPOON
CHICAGO TRIBUNE
THE PARIS REVIEW
SALMAGUNDI

W. H. AUDEN *explained, in the essay from which this questionnaire is taken, that all "the judgments, aesthetic or moral . . . however objective we try to make them, are in part a rationalization and in part a corrective discipline of our subjective wishes."*

LANDSCAPE: Limestone uplands like the Pennines plus a small region of igneous rocks with at least one extinct volcano. A precipitous and indented sea-coast.

CLIMATE: British.

ETHNIC ORIGIN OF INHABITANTS: Highly varied as in the United States, but with a slight nordic predominance.

LANGUAGE: Of mixed origins like English, but highly inflected.

WEIGHTS & MEASURES: Irregular and complicated. No decimal system.

RELIGION: Roman Catholic in an easygoing Mediterranean sort of way. Lots of local saints.

SIZE OF CAPITAL: Plato's ideal figure, 5004, about right.

FORM OF GOVERNMENT: Absolute monarchy, elected for life by lot.

SOURCES OF NATURAL POWER: Wind, water, peat, coal. No oil.

ECONOMIC ACTIVITIES: Lead mining, coal mining, chemical factories, paper mills, sheep farming, truck farming, greenhouse horticulture.

MEANS OF TRANSPORT: Horses and horse-drawn vehicles, narrow-gauge railroads, canal barges, balloons. No automobiles or airplanes.

ARCHITECTURE: State—Baroque. Ecclesiastical—Romanesque or Byzantine. Domestic—Eighteenth Century British or American Colonial.

DOMESTIC FURNITURE AND EQUIPMENT: Victorian except for kitchens and bathrooms which are as full of modern gadgets as possible.

FORMAL DRESS: The fashions of Paris in the 1830's and '40's.

SOURCES OF PUBLIC INFORMATION: Gossip. Technical and learned periodicals but no newspapers.

PUBLIC STATUES: Confined to famous defunct chefs.

PUBLIC ENTERTAINMENTS: Religious Processions, Brass Bands, Opera, Classical Ballet. No movies, radio or television.

AVIATION WEEK and Space Technology *is the magazine of record for the defense and aerospace industries, and is available by subscription only to individuals in related industries, the sciences, and the government.*

GOVERNMENT: Totalitarian bureaucracy. All citizens are employed by the government, and thus no one works very hard. No presidents, kings, or prime ministers. Only committees with rotating chairmanships.

SOURCE OF PUBLIC INFORMATION: Leaks. All information is classified.

LANGUAGE: Federalese. Vocabulary limited to words like "implement" and "finalize." Since all activity consists of committee meetings, nothing is ever finalized or implemented.

CAPITAL: None. No central direction required.

FURNITURE: Largely wooden swivel chairs, with waffle-pattern seat pads for official branding of the bottoms of occupants.

CLIMATE: Fog.

LANDSCAPE: All downhill.

AGRICULTURE: Lotus cultivation. One forbidden apple tree.

MILITARY FORCES: Consist entirely of secretaries of defense, undersecretaries of defense, and civilian systems analysts. Weapons are only studied, never designed or built. There are no forces to use them if, by mistake, a decision does emerge.

ARCHITECTURE: Bolshevik modern.

ART: Government-approved line drawings or stick figures. Usually depictions of committee meetings.

EDUCATIONAL SYSTEM: Personal stereo players and tape cassettes supplied by government. Students run during sleep for subliminal indoctrination. No homework or study.

ENTERTAINMENT: Public hearings. Jokes about bureaucracy.

DRESS: Baggy Mao suits or loose-fitting bathing costumes.

RELIGION: Vague, convoluted loyalty oaths.

LAW ENFORCEMENT: Lie detectors and whistle blowers.

JUDICIAL SYSTEM: Supreme Court issues numerous rulings based on interpretations of transactions of committee meetings. Sits once every ten years.

TRANSPORTATION: Consists solely of unregulated airlines as a result of misunderstanding in a Supreme Court decision. Routes are changed daily on the basis of previous day's traffic. Fares are set each day, but are not revealed to the public.

ECONOMIC SYSTEM: All income is paid to the government in taxes. After committee discussions over several months, all revenues are paid back to citizens as entitlements, which are then paid back to the government the following year in taxes. The government does all manufacturing, which consists predominantly of swivel chairs.

NUMBER SYSTEM: Base one billion arithmetic. All quantities less than one billion are banned.

WEIGHTS AND MEASURES: The system has never been finalized.

TIME *is America's oldest and largest newsweekly.*

LANDSCAPE: Martha's Vineyard abutting the Dolomites.

CLIMATE: Rome in May.

LANGUAGE: Correct English and any kind of Italian.

WEIGHTS AND MEASURES: Who cares?

SIZE OF CAPITAL: The central *arrondissements* of Paris, whatever that adds up to.

GOVERNMENT: Constitutional monarchy.

SOURCES OF NATURAL POWER: Solar and will.

ECONOMIC ACTIVITIES: High-tech industry, services of all kinds, gardening, barter, and a little gambling.

MEANS OF TRANSPORT: Helicopters (silent).

ARCHITECTURE: Georgian, Palladian, New England Shingle.

FORMAL DRESS: Edwardian.

SOURCES OF PUBLIC INFORMATION: Bards and the newsmagazines.

PUBLIC STATUES: Female only.

FOOD: Caviar and pasta.

NATIONAL ANTHEM: The "Marseillaise."

NATIONAL MOTTO: "Liberty, Merit, and Fraternity, within reason."

REQUIRED READING: Shakespeare, P. G. Wodehouse.

CURRENCY: Gold eagles.

POET LAUREATE: T. S. Eliot (*pace* Auden).

COURT PAINTER: Gustav Klimt.

MARITAL ARRANGEMENT: Monogamy with a five-year option to renew.

CHILD-REARING SYSTEM: Nannyism.

MOST SEVERE PUNISHMENT: Expulsion from Eden.

OFFENDERS SUBJECT TO THIS PUNISHMENT: Puritans, bores, possessors of nasal voices, users of clichés (especially "reordering priorities" and "getting in touch with my feelings"), among others.

LIFE EXPECTANCY: As long as you expect.

BOWLING *is the official bimonthly magazine of the American Bowling Congress, published in Greendale, a town in southeastern Wisconsin.*

LANDSCAPE: Rolling hills, wooded, with lakes, like parts of northern Wisconsin off Highway 45 or southwestern Pennsylvania off Highway 40.

CLIMATE: Every day is August 3. A slight drizzle in the morning burns off by noon. Temperatures reach a high in the eighties and drop to a pleasant chilliness perfect for bonfires at night. (Sweaters are optional.)

POPULATION: Beer drinkers. These are the folks who have no fear of alcohol but do not need to drink to be sociable, as martini drinkers do. They are a dedicated lot who completely disregard ex-jocks and advertising budgets and will never give up their native brew (Point and Iron City).

LIFESTYLE: Communal, with reservations. You can join as long as we know you are coming. Although all duties are shared, parents are responsible for their own kids.

DAILY ACTIVITY: One adult male and one adult female chosen by lot the night before escort the children to the lake while the rest of the adults sleep in and gradually arise to coffee and the cold floor of the cabin. The adults on guard take fruit and rolls to the lake (which is only three feet deep for the first 100 yards) and oversee the kids, blow up the toys, and tell the kids to quit screaming and not to drown self or another. About noon, the rest of the folks make their way to the lake; one of them carries the cooler. Inside are piles of amber long-necked bottles of beer, so cold and wet from melting ice that the label slides off in your hand as you pull the bottle to your lips. Acceptable activities include reclining, rafting, playing volleyball and horseshoes, and listening to the radio (actually two radios, one tuned to a "golden oldies" station, the other to a Milwaukee Brewers–Chicago White Sox game).

Polite discourse on the New Baby Boom, the Bomb, Education Today, the Church and the New Morality, and the Best Infield of All Time is encouraged. As the day wears on, the kids get tired and slightly sunburned, half the women get totally sunburned and the other half tan perfectly, and one adult male cuts his foot on a rock. As the sun sets, the kids go for a canoe ride with their dads. Another beer is hoisted to the lips; it is so cold and wet that the label falls off. The Brewers win in the bottom of the ninth. (Yount doubles, Cooper singles, and Simmons sacrifices in the winning run.)

RULES: Nothing is written; everything is understood.

RITUALS: Everyone says "please" and "thank you" and never thinks twice about it.

PUBLIC STATUES: Johnny Appleseed, Abe Lincoln (as boy and man), and Lou Gehrig or Gary Cooper.

FORM OF GOVERNMENT: Town meetings. Beer and punch served at the conclusion.

PUBLIC ENTERTAINMENTS: Community theater, bingo, and amateur sporting events.

BANNED SUBSTANCES: Bumper stickers, alligators, anything that can't be grown or bought at any self-respecting K-Mart, food processors, microwaves, permanent waves, ultraviolet waves, books on health and dieting, erasable pens, headbands, vegetables that aren't green, and mouthwash.

MOTTO: "It's not the size of the wave, it's the motion of the ocean."

W *is a biweekly consumer version of* Women's Wear Daily *that features articles on society, travel, and fashion for the woman of the* haute monde.

LANDSCAPE: A wild English garden.

CLIMATE: Enchanting.

ETHNIC ORIGIN OF INHABITANTS: Well bred.

LANGUAGE: Witty and to the point or witty and obscure.

WEIGHTS AND MEASURES: Hardly a proper question to ask a lady.

RELIGION: Fun! Beauty! Color!

SIZE OF CAPITAL: Larger than Versailles, smaller than Paris.

FORM OF GOVERNMENT: Royal.

SOURCES OF NATURAL POWER: Knowing where the bodies are buried gives one tremendous power.

ECONOMIC ACTIVITIES: Having wonderful rich friends.

MEANS OF TRANSPORT: One's own plane, railroad car, yacht, etc.

ARCHITECTURE: Oh, it must be old.

FORMAL DRESS: Always.

SOURCES OF PUBLIC INFORMATION: Gossip. Of course.

PUBLIC STATUES: Balenciaga, Chanel, Dior, Vionnet, and, although he is not dead yet, Yves St. Laurent.

PUBLIC ENTERTAINMENT: Don't be vulgar. I like my entertainment private.

COSMOPOLITAN *is a magazine for women who want to "realize the very best of themselves."*

In the south, the air will be like that of the Provence region of France . . . sweet, tender, and a tiny bit friskier at night. The mean temperature will be 77 degrees. The skies between

four and seven every day will resemble those over Botswana
. . . lots of pinks, lavenders, and mauves behind whipped-
cream clouds. The vegetation will be jungle-lush, but it
won't remind anybody of Hawaii. There may not even be
any pineapples. The air will be fragrant with gardenias and
jasmine. You can have as many armloads of gardenia blos-
soms as you like to float in your private pond.

In the north, there will be two seasons, fall and winter, but
fall will last only two days. The moment you arrive (in very
woodsy country like the upper Hudson River valley), au-
tumn leaves will be at their showiest . . . reds, gold, russet.
(There will be lots of red maples, because nobody ever gets
enough of them outside Eden.) After forty-eight hours, the
leaves will leave the trees, the temperature will drop, and
twelve inches of snow will float down to transform everything into a winter wonderland. The alpine chalets will have
wide fireplaces (the firewood will replace itself as soon as it is
used up and leave no ashes; there will be no fake California
gas logs or composition logs), deep, cushy couches and
chairs, oak-beamed ceilings, and hand-woven mohair
throws. Everybody will be a world-class skier and never
break anything.

The population will consist of as many men as women, but
emotionally everyone will be androgynous. Men will have
tender, somewhat passive dispositions, and women will be
forthright and energetic—but sometimes it will be the other
way around. Guile will not exist.

The food will be ambrosia, probably vegetables and fruit
or chocolate chip cookies and pasta primavera. (We are not
going to kill anything to eat or wear or mount as a trophy.)
Whatever it is, it will *never* make anybody fat or even chub-
by. In Eden, calories literally will not count. Beverages will
be the best wines of France and double chocolate milk-
shakes. There will be no alcohol other than wine, no drugs,
no caffeine, and no cigarettes. There will, however, be a few
Havana cigars in a far corner of Eden for sybarites like my
husband.

How will we look? Sensational, of course. Since there will
not be any preconceived standards of beauty, each of us will
be considered beautiful. (Not worrying about how we look

will in *itself* constitute paradise for many of us.) We will all select the age we want to be—tiny tot, teenager, thirties, ninety-five—and switch back and forth as often as we like, but only for short periods. Old age will be valued for its wisdom and mellowness. There won't *be* any downside to old age, because in Eden there will be no illness, pain, or disease.

Deciding who you want to pal around with will take a lot of time and bring infinite pleasure, because you'll have a crack at *everybody*—all ages, intellects, colors, accomplishments, and personalities. Whomever you like will automatically like you back. You will enjoy innumerable gambits, forays, discoveries, and explorings with your special pals. An exploration might take weeks or years. Since there won't be any jealousy, nobody will be upset if you are gone for so long. There will be no betrayals of friendship or love.

Housing in southern Eden in the summer will consist of two- to four-story *palazzi* like those in Italy or other Mediterranean countries, with marble floors, wide staircases, enchanting views of endless gardens, satiny wood paneling, exquisite furniture and trappings. Sheets will be silk or linen, changed daily. Clothes—loose-fitting togalike garments—will be of silk, linen, gossamer wool, or Egyptian cotton. Chests of jewels will be available for playing dress-up; everybody will have as many emeralds, sapphires, rubies, and diamonds as he or she pleases, but nobody will take them too seriously. There won't be any money, because no one will need anything—it will all be there in abundance. Every kind of music will be available, played by robot musicians. The great and not-great works of literature will also be available, and there will be unlimited time to read. No television. Small chariots run by diesel power will be Edenites' means of transport.

Exquisite little robots who look soft and touchable will do *all* the work. Everything. Nobody will program them. They will just know what to do. They will handle all domestic chores, build the palaces and lodges, build and operate the chariots, weave the cloth, design the clothes, etc., etc. They will never break down.

There won't be any sex. Sex is what people *not* in Eden are given to console themselves for all the heartache, pain, and loneliness they endure. Since there won't be any heartache, pain, or loneliness in Eden, we won't need sex. Note: I have not included apple trees in the flora and fauna, so Adam will not be tempted and his ribs will remain intact. Anyway, his Eve will already be there. As for babies, they will be found under giant lily pads. Robots will take care of the babies, who will never cry; they will all grow up perfect.

There won't be any form of government. People will instinctively do what makes them and other people happy.

GRAND STREET *is a literary quarterly based in New York City that publishes original fiction, poems, articles, photographs, and translations.*

Eden is somewhere like the lobby of the old Astor Hotel, which used to be on Broadway between Forty-fourth and Forty-fifth streets: bar over there, newsstand here, lots of bedrooms upstairs, and a drugstore outside on the corner. No four-wheeled vehicles, no dogs or cats, no weather, no nature whatever. Except human nature, mostly in the form of out-of-towners, many surprisingly bookish. I envision as well Hazel Scott talking with H. L. Mencken, Peter Arno with John Maynard Keynes. Not far away is a theater showing only Japanese movies.

SAVVY *is a magazine for executive women that places particular value on entrepreneurship.*

LANDSCAPE: The northern Pacific coast, where the ocean slams against the rocks, and the rocks are filled with tide pools, and the tide pools are filled with anemones. The coastline and its sentinel of redwoods, the wild rivers, and the fir-forested mountains are politically undisputed.

CLIMATE: Determined by ocean winds within two miles of the coast—foggy, rainy. Over the first line of mountains, the weather of Pasadena, California, where there is no smog.

LANGUAGE: For close friends, a sensual, gentle Spanish; for lovers, Portuguese; for acquaintances, Japanese. English is written and spoken for business; Russian, for science. Klamath and Wiyot dialects are needed for survival in the wild. No one ever speaks French.

FOOD: Because everyone was breast-fed, there is no problem with cholesterol, and vast amounts of butter and cheese and cream and eggs are common in the daily diet.

MUSIC: Whistling and spontaneous singing of songs popular before 1970.

PUBLIC ENTERTAINMENTS: Feeds of deep-pit roasted beef, venison, lamb, grilled salmon, or mussels, attended by huge groups of extended families. They often feature open-air performances of Shakespeare, during which everyone—à la *The Rocky Horror Picture Show*—shouts all the lines. These are followed by all-night country dances in big clean halls with bright lights and lots of beer.

HOLIDAYS: Celebrated with parades led by elementary-school and high-school bands playing slow Iberian processionals and fast American recessionals. Children carry flowers and there are fire engines—but no cars, no grand marshals, no floats, and no public officials.

TRANSPORTATION: Pickup trucks, jeeps, bicycles; electric cars in town; fast Japanese-manufactured trains. Trips around the territory are made in Gulfstream jets.

CLOTHES: Constant recycling of clothing through "exchange" shops; thus, an abundance of "new" clothes. Style is a fluid, personal expression, and, depending on one's mood, dress ranges from jeans and plaid flannel shirts to suits of the 1940s to Empire-period costumes with exposed bosoms.

WAR: Unknown, but feuds are plentiful; only those whose pride or property is at direct risk take part. Feuds are a source of gossip, news, and the tension needed to appreciate serenity and arouse passion.

CONTROLLED SUBSTANCES: Gummed surfaces. Nothing may be affixed to anything else unless the elements to be joined are mutually designed for that purpose. There are no bumper stickers, no postage stamps, and no Avery labels.

RELIGION: Fierce, joyous, and outer-directed. No gurus, no horoscopes, no mantras. People pray for the grieving and bring them casseroles.

FORM OF GOVERNMENT: Adapted from the English Parliament. Two Houses, one made up of natives, property holders, and entrepreneurs, the other of renters and newcomers. Elections are frequent, governments collapse regularly, and bribes and barter are common methods of getting things done.

NEW YORK NATIVE *is a weekly newspaper published in New York City for the gay community.*

Eden is neither a place nor a state of mind, but a palpable sense of belonging, of being a welcome, necessary, and contributing member of a congenial social order. It can be dangerous to be an insider. Nonetheless, that is what many of us want, particularly we racial, sexual, and economic outlaws who view ourselves as having been twice cast out of the Garden: once by mythology, once by mythologists. These notes, therefore, take the form of musing on the practices and characteristics of an Arcadia for the unappreciated. My particular Eden is a gay and lesbian homeland (sympathetic others welcome, too); it is surrounded by complementary city-states of other people's devising—not ghettos, necessarily, but free zones for trade in divergent attributes and ideals.

LANDSCAPE: Wide beaches along an aquamarine sea, steep mountains, dramatic vistas, rain forests, majestic plains in the interior, a small desert or two.

CLIMATE: Tropical and predictable, with steady, cooling trade winds. Intense sunshine blazing through azure skies, startling for their clarity. Occasional violent thunderstorms.

TEMPERAMENT OF THE POPULACE: Peaceable, urbane, rational, inquisitive, given to peeking through spyglasses into neighbors' windows.

SEXUALITY: Openly expressed and enthusiastically practiced with friends, strangers, and lovers. Partnership ceremonies available (but not promoted) for couples and ménages, gay and otherwise.

RELIGION: Secular Buddhism with traces of Taoism. Selective totemism.

EDUCATION: Thorough and progressive. Free throughout a citizen's lifetime.

OWNERSHIP OF PROPERTY: An alien concept, as among many aboriginal tribes.

TRADE: Heavily dependent on barter. Small, locally obtainable pebbles occasionally used as currency.

ENFORCEMENT OF ORDER: Limited to the prevention of violent crimes.

STRATEGIC VALUE: None.

MILITARY: All retired and disarmed.

PRINCIPAL HOLIDAYS: Halloween, New Year's Eve, Gay Pride Day.

SOURCES OF POWER: Sun, wind, water, a little petroleum. No nuclear.

ARCHITECTURE: In town—Edwardian houses, Victorian gingerbread cottages, small postmodern skyscrapers, occasional Egyptian and Greek facades (but not on institutional buildings). In the country—clapboard houses, wigwams, and enthusiastically tinted stucco shacks. No glass in the windows, only louvers.

INTERIOR DESIGN: Traditional Japanese.

LANDSCAPING: Zen gardens, banyan trees, dazzling tropical flowers, small Roman temples.

PUBLIC ART FORM: Sand painting.

PUBLIC ENTERTAINMENTS: Opera, movies, buskers, political rallies, gymnastic demonstrations; vocal recitals and performances of reggae, jazz, New Wave, and classical music in the parks.

SOURCES OF INFORMATION: Many newspapers, magazines, journals, books, newsreels, and television and radio stations, all with wildly conflicting points of view. Some serious, some trashy; very much like the American press.

MEANS OF LONG-DISTANCE COMMUNICATION: Letters, telegrams, personal computers. No telephones.

LOCAL SAINTS: Hadrian and Antinoüs, Emma Goldman, Gertrude Stein, Magnus Hirschfeld, Hannah Arendt, Flannery O'Connor, Tennessee Williams, Harvey Milk, Christopher Isherwood.

LIVING NATIONAL TREASURES: Allen Ginsberg, Tobias Schneebaum, Edmund White, the Sisters of Perpetual Indulgence.

READER'S DIGEST *is published in fifteen languages and is purchased by 28 million people each month.*

The quintessence of editing is to achieve maximum clarity and feeling in a minimum of words. (Few writers display this talent of their own volition, hence the deep service editors render to readers.) No magazine practices this more perfectly than *Reader's Digest*, and in that context my concept of Eden can be condensed to a single phrase: Susie, my wife.

FORBES *is one of the nation's leading magazines on business and finance.*

LANDSCAPE: Handsome plains punctuated by assertive hills and stands of fine old trees. Near a great river leading to the sea. Less than one tankful's drive from serious mountains and splendid beaches. A place, in short, rather like the northwest Bronx.

CLIMATE: Four seasons—bone-chilling winters, hopeful springs, beastly summers, and poignant autumns. Rather like the northwest Bronx.

ETHNIC ORIGIN OF INHABITANTS: Highly varied, rather like the northwest Bronx.

WEIGHTS AND MEASURES: Everything metric, but lots of slang terms for various portions, e.g., a gaffe of gin (10 milliliters), a fiasco of gasoline (fill 'er up).

RELIGION: Reformed Druid. Annual orgies, strictly voluntary, including painting oneself blue and frolicking in the woods. No human or animal sacrifice. The issue of whether women may celebrate the Druidical sacraments is long since settled. They may.

CAPITAL: Deserted ten months of the year.

FORM OF GOVERNMENT: Participatory fascism. Powerful enough to keep essential services going, but sufficiently corrupt to be only rarely a menace. Rather like the northwest Bronx.

ECONOMIC ACTIVITIES: The largest component of Eden's gross national product derives from the production of musical instruments, especially terrific pianos and harpsichords, and the exchange of services related to their use in concert by master players. Agriculture is among the most profitable lines of work. The cultivation of zucchini is illegal.

FORMAL DRESS: Absolutely. This Eden greatly values dressing up (and down). Males are taught to ask themselves: What would Fred Astaire wear? Depending on their age, females are taught to think Florence Eiseman, preppie, or Ralph Lauren.

PUBLIC STATUES: None. But most bus stops and public squares have a large, indestructible kiosk for the posting of bills, notices, and offers of piano instruction, and for the display of graffiti.

PUBLIC ENTERTAINMENTS: Street music of all kinds—military bands, steel bands, break dancers, jugglers. Some movie houses thrive by selling advance seating at whatever price the market will bear and serving the holders of such seats Colombian coffee in the lounge.

MOTHER JONES *is a monthly magazine named after Mary Harris Jones, orator, union organizer, and hell-raiser.*

LANDSCAPE: A precipitous, indented seacoast, like southern Ireland or northern California. There is at least one live volcano, which provides the only *frisson* of danger. There is no war, no political terrorism, no murder, and no nuclear weapons.

CLIMATE: The days are crisp and sunny, like winter in San Francisco. The nights are warm, as in the tropics, but the air is cooled by coastal breezes.

SOCIAL CLASS: Class X, of course.

LANGUAGE: The vocabulary of English, the tonality of Chinese, the melodic inflections of Italian, the glottal stops of Swahili.

RELIGION: Zen-like in its detachment from materialistic striving, with heavy witchy overtones. Nature is deified. Her gods and goddesses play among the mortals.

SIZE OF CAPITAL: There is no capital.

FORM OF GOVERNMENT: Passionately democratic. Both sexes and all minorities are fairly represented. The economy is planned by local and national information-feedback networks. Talent, dedication, and even competitiveness are fostered and richly rewarded, but by nonmonetary means.

SOURCES OF NATURAL POWER: Predominantly solar. No nukes.

ECONOMIC ACTIVITIES: The hierarchy of rewards for productive and nonproductive (or reproductive) work that exists today has been reversed. Private life, education, health, art, and science are recognized as the primary values. Super high-technology commodity production provides for the basic needs of all individuals, leaving them free to devote themselves to those values. Society has been largely demonetized; the marginal money economy serves as a seedbed of creative ideas.

FORMAL DRESS: Fashion is an art, drawing on ethnic history as well as on new trends. But punk is dead.

PUBLIC STATUES AND ENTERTAINMENT: Everyone is celebrated during his or her lifetime with joyous tributes. There are elaborate public plazas surrounded by state-of-the-art stereo equipment that plays reggae, rock-and-roll, Mississippi blues, Beethoven, and Andean flute music.

THE FAMILY: Raising children is considered the most intellectually fascinating and emotionally satisfying occupation, and the state lavishes its resources on it. Men and women share the experience equally.

GENDER: Androgyny is widespread. Women are more autonomous and men more sensitive than they are now, but there are still distinct genders.

SEX: Sexual preferences vary widely and sexual experimentation abounds, ranging from celibacy and monogamy to polyandry, polygamy, omnigamy, and wild, uncategorizable libertinism.

NATIONAL LAMPOON *is a humor magazine founded by three alumni of the* Harvard Lampoon.

LANDSCAPE: J. M. Barrie's Never-Never Land is about ideal.

CLIMATE: Lots of weather, all controlled, like in a shopping mall. We hold the controls.

LANGUAGE: Swiss, English, Dolphin . . . whatever. Our Eden has a 100-year moratorium on regarding language as the expression of anything important. The moment someone says or writes something, it is dismissed as folderol.

WEIGHTS AND MEASURES: In an effort to reinstate babies to their proper place as the basis of all civilization, the first baby born each year would become the standard for weights and measures. "That weighs about one and a half Debbies," we would say, or "It's about seventeen Maxes long."

RELIGION: Voodoo, but in an easygoing, Mediterranean sort of way.

FORM OF GOVERNMENT: A huge, impersonal bureaucracy, symbolized by a huge, yellow, smiling face on wall posters and currency.

SOURCES OF NATURAL POWER: Pyramids. Also, there's a guy named Al in everybody's basement who pedals a bicycle hooked up to a generator twenty-four hours a day. When he starts to get sluggish, you hit him on the head with a giant spoon specially designed for the purpose.

ECONOMIC ACTIVITIES: Strip mining, working with asbestos fibers, investment banking.

LIMOUSINE ROUTES: Must pass through ghettos.

MEANS OF TRANSPORT: If you want, Al will unhook his bicycle from the generator and run down to the store. Also, everyone has a big old Cadillac and runs into everyone else's mailbox with it.

FORMAL DRESS: Early Halloween. Masks a must.

SOURCES OF PUBLIC INFORMATION: *Entertainment Tonight* is broadcast twenty-four hours a day, and all news events have to be inferred from celebrity reaction to them.

PUBLIC STATUES: Confined to famous defunct sculptors and cartoon characters that never quite caught the public's fancy.

PUBLIC ENTERTAINMENTS: Lawyer-baiting, bowling on LSD, shooting at random objects in the shadows, riding motorcycles and off-road vehicles at town meetings, drunken barking at celestial objects, Hovercraft free-for-alls, jetpack poker, bullfighting, blessing of tuna cans, and watching Edy Williams's films.

SOURCE OF ORGAN TRANSPLANTS: Ed McMahon.

HOLIDAYS REQUIRING FAMILY GET-TOGETHERS: None. Oh, all right, Sam Shepard's birthday.

ANNUAL MAGAZINE SPECIAL: *People* magazine's "Mother Teresa Swimsuit Issue."

CHICAGO TRIBUNE *is the largest-selling daily newspaper in Chicago and throughout the Midwest.*

LANDSCAPE: San Francisco without cracks in the earth.

CLIMATE: A Chicago spring; something seen so rarely is undoubtedly magnificent.

ETHNIC ORIGIN OF INHABITANTS: Varied, as in Shinar. There are only minorities, and political alliances are forbidden.

LANGUAGE: Southernese, East Texas variety.

WEIGHTS AND MEASURES: Limited. A pinch, a handful, fill this bag, and need a truck.

RELIGION: Abundant, but silent and tolerant.

SIZE OF CAPITAL: Small enough not to need a phone company.

FORM OF GOVERNMENT: None preferred, but benevolent dictatorship acceptable.

SOURCES OF NATURAL POWER: Wind, water, sun, and raw vegetables.

ECONOMIC ACTIVITIES: Farming, fishing, seven card stud, and other games of chance.

MEANS OF TRANSPORT: Bicycles, horses, trains, and boats small enough for bass fishing.

ARCHITECTURE: American colonial.

DOMESTIC FURNITURE AND EQUIPMENT: Whatever holds up, plus microwaves and refrigerators with ice makers.

FORMAL DRESS: None permitted.

SEMIFORMAL DRESS: Great Gatsby, casual pioneer.

Sources of public information: Good American news-papers.

Public statues: Pigeons, legendary editors, and Brooklyn Dodgers who are in the Hall of Fame.

Public entertainments: Parades, pre-1955 movies, all music not appealing to teenagers.

THE PARIS REVIEW *is an international quarterly that publishes fiction, poetry, art, and interviews with contemporary writers.*

An island. Something along the lines of the Seychelles—with a coastline of granite rocks, like Henry Moore sculptures, rising out of a warm tropical sea.

A few incidentals: a large and perfectly balanced boomerang, some bright-colored bathtub toys with small propellers and keys to wind them up, the ingredients and tools for making and setting off large aerial fireworks (along with an instruction booklet), athletic equipment, and a substantial amount of fishing gear, including a number of small red and white bobs.

The island compound would feature a dining pavilion among the palm trees, or a hall, rather, a somewhat baronial edifice with excellent acoustics, so that conversations, even very whispery ones, would not drift up into the rafters and get lost among the ceremonial flags. On hand would be an excellent butler, quite deaf, but faithful, and willing to help with the fireworks.

The compound would contain a number of guesthouses. These small mushroomlike structures, set apart from each other, would all have views of the sea. They would be well appointed inside, each one having a white fan turning slowly on the ceiling and a large porcelain washbasin with a neatly folded, fluffed-up towel alongside. Every afternoon I would know my guests were being installed into these accommodations by the sounds of the houseboys chattering excitedly among themselves as they carried the baggage from the quay.

I would not see my guests before dinner, my own day being quite somnolent. Oh, a little boomerang tossing, perhaps, the construction of an aerial bomb or two, some bait-casting in the mangrove swamps, and surely a bit of a tub before dinner. (It's not that I would feel unfriendly toward my guests, simply that my personal pursuits, especially sitting in a tub winding up a small blue tugboat, would not be especially conducive to their companionship.)

The guest list would be composed of people I have never met. Not only that, they would be dead. Ludwig II, the mad king of Bavaria, dined alone with busts of various dignitaries—Louis XIV and Marie Antoinette among them—set on chairs down the length of the banquet hall at Linderhof, and carried on an animated if slightly one-sided conversation with them. *My* guests would be the real shades.

Many of them would be seagoing people—the captain of the deserted brigantine *Mary Celeste*; Joshua Slocum, who also disappeared at sea; Richard Haliburton, who may have fallen off the stern of a Chinese junk; and the captain of the *Iron Mountain*, that paddle-wheeler whose barges once floated down the Mississippi. Amelia Earhart, of course, and Judge Crater (what an interesting guest *he* would be). Ambrose Bierce, who said, "To be a gringo in Mexico, ah, that is euthanasia," and who then disappeared on a reportorial assignment in Mexico, would dine with me. Speaking of Mexico, so would the mysterious B. Traven. And Captain Kidd, to discuss the whereabouts of his vanished treasure. Jimmy Hoffa, to ask if he was really shredded. Shubert, to inquire about the "Lost Symphony," and perhaps to persuade him to play a bit on the standup Yamaha in the corner. Al-hakim, whom the Druse believed to be the reincarnation of God and who disappeared from his palace in 1021, would also be there. And while one couldn't get *all* the lost tribes of Israel into the guesthouses, at least a few lieutenants would be invited.

Some of my dinner partner choices would be more quixotic. I'd like to hear personally from George Stjernhjelm why he was so convinced that Adam and Eve spoke Swedish. I've always wanted to know why Thomas Cromwell, Oliver's great-uncle, was so anxious to get Henry VIII to marry Anne, the daughter of the duke of Cleves. (The king took one look and hated her. The marriage took place but was never consummated, and Cromwell lost his head. Frightful error of judgment.) So he could have a brandy or two at dinner and perhaps give an odd little talk on matchmaking. And General James Longstreet. Why, I would ask, did he not roll up Cemetery Ridge when he had the chance?

Finally, I've always wondered what it would be like to wear heavy armor and joust in a tournament—to look through a small slit in a helmet, see one's double across a quarter mile of tilting green, and feel the great horse under me beginning to move. The Black Prince might describe that. Henry II of France was killed in one of those tournaments, so he might not be as enthusiastic a raconteur as the Black Prince, who died in his bed. But a lively discussion between them about the pros and cons of jousting might ensue at the banquet table.

I don't know how much of this it would be possible to take. It could be numbing, especially if the captain of the *Mary Celeste*, for example, turned out to be defensive and stuffy. So my Arcadia would also have a swift means of escape—preferably a drug-runner's cigarette boat with a deep rumble of a motor in it, which, after a time, would tie up at a New York pier where, waiting in a fine mist, there would be a yellow cab.

SALMAGUNDI *is a quarterly journal of the humanities and the social sciences published by Skidmore College.*

DISCOURSE: Usually civil, but tense, with argument and feeling.

LANGUAGE: Robust and resonant, neither thin nor overly fastidious.

SCHOOLS: Those in which students study and professors profess with no possible confusion of function.

PENAL SYSTEMS: Those that punish.

ATTITUDE TOWARD LOVE AND MARRIAGE: Reverential.

PSYCHOANALYTIC MODEL: Ordinary conversation with the object of truthfulness rather than definitive explanation.

SOURCES OF POETIC INSPIRATION: O. Mandelstam (in translation!), Robert Lowell, Ben Belitt, Seamus Heaney.

CRITICAL MODELS: Lionel Trilling, R. P. Blackmur.

ATTITUDE TOWARD RELIGION: Still the future of an illusion.

ATTITUDE TOWARD PLAY: A fundamental endowment sadly on the way to becoming a fetishized commodity.

ATTITUDE TOWARD HIGH SERIOUSNESS: Better than low seriousness.

ATTITUDE TOWARD HAPPINESS: All happy families are not alike.

BOOKS: *Triumph of the Therapeutic; The Culture of Narcissism; Lying, Despair, Jealousy, Envy, Sex, Suicide, Drugs and the Good Life.*

MACHINE OF CHOICE: Hand-operated guillotine.

POLITICS: Mistrust of the powerful, willingness to play for low stakes.

ATTITUDE TOWARD DOUBT: Simply decide in favor of what is correct.

ATTITUDE TOWARD VIRTUE: That of a busy surgeon with a job to do.

ATTITUDE TOWARD COMPULSIVE IRONY: An attractive alternative to self-loathing.

SATIRIST, WISE MAN, SOURCE OF INVENTIVE ONE-LINERS: Karl Kraus.

◆

III

Promoting a New and Improved Product

Advertising is the language of democracy, said Daniel Boorstin. Observers as far back as Tocqueville have noted our curious obsession with image. In the last century, every other presidential candidate claimed to have been born in a log cabin—a feeble attempt to tap the favorite myth of the self-made man, the rugged individualist, or as he is known today, the entrepreneur. In this century, the candidates are still working the same angle: they tell us that they are simple haberdashers or peanut farmers, or that they have wives who wear nothing more glamorous than a cloth coat.

Technology has so mixed our national fixation on image with the come-ons of the market that the cackle of pitchmen has become a kind of white noise in our culture. Today, very little happens in this country that isn't touched up (just a little, if you don't mind) by the wizards of Madison Avenue. Occasionally, though, a subject with some extant innocence will reveal itself and, with apologies to all concerned, *Harper's Magazine* then hires the newest talents in promotion to put together a portfolio or plan a strategy.

You Can Have It All!

The recent public debate on our nation's scandals exposes a fundamental irony. Amid the moralizing columns of pundits and two-minute homilies by newscasters warning "Thou Shalt Not" fall the whispers of advertisers: "Who Says You Can't Have It All?" and "Obsession" and "You Deserve a Break Today" and "The Pride Is Back!"

With sweet words, Madison Avenue seeks to profit from our longing to lead ourselves into temptation. The schizophrenia of public puritanism and private libertinism creates a host of charming—and uniquely American—effects. Inside traders are seen contemplating the pages of Holy Scripture. The President publicly offers his urine for official inspection. Mafia bosses make a public show of attending church. Preachers swear off adultery.

In the interest of moral instruction and clarification, *Harper's Magazine* asked leading advertising agencies to develop a campaign *promoting* the seven deadly sins: Wrath, Lust, Avarice, Gluttony, Sloth, Envy, and Pride. Each agency pitted in-house teams against one another to perform this public service, to provide grist for tomorrow's sermonizers, and to reconcile God and Mammon.

---- ◆ ----

FALLON McELLIGOTT
THE MARTIN AGENCY
NW AYER
SAATCHI & SAATCHI DFS COMPTON
J. WALTER THOMPSON
OGILVY & MATHER
TBWA ADVERTISING

THE GLUTTON SOCIETY
Helping people make the most of themselves for over 100 years.

GLUTTONY

Agency: Fallon McElligott. *Art Director:* Dean Hanson.
Copywriters: Jarl Olson, Mike Lescarbeau.

Do you remember all of the things you told me you wanted as a child?

Well, your list may have changed, but I'll bet it hasn't gotten any shorter.

Perhaps you shouldn't be worried about that.

Greed has always motivated men and women. It has motivated inventors to make better mousetraps, artists to create greater art and scientists to find cures for diseases and pathways to the moon.

Just be sure to use your greed to good ends. Be greedy for knowledge. Be greedy for the kind of success that helps you, your family and your friends. Be greedy for love.

Just don't be greedy in ways that hurt others.

Remember, I'll always be the first one to know if you've been bad or good. So be good for goodness sake.

The world's foremost authority speaks out on the subject of greed.

AVARICE

Agency: The Martin Agency. *Art Director:* Hal Tench. *Copywriter:* Mike Hughes. *Photographer:* Jim Erickson. *Production:* Chet Booth.

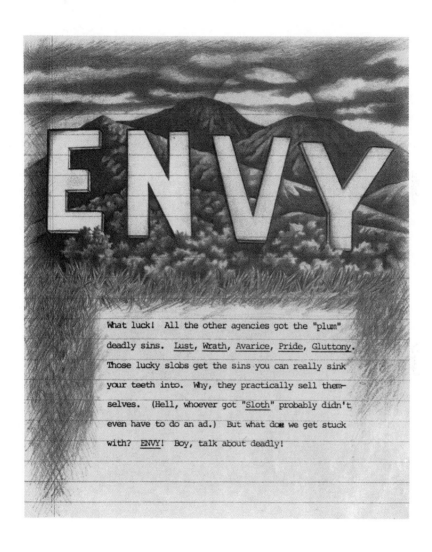

What luck! All the other agencies got the "plum" deadly sins. <u>Lust</u>, <u>Wrath</u>, <u>Avarice</u>, <u>Pride</u>, <u>Gluttony</u>. Those lucky slobs get the sins you can really sink your teeth into. Why, they practically sell themselves. (Hell, whoever got "<u>Sloth</u>" probably didn't even have to do an ad.) But what does we get stuck with? <u>ENVY!</u> Boy, talk about deadly!

ENVY

Agency: NW Ayer, Inc. *Art Director:* Keith Gould.
Copywriter: Patrick Cunningham.

The only emotion powerful enough both to start a war — and stop one.

WRATH

Agency: Saatchi & Saatchi DFS Compton. *Creative Director:* Dick Lopez. *Copywriter:* Jeff Frye.

IF THE ORIGINAL SIN
HAD BEEN SLOTH,
WE'D STILL BE IN PARADISE.

SLOTH

Agency: J. Walter Thompson. *Art Director:* Jean
Marcellino. *Copywriter:* Chuck Hoffman.

It's Time To Start Feeling Good About Yourself—*Really* Good!

"PRIDE goeth before a fall"—we've all heard it. But how *TRUE* is it?

It's mostly *BUNK*, agree today's top mental health experts.

Pride: the sin you can feel good about

You've heard all the bad-mouthing. At home. In Sunday school. In literary magazines. "Pride's a sin!" they proclaim. Well, don't you believe it.

"Pride's gotten a bad rap," says psychiatrist/ornithologist Bernard Warbler.

"It's time this country wakes up and faces facts. Pride, *to whatever extent*, is healthy and natural. The psychiatric community is in complete agreement on this point."

So stick out your chest, for heaven's sake. PRIDE—it's today's "buzz word" for mental health!

Henry VIII

Failure after romantic failure, it was Henry's pride that kept him searching for Mrs. Right. At 52, he finally found her—the lovely Catherine Parr.

William Plover
Dictionary Editor

The most misunderstood word in the English language?
"Hubris," or excessive pride, is a word that's quickly leaving our vocabulary. *Good riddance!* The concept of "excessive" pride no longer works—and people are taking notice.

Dictionary editor William Plover: "'Hubris,' of course, comes to us from ancient Greece, and most word-watchers think it's come far enough. It's quite clear, early translators misunderstood the sense of 'wellness' implied by the Greeks. Resulting in centuries of lexicological slander, if you will. To me, hubris is a rather pleasant word."

Next time you run across "hubris" in the dictionary, cross it out—or write a new definition. You'll feel better for doing so!

A poet celebrates pride

And on the pedestal these words appear:

My name is Ozymandias, king of kings:
Look on my works, ye Mighty, and despair!

—*Percy Bysshe Shelley,*
"Ozymandias"

Shelley was an early advocate of prideful living. His famous king Ozymandias wasn't afraid to put his words—or himself—up on a pedestal.

Shelley's wife, Mary Wollstonecraft Shelley, believed pride enabled men to do the extraordinary. Her novel Frankenstein was a classic celebration of a doctor's pride so great, it was larger than life itself.

Dr. Frankenstein's pride allowed him to create a human being—a task no fictional character had ever before accomplished.

Putting yourself on a pedestal—it's never been more convenient

But how can *you* live more pridefully?

It's easier than you think. We're the Pride Council. A trade association dedicated to bringing fine products—"Prouducts™"'—to the American people. At prices that make pride easy to swallow.

ACT NOW! HERE'S HOW!

Just read the coupon below. You'll find carefully screened and selected companies that can help you design the look-down-your-nose lifestyle you've always dreamed of having.

Don't *dally*—send in your coupon today!

It would be a sin not to.

The Pride Council
Pride. It's not a sin anymore.™

PRIDE

Agency: Ogilvy & Mather. *Creative Director:* Jay Jasper.
Art Director: Carrie Wieseneck. *Copywriter:* Jim Nolan.

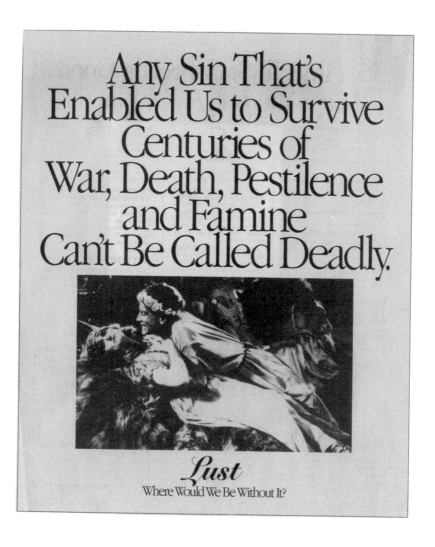

LUST

Agency: TBWA Advertising, Inc. *Art Director:* Geoff
Hayes. *Copywriter:* Evert Cilliers.

He's Back!!!

The Eighties have witnessed the flowering of the art of publicity. Consider the professionals credited with George Bush's presidential victory: spin doctors, ad makers, speechwriters, gesture coaches, sound-bite writers. Whether it's an executive coping with an industrial accident or a rock star pitching a new album or a lawyer arguing a novel insanity defense, the demands of the modern media require a coterie of image advisers. One wonders how these professionals would manage the Western world's most anticipated reappearance—the Second Coming of Jesus Christ, as predicted in the Book of Revelation.

To examine the current state of the public-relations art, *Harper's Magazine* hired consultants to offer Jesus frank advice on six tasks critical to winning over American public opinion: developing a media strategy, writing a monologue for a guest-host appearance on *Saturday Night Live*, redesigning the cover of the New Testament and writing the jacket-flap copy, designing a contemporary wardrobe, and developing a storyboard for a one-minute television commercial. Equipped with this portfolio, Jesus should be as influential in His Second Coming as He was in His first.

---◆---

RON SUSKIND
AL FRANKEN
MICHELE LANCI-ALTOMARE
GERRY HOWARD
ADELLE LUTZ
PHYLLIS K. ROBINSON

---◆---

■ Advance Memo ■

ASSIGNMENT: Write a memo outlining the media strategy and schedule for Jesus Christ's tour of the United States. CONSUL-TANT: Ron Suskind, formerly an advance man for John Anderson's 1980 presidential campaign and a field director for Charles Robb's 1981 gubernatorial campaign in Virginia, is a reporter for the Wall Street Journal.

MEMO: U.S. Tour
TO: Jesus Christ
FROM: Ron Suskind, consultant and advance director

INTRODUCTION

Remember rule one—issues divide, images unite. Your visibility is without precedent (stained glass, Shroud of Turin, postcards, etc.) and Your name recognition is second only to Princess Di. But data indicate intense confusion over where You stand on certain unavoidable issues.

According to Your notes, You're here to "judge the living and the dead." My staff and I assume You've already dealt with the dead. So, now it's time to build support among the living. To this end, it would be better to start slow, with smaller issues, and build a mandate—like Your first campaign.

For the first three days, we've planned several miracles of the modest water-to-wine variety that should verify Your authenticity but stop short of conjuring up the divisive flood-and-fire imagery of Armageddon. We want to show a willingness to perform miracles while, at least in the beginning, respecting existing laws of physics. To encourage spontaneity, Your itinerary will note various "miracle opportunities"—miracle ops. We don't want You to become a captive

139

of Your media strategy. These miracles will be opportunities for growth and flexibility. Most importantly, small miracles will serve to lower expectations.

Another immediate problem: overexposure. The papal visit of 1987 illustrated risks of intense early coverage. By day six, John Paul II was buried on the national page of the *New York Times* (next to A.P. digest), overwhelmed by the more skillful media strategies of Oliver North. Thus, we suggest reserve: a half-day itinerary. Each day will have one theme, one media strategy, one meeting with an opinion leader, and one public event. We'll float the miracles as needed. A few hours of rapid-fire stops and at the end of each day board Your jet (Nazarene One), with traveling staff, bound for an undisclosed location. The mystery of Your whereabouts will lend to enthusiasms that "I am in your midst" (Luke 22:27). Interest tends to build the longer You are missing—as the last 1,959 years clearly indicate.

DAY ONE

Theme: Traditional values.

In reintroducing You, we don't want to create converts so much as tap existing support. To evoke a yearning for simpler days (from A.D. 1 through Eisenhower), it is important to rely on those oft-recited parables. Of course, they'll need to be reworked (boiled to thirty seconds, max), and You should try to moderate judgmental tone—for instance, "The last shall be first, but the middle might also fare nicely." Just a suggestion. The key here is to play upon a millennium of Sunday-school assumptions about Your *ability* to answer all mankind's questions without stating specific truths that might offend special interests.

Media Strategy: Two-minute bio spots aired nationally; prime-time buys will deal with early days, battle with Satan, record of inerrancy.

Arrival: 7 A.M., New York. According to the Book, Your arrival schedule is still unclear ("He comes amid the clouds," Revelation 1:7). However, of the three New York–area airports, we suggest La Guardia. (Avoid Newark, where we've tentatively planned to introduce the Antichrist.) We've discussed a grand entrance, but remember our media strategy calls for a modest start with eye to building momentum. Might be better if You fly Eastern—a sign of Your humility. Meet entourage at Ionosphere Club before first press conference. Talking point: "It is I, Jesus . . . I am the Root and Offspring of David, the Morning Star shining bright" (Revelation 22:16). Strike tone of "happy to be back," including breezy sound bite to emphasize affability: "My flight was on time (*pause*), a small miracle." Board glass-domed vehicle (Donkey One) for ride to Triborough Bridge.

Event: 9 A.M. Walk across East River (miracle would be to swim it) for parade down 116th Street, main thoroughfare of Spanish Harlem; more people, per capita, named for You here than anywhere in America.

Miracle Op: Multiplication of loaves; granted, a reprise, but worked well first time and offers added strength of familiarity.

Meeting: 1 P.M. Midtown meeting with Edward Koch, a skeptic, and Mario Cuomo, a syllogist. To Koch: "A city set on a hill cannot be hidden. Men do not light a lamp and then put it under a bushel basket. They set it on a stand where it gives light to all in the house" (Matthew 5:14–15). To Cuomo: "If anyone wants to rank first, he must remain the last of all and the servant of all" (Mark 9:35). These citations from Scripture (each stressing traditional values) offer a proper mix: suggesting omnipotence yet cryptic enough to keep pundits busy for one news cycle. Afterward, copter to La Guardia. Nazarene One to undisclosed location.

DAY TWO

Theme: Someone to watch over me.

The concept of a personal God is problematic. The idea that a deity watches 5 billion of us *intimately* is tough. Yet, the sense of a Supreme Being watching over human actions is a crucial proscriptive force that moderates destructive appetites and forms a framework for prayer. A solution is to win over several opinion leaders, as well as the media, with a well-placed proverb, followed by an apropos miracle, indicating that, somehow, You've been closely monitoring the progress of each member of the flock. This is a natural way to build support among undecideds.

Media Strategy: Suspend paid-media spots to emphasize free-media press conference in Washington. See below.

Event: 3 P.M., Washington. Arrive by Donkey One at north steps of Capitol for press conference with national press corps. Leader of corps is a man named Sam Donaldson, sardonic and versed in human sacrifices. He is trained to ask the question You most wish to avoid. He will try to test and embarrass You, probably with one of those theological chestnuts. Our sources indicate he will ask: "If You are omnipotent, can You create a rock You cannot lift?" Think about it.

Miracle Op: This press conference is held outdoors for a reason. Easy miracle ops. Use forces of nature. Heavy rain is too pedestrian. Last year's drought didn't faze anybody. We suggest hail.

Meeting: 6 P.M. Talk with prominent televangelists. These guys hold sway over millions and yet are held in contempt by millions more. Have built strong (useful) grass-roots organizations. But there are strings attached. They want top spots in the Kingdom. While they are Your natural constituency, forging too cozy an alliance could alienate others; however, too harsh a snub could provoke cries of "false prophet." Handle gently. We suggest You attract their support with intimations of apostle appointments. Good luck.

DAY THREE

Theme: Distancing from Father.

Your Father, our numbers indicate, has very high positives and that causes You some problems. He's considered more of a doer, You more of a talker. He's a deity's deity— wrath, compassion, says what He means, first week in office created cosmos, oceans, continents. Next to that, Your program of forgiveness, repentance, love—albeit widely admired—brings up "wimp factor." Taking a leaf from the George Bush campaign, we suggest the phrase "mistakes were made." It associates You with the good of His programs, while allowing You to show strength and autonomy by criticizing certain acts of the past.

Media Strategy: Heavy buys in top markets; ads deal with current array of urban problems (fitting with the theme of "mistakes") and end with presumption that You can lead mankind from the darkness.

Event: 7 A.M., Iowa. With live feeds going to morning shows, You stand in wheat field upon earthen mound (Astroturf over low riser, as a precaution) for Mistakes Were Made speech. As per Your request, You will write this one. Still, one sound-bite suggestion: "Yes, the Creator has made some mistakes. But to forgive is human; to err, divine." Shows both humility and humor.

Miracle Op: As You know, farmers are history's malcontents. You might tell them that the weather will no longer be arbitrary and call forth a spring shower. But to show You're not soft on farmers, we suggest a short, scorching sun blast, igniting random fires. It's this type of "swift sword" miracle op that has boosted Your Father's favorable ratings. Our work with focus groups indicates that targeted wrath will be well received.

Meeting: 11 P.M. Appearance on *Nightline*. Host Ted Koppel doubts everything, yet is expert in Byzantine logic. Our sources suggest two possible guests opposite You: Madalyn Murray O'Hair, a cartoon atheist; and Harvey Cox, folksy professor of theology at Harvard University. Expect some of the classics: How could God allow the Holocaust? We suggest the standard seminary response: "God permits evil to lead us to a greater good." Then get off the negative and stress positive: "And it's the greater good that I would rather talk about tonight, Ted." Or go with that line from Archibald MacLeish's play *J.B.*, "If God is God, He is not good; if God is good, He is not God." Expect a curveball conundrum: What were You doing before You created the world? Remember Calvin's best answer: "Building Hell for the curious." Wave off the angels-on-the-head-of-a-pin question, but if pushed to explain the chastity issue, remember Augustine's prayer: "Dear God, give me chastity and continence, but not yet."

Completion of *Nightline* appearance may mark best time for an image adjustment—an opportunity to assert Your emerging role with grander miracles befitting a Savior. Tracking polls through the first three days will give us data to plan the next three. Of many memos, this is but the first. Second coming. If all goes well, we'll be in Jerusalem by Pentecost. See You sunrise at the Ionosphere Club.

■ 'SATURDAY NIGHT LIVE' MONOLOGUE ■

ASSIGNMENT: Write the opening monologue for Jesus Christ's appearance on Saturday Night Live *as guest host. CONSULTANT: Al Franken is a writer and performer for the show.*

DON PARDO: (*voice-over*) Ladies and gentlemen, Jesus Christ of Nazareth!

(*Jesus enters to applause. Very possibly a standing ovation. He walks down the stairway to "home base" and acknowledges the applause.*)

JESUS: Thank you. Thank you. Thank you.

(*End music. Applause continues. Probably lots of whooping.*)

Thank you. Thank you. Thank you.

(*Applause stops.*)

Wow! *Saturday Night Live!* You know, I have to admit, I'm a little nervous. I've never really tried to be funny before. The executive producer, Lorne Michaels, gave Me some good advice. He said, "Just go out there, have a good time, and be Yourself. And whatever You do, don't preach!" So don't worry. I'm not going to tell you how to live. After all, we're here to have a good time!

(*More whoops.*)

Now Lorne also told me I shouldn't approach this like a comedian. I mean, let's face it, if I come out here and compete with Steve Martin, I'm going to come out a poor second. He said, don't do jokes like, "I just came down from Heaven and—boy!—are My arms tired." He said people will start thinking, "Oh, here's some old Jew telling jokes." So, the writers wrote me a few jokes, and Lorne said, "Don't worry, nothing's written in stone." I said, "No, no, written in stone, that's Moses." But *seriously*, I guess the best advice I got was to come out here and show that I have a sense of humor about Myself. You know, do something a little self-deprecating. Which is kind of tough for Me. After all, I *am* God.

(*Applause, whoops.*)

In fact, that's something I'd like to clear up. I just saw *The Last Temptation of Christ*, which is supposed to explore the question of whether I'm man or God. Can you believe that? Man or God? I'm here, aren't I? Course, I'll tell you one thing, if Mary Magdalene looked like Barbara Hershey, I might have thought twice about this celibacy thing. I mean, the real Mary Magdalene was about four foot two, 135 pounds. And with bad teeth yet. By the way, the censors didn't want Me to do that last joke about Mary Magdalene and celibacy. They said it was sacrilegious. I said, "Hey, I'm Jesus." They said I'd offend a lot of Fundamentalist Christians. Now, I said I didn't want to preach, but I have to tell you I don't really care that much for the Fundamentalists. If anyone's interested, I think the folks that come closest to getting the whole thing right are the Mennonites. And they're not even watching.

But, anyway, we've got a great show for you. I'm in a lot of sketches—the money-changing sketch, the water-to-wine-miracle sketch, and the Last Supper sketch—where I play Myself. But I'm most proud of this diner sketch we're doing, where I play an old man with a Cuban accent. It's a character I do, and I think it shows a little of My range.

And, finally, our big surprise. Tonight's musical guests: Paul, George, and Ringo!

(*Whoops.*)

And who's playing with them? That's right. Me!

(*Whoops.*)

We'll be right back! I love you all!

(*Applause. Fade.*)

■ BOOK COVER DESIGN ■

ASSIGNMENT: Create a cover image for the mass-market publication of the New Testament. CONSULTANT: Michele Lanci-Altomare, formerly at Simon & Schuster, is a graphic designer for Price/Stern/Sloan Publishers in Los Angeles.

■ Jacket Flap Copy ■

ASSIGNMENT: Write the dust-jacket copy for the mass-market publication of the New Testament, to tie in with the Second Coming. CONSULTANT: Gerry Howard is an editor at Norton.

Here is Jesus Christ's own story in the immortal words of the New Testament—the first and most overwhelmingly successful book in publishing history.

At the age of thirty Jesus was an obscure Jewish carpenter in a backwater province of the Roman Empire. By His death at age thirty-three from a brutal flogging and crucifixion, He had largely completed His meteoric ascent to the heights of divinity. Since His demise and subsequent Resurrection, Christianity's growth has proceeded unabated and inexorably down through the ages; today, countless millions in every corner of the globe call Him Savior. In an age devoted to the creation and near-worship of celebrity, His name recognition worldwide is uncontested. To call someone a "Christ figure" confers the highest praise.

Still, who was this man? This question assumes tremendous urgency on the eve of His Second Coming—an event widely regarded as possibly the most significant occurrence in human history. (Perhaps it will even herald the end of human history.) No account of the life of Christ has ever surpassed the New Testament in drama, eloquence, veracity, and influence. In four novellas, Matthew, Mark, Luke, and John each retell the compelling personal saga of Jesus, a breathtaking rags-to-heavenly-riches story of struggles and triumphs, of faith and betrayal, of suffering and death—and Eternal Life.

From the start, the life of Jesus was rich in paradox and contradiction. His birth in a manger in the tiny town of Bethlehem could not have been more humble; nonetheless, the very heavens heralded His arrival and kings traveled great distances bearing Him gifts. As He grew, Jesus confounded religious scholars with His precocity, and the stirring eloquence of His sermons and parables led many Israelites to proclaim Him as the Messiah. In the face of persecution He attracted followers of inspiring loyalty, yet, ironically, His closest associates perpetrated His downfall—Judas, who betrayed Him with a kiss, and Simon Peter, who denied Him thrice. The passion and death of Jesus are unique for their bloody physical violence and searing spiritual suffering, but His supreme sacrifice represents an inspirational victory for all mankind.

The New Testament has rightly been called "The Greatest Story Ever Told." Its riches are inexhaustible; believers and infidels alike can debate its story and message endlessly. As the Last Judgment approaches, there is no better time for readers of all persuasions to reacquaint themselves with this timeless book (in point of fact, time is running out). This deluxe commemorative edition is the only version that carries Christ's personal blessing and is durably bound for *many* years of use. As gripping as a suspense novel, as gorgeously told as an epic poem, as sweeping as the most lavish miniseries, the New Testament lives—as does Jesus Christ Himself.

The great and famous pay homage to the New Testament:

"Just as my administration is devoted to creating a kinder, gentler America, Jesus Christ is coming to earth to bring us a kinder, gentler eternity—and here is His blueprint from which we can all learn."

—President George Bush

"The great biblical epic of our time—and for all time. I could not put it down or put it out of my mind."

—Pat Conroy

"I salute the real 'Chairman of the Board,' a beautiful human being—if I can put it like that—who has always done things His way."

—Frank Sinatra

"I think of Jesus Christ as my close personal friend, and this book shows why He is regarded as the ultimate mover and shaker. I look forward to working with Him on the problems that beset me and New York City when He's settled in."

—Donald Trump

■ Fashion Designs ■

ASSIGNMENT: Design a contemporary wardrobe for Jesus Christ. CONSULTANT: Adelle Lutz is an actress and costume designer with the New York City firm Todo Mundo, Ltd.

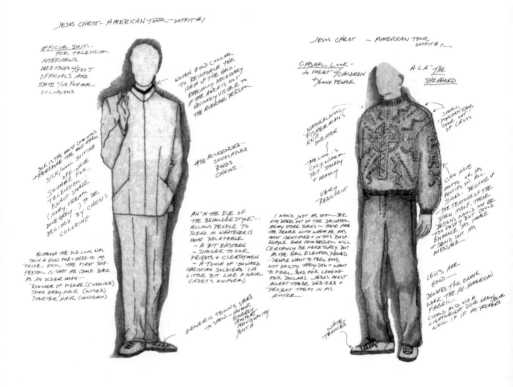

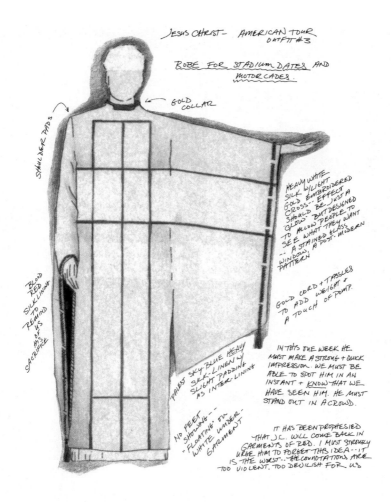

JESUS CHRIST — AMERICAN TOUR
OUTFIT #3

ROBE FOR STADIUM DATES AND
MOTORCADES.

GOLD COLLAR

SHOULDER PADS

HEAVY WHITE SILK W/ LIGHT GOLD EMBROIDERED CROSS — EFFECT SHOULD BE "JUST A GLOW" BUT DESIGNED TO ALLOW PEOPLE TO SEE WHAT THEY WANT — A STAINED GLASS WINDOW, A POST-MODERN PATTERN

BLOOD RED SILK LINING TO REMIND US OF HIS SACRIFICE

GOLD CORD + TASSELS TO ADD WEIGHT + A TOUCH OF POMP.

PALEST SKY-BLUE HEAVY SILK-LINEN W/ SLIGHT PADDING AS INTER-LINING

NO FEET SHOWING — "FLOATING" IN WHITE UNDER-GARMENT

IN THIS ONE WEEK HE MUST MAKE A STRONG + QUICK IMPRESSION. WE MUST BE ABLE TO SPOT HIM IN AN INSTANT + KNOW THAT WE HAVE SEEN HIM. HE MUST STAND OUT IN A CROWD.

IT HAS BEEN PROPHESIED THAT J.C. WILL COME BACK IN GARMENTS OF RED. I MUST STRONGLY URGE HIM TO FORGET THIS IDEA — IT IS THE WORST — THE CONNOTATIONS ARE TOO VIOLENT, TOO DEVILISH FOR US

■ TELEVISION COMMERCIAL ■

ASSIGNMENT: Develop a storyboard for a one-minute television commercial to announce the Second Coming of Jesus Christ. CONSULTANTS: Phyllis K. Robinson (creative director) is president of her own advertising- and marketing-strategy firm and a

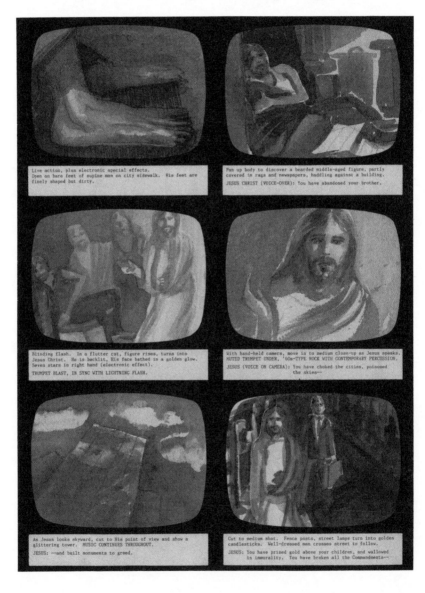

Live action, plus electronic special effects. Open on bare feet of supine man on city sidewalk. His feet are finely shaped but dirty.

Pan up body to discover a bearded middle-aged figure, partly covered in rags and newspapers, huddling against a building. JESUS CHRIST (VOICE-OVER): You have abandoned your brother.

Blinding flash. In a flutter cut, figure rises, turns into Jesus Christ. He is backlit. His face bathed in a golden glow. Seven stars in right hand (electronic effect). TRUMPET BLAST, IN SYNC WITH LIGHTNING FLASH.

With hand-held camera, move in to medium close-up as Jesus speaks. MUTED TRUMPET UNDER, '60s-TYPE ROCK WITH CONTEMPORARY PERCUSSION. JESUS (VOICE ON CAMERA): You have choked the cities, poisoned the skies—

As Jesus looks skyward, cut to His point of view and show a glittering tower. MUSIC CONTINUES THROUGHOUT. JESUS: —and built monuments to greed.

Cut to medium shot. Fence posts, street lamps turn into golden candlesticks. Well-dressed man crosses street to follow. JESUS: You have prized gold above your children, and wallowed in immorality. You have broken all the Commandments—

member of the Copywriters Hall of Fame. Michelle Farnum (illustrator) is senior vice president and associate creative director at DDB Needham.

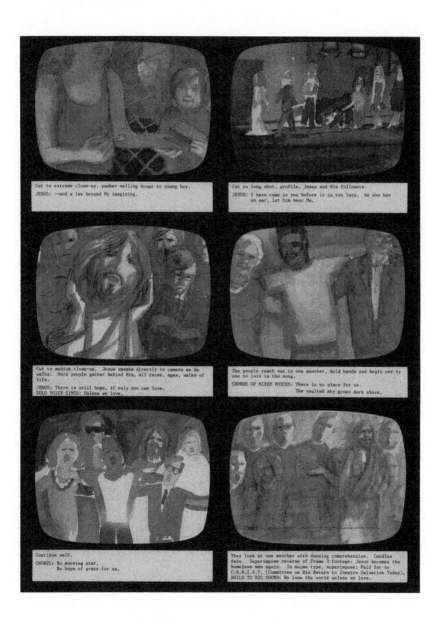

Manufacturing the Next President

Only a half century ago the stage of a presidential campaign was as big as the country itself. Speeches rang out against the backdrops of open sky, small towns, mountain ridges, and railroad depots. Today the stage measures the few inches of a television screen. In this miniature arena, our political giants feint and parry for thirty seconds of good exposure. And offhand remarks as banal as Ronald Reagan's "I paid for this microphone" and Walter Mondale's "Where's the beef?" are elevated to the status of oratory.

Every four years the campaigns are further distilled into television extract and squeezed onto the minimalist proscenia of Iowa and New Hampshire. The candidates surround themselves with the impresarios of the contemporary political theater—strategists, pollsters, and media consultants, who dress them in the costumes of wisdom and power.

Anticipating a fierce television campaign during the 1988 race, *Harper's Magazine* asked several adepts in the political arts to simulate the process of the Democratic nomination. Improvising a series of scenes, the participants carried the logic of their strategies through Iowa, New Hampshire, and the South to next summer's convention.

The following forum is based on a discussion held at the National Press Club in Washington, D.C. Lesley Stahl served as moderator.

LESLEY STAHL
is senior White House correspondent for CBS News and moderator of Face the Nation.

ROBERT BECKEL
was the campaign manager for Walter Mondale in 1984. He is a political analyst and president of Robert Beckel and Associates, a public-affairs firm, in Washington, D.C.

RON BROWN
is the chairman of the Democratic National Committee. He is a partner in the law firm Patton, Boggs, and Blow in Washington, D.C.

HARRISON HICKMAN
is a partner in the polling firm of Hickman-Maslin Research in Washington, D.C.

RAYMOND STROTHER
was the media consultant to Gary Hart in 1984 and 1987. He is president of Raymond Strother Ltd., a political-consulting firm, in Washington, D.C.

Iowa: Breaking Out

LESLEY STAHL: It's January 15, 1988, one month before the Iowa caucuses, when roughly 100,000 Democrats will turn out. The polls confirm that it's a race between Dick Gephardt and Mike Dukakis, although support for both is soft. Jesse Jackson has a nice chunk of votes, and all the others are bunched at the bottom.

Harrison Hickman, you are Paul Simon's strategist; he comes to you and says, "Look, Harrison, I'm an asterisk. I have 4 percent of the vote. You gave me this bow-tie strategy. Thanks to you, I have more bow ties that Imelda Marcos has shoes. I've got one month to go. Harrison, how do we get this campaign off the ground?"

HARRISON HICKMAN: Start with your strength. Draw out the differences on fundamental Democratic issues between you and, in this case, Gephardt.

Simon should go to, say, a school in Iowa and talk about his nearly perfect voting record on education. Then mention that Gephardt voted for tuition tax credits for private schools and later changed his position.

STAHL: Aren't you concerned about how a show of liberalism will play in the South? What will you tell Simon?

HICKMAN: I'd say, "Paul, you're not going to create any problems in the South you don't have anyway. Besides, you don't get to play in the finals if you don't win the semifinals. Just to keep the campaign alive you have to break through in Iowa. The best way to break through is to preach the old-time Democratic gospel to these caucus attendees."

STAHL: Bob Beckel, you're on the Paul Simon campaign, too. What is your advice?

ROBERT BECKEL: I'd say, "Paul, we've got to change the dynamic here. Our polls show Dukakis and Gephardt jockeying for first. They're going to do what people at the top notoriously do: Be careful.

"So, Paul don't be cautious—sound tough. But be careful because Paul Simon suddenly sounding tough would be like Truman Capote suddenly sounding like John Wayne.

"It's time to take a page out of George McGovern's book. At the time of the last debate in Iowa during the 1984 presidential campaign, McGovern had only 3 or 4 percent of the Iowa polls. Then standing on a stage flanked by Mondale and Hart, he looked directly into the audience and said, 'Now, look, you people here in Iowa. You remember your traditions. You remember your liberal roots. Don't throw away your *conscience.*'

"McGovern went from three to ten points overnight. So, play a hard populist appeal: Go left and challenge them on the basis of conscience."

STAHL: Ray Strother, what's your advice to Simon?

RAYMOND STROTHER: When I was with Hart, we faced the same problem. We marshaled all our resources. We pulled out of every place except the three major cities in Iowa. We made an intense effort to generate something that would come close to second place.

Since no one thought we could do it or was paying any attention, the expectation level never got very high. So no matter what we did, we accomplished something. And Hart came in second in Iowa. It was not done with media particularly, but with organization, with footwork, with knocking on doors—all those sweaty things one must do to win these ridiculous races.

Simon should raise the expectation level of the two front-runners. Cast them as *giants*, impossible to overtake. Try to characterize Dukakis as a candidate with an easy 38 percent. So, when he falls short, the media will do you the favor of declaring him a loser. Then start talking about New Hampshire the same way. Inflate the expectation to

58 or 62 percent, and you can virtually drive Dukakis out of the race if he doesn't get it.

STAHL: Ron Brown, you're on the Simon campaign and your polls reveal that many of Jackson's supporters list Simon as their second choice. Your pollster urges you to persuade these voters that a Jackson vote is a wasted vote. What's your strategy?

RON BROWN: Simon has to do it, but it's dangerous. I would suggest a nonattack strategy, touting Simon's liberal progressive Democratic history. He must make the Iowa caucus a battle for the soul of the Democratic Party.

He must concentrate on a "progressive" approach, arguing that he is the only candidate who can carry that message through the November election to the White House.

STAHL: Bob Beckel, you're Dukakis's adviser. The other campaigns have mounted negative campaigns. In every debate Dukakis is ganged up on, except by Simon, who's inching up in the polls. What do you do?

BECKEL: First, we decide whether Simon's new voters are coming out of our hide or out of somebody else's. If they're coming out of somebody else's hide, we'll encourage it and say what a nice guy Paul Simon is. If they're coming out of our hide, we mount a counteroffensive.

If, as a front-runner, we get defensive, we're in serious trouble. It will erode our base. A lot of people believe Iowa caucus voters make up their minds three or four weeks before the actual vote. They're wrong. The Iowa caucus voter is very volatile. So we can't be defensive. But I would also tell Dukakis this:

"Mike, we started out being able to get away with coming in third in Iowa about six months ago. Then something funny happened around July and August of 1987. Suddenly these fools in the press began to dub us the front-runner, even though we had only 6 percent in the opinion polls.

"Like every good Republican, we've been trying to convince everybody else that Jesse Jackson is the front-runner. But nobody bought it. When we raised five million bucks—despite our 6 percent—we were crowned the front-runner. So we take on all the problems of a front-runner yet we have no voter base."

At the next debate, Dukakis should say, "You know, I've been sitting here taking these digs from all of you, except for my friend Paul Simon, who is showing a lot of sense. Paul has stuck to the issues. The rest of you have decided to boost your campaigns by attacking me. Well, the gloves are off. It's time to start talking issues. So, Dick, let's go back to your tax-cut vote for Ronald Reagan in 1981."

STAHL: Ray Strother, you're Albert Gore's man, and your campaign has decided to go negative, but Gore refuses. Let's hear you explain why he should.

STROTHER: I would start by asking Gore how much he likes the Senate, and how much would he enjoy spending the rest of his life there.

First, don't say "go negative," say "go contrastive." Second, his message should intimate: "I am not a typical Southern politician." Perhaps Gore should cast the other candidates as people of the *past*, whereas, he, because of his age, is the only candidate of the future. In essence he should adopt the Gary Hart message of 1984, and try to lump the others together because they're older.

BROWN: It would be a mistake for Gore to go negative this early. He is not expected to do well in Iowa. Gore should try to diminish the importance of Iowa. His message should look ahead to Super Tuesday and steer attention away from Iowa's results. To go supernegative in a state where it's unlikely he would do well anyway would be a mistake.

HICKMAN: Gore's going to have a problem diverting attention. Even though he might play down Iowa, the evening news will still lead with: "The winner today was . . ." Gore is still going to get just 1 or 2 percent. Realistically, he can't change the expectations.

He must go somewhere and win—whether it's New Hampshire or another early state. He has to prove he's a candidate who can win. I think the South is probably the only place where he has the chance.

BECKEL: This underscores the irony of the Super Tuesday problem that we Democrats have created for ourselves. It's a big fallacy that Southern politicians can say, "Forget what happens in Iowa and New Hampshire. Y'all wait down here now for the South's favorite son."

In creating Super Tuesday, the Southern legislators altered the historical primary dates so they can all get together. Why? To *moderate* the process and get us a good old conservative boy who could run in a general election. But it's going to backfire because the North will do the real elimination of the candidates. The South will simply ratify the Northern choice.

HICKMAN: Reubin Askew and Fritz Hollings got in that situation in 1984. Scoop Jackson had that problem in 1976. It's true: Candidates who don't win early, who don't play at the top, get eliminated.

STAHL: So what can Gore do?

HICKMAN: He can try to reshuffle the deck and shake up the votes. Try to get people to reconsider. But if he goes too negative in a multicandidate field—especially in presidential politics—he might shake too many apples off the tree. They'll fall, but many of them will fall into somebody else's yard.

If you're too negative, people say, "Yeah, Gore's right about Dukakis, but he's too negative. I'll vote for Simon or Gephardt or somebody else." It's very delicate. You must do it with a scalpel rather than with a butcher's knife.

BROWN: That's the danger of a real negative campaign: You run the risk of turning a long-shot candidacy into a no-shot candidacy.

BECKEL: You're going to have a no-shot candidacy *anyway*. If he ends up with 4 percent in Iowa, Gore can pack it up and go back to the foothills. If I were Al Gore, my strategy would be to end up fourth in both Iowa and New Hampshire.

I'd identify the two candidates right in front of me. If they are Babbitt and Simon, I'd contrast myself with them. I wouldn't go after Dukakis because—Harrison's right—the apples will fall in somebody else's yard. I'd chase the weakest guys, the two who are bunched nearest me. Go after them hard on a "contrastive" and pray for fourth place.

STROTHER: Contrary to what you said, Bob, Gore could plan his strategy around Super Tuesday. He could use Iowa as an *arena* to slug it out and to send a message to the rest of the country. You have to realize something about Southerners: They always want someone to send America a message. Gore should send a message that the conclusion of the Iowa caucus and the New Hampshire primary is not the end of the race. The real conclusion is weeks away—in the South on Super Tuesday.

Iowa: Riding the Pig

STAHL: You're still in Iowa, but you're not on television. You're on the phone, trying to seduce the "workhorses," those men and women who motivate delegates to turn out at the precinct houses on that cold February night.

Bob, you're with Dukakis, and you tell your candidate he must phone one particular workhorse every day. Let's say her name is Jamie Terrell. If her heart's in it, Terrell can get you twenty people to turn out.

Jamie Terrell is well educated and has a proven record. She is undecided but Gephardt is really working on her. Hanging in her kitchen is a chart chronicling the calls and visits from the candidates. She's a pig farmer and she collects porcelain pigs.

What do you want Dukakis to do to woo her into your camp? You be Mike and I'll be Jamie. Woo me. Bring me a porcelain pig.

BECKEL: "Jamie, I wouldn't want to insult your intelligence and ask you how the pigs are doing, but I'm here because you may be the most important person in my life right now—and that includes my wife. You've heard from all of us, and you're probably sick of seeing us here in your kitchen.

"We've talked about the issues. I'm for the small farmer; Gephardt is for the small farmer. I'm not here to take it away from anybody else, but I am here to tell you this: I'm going to win this race. I'm going to beat Gephardt in New Hampshire. Here are my polls. Jamie, this is what it comes down to. You're a smart person. You're a good politician. Come with me. I'm going to beat Gephardt here, and then I'm going to beat him in New Hampshire. He'll be dead by the time I get South. Jamie, come with a winner."

STAHL: Would you offer her a position at the convention, maybe secretary of defense?

BECKEL: The problem is I've already offered that job to at least twenty Southern congressmen.

STAHL: Ron, you're Gephardt's guy, and you know Dukakis has pressured Jamie with this "I'm going to win" strategy. You've also been working on Jamie. She has a whole cabinet of porcelain pigs just from you.

BROWN: I'd probably bring one more, and then play a different card: "Jamie, you know I've been here from the beginning. We've talked many times. These Johnny-come-latelies have been running in and out of your kitchen these last days. But where was I back in the summer of 1987? I was here in your kitchen—early."

STAHL: Ray, you have Gore call, and Jamie says, "You know, I really like you, Al. And I'm going to tell you something I haven't told the others. My people feel that there is not a *real* man in the race. We're having a pig festival up here this weekend. And we're going to have two contests: the rail splitting in the morning and the pig ride in the afternoon. I think if you participated in some of these contests, it would do you a lot of good."

STROTHER: "Sure, I'll be there. There's no doubt about that. However, I have a bad back so I can't ride the pig, but the rail splitting is a fabulous photo opportunity. I will be there."

STAHL: By the way, Al, what are you planning to wear?

STROTHER: "I'm going to wear my L.L. Bean jeans, my L.L. Bean plaid shirt, and just a little suntan lotion."

STAHL: Ron, is Jesse Jackson going to split the rail and ride the pig?

BROWN: He's going to be there in his well-worn overalls. He's not going to ride the pig, but he's going to split the rail.

STAHL: Why isn't he going to ride the pig?

BROWN: He is anxious to establish himself as a dignified, mainstream, nongroveling, unifying force in the Democratic Party.

STROTHER: You have to understand, we ride pigs because of the media, because of Lesley Stahl.

STAHL: Bob, Dukakis comes to you and he says, "You know, everybody's going to be up there at Jamie Terrell's pig festival. I really think I should ride the pig. I've got a friend who has a pig farm. He says if I could just practice for a couple of hours, I could learn how."

BECKEL: "Mike, let me remind you that it was only seven months ago that you came to Iowa and told these people to grow endive. I know you've come a long way since then, but I'm not sure you've made it to pig riding yet.

"You get on that pig and you know the picture the press is going to run. Not you staying on the pig, Mike, but you falling off the pig. Just imagine those L.L. Bean clothes with a whole mess of pig crap all over them and you lying there in a puddle. That's the picture they're going to see in the South. Then try to sell yourself to a Georgia farmer as someone who knows something about farming. Mike, stay off the pig."

STAHL: Harrison, does Simon wear his bow tie with his overalls? Do you let him ride?

HICKMAN: Quite frankly I don't think Paul Simon would even be there. While everyone else is riding the pig, he would visit the other key people who are undecided.

At this point in the race you figure out a way to get in a media story on the weekend. If not in the pig festival story, you can get in other media around Iowa.

Iowa: Louis Farrakhan Calls Jackson

STAHL: Ron, it's two days before the caucus, and you learn that Louis Farrakhan plans to endorse Jesse Jackson for President. Farrakhan promised Jackson that he wouldn't do that, but he feels he must. What do you do?

BROWN: As a strategist, I would try to keep Jackson out of it, but I'd try to stop a Farrakhan endorsement. I'd remind him of his pledges, and that if he wants Jackson to be a credible candidate, he will have to stay out.

I think Jackson's public position would be: "I discussed this matter with Minister Farrakhan early on. We had an agreement, and that agreement should not be breached. I cannot stop anyone from endorsing me. You certainly cannot make judgments about where I stand on the issues based on every individual who endorses me."

To the press I'd restate the world of difference between Jackson's positions and Farrakhan's. I would point out that various fringe political figures in this country have endorsed other candidates. Why isn't the press asking those candidates the same questions?

BECKEL: If I were Jackson's campaign manager, I'd say, "Here is an opportunity to get rid of this ghost. Stand up and make it clear once and for all. Farrakhan, you're done, finished. I don't want your support." And then I'd jump in my car and roll out of there as fast as I could.

STAHL: What about the other candidates?

STROTHER: We have to do what we were afraid to do last time—engage Jackson directly. Somehow we thought it was better to ignore him. But Jackson should not be spared criticism of his bad ideas, including a weak rejection of

Farrakhan. Jackson has to deal with that as much as Paul Simon would if Ed Vrdolyak of Chicago endorsed him. It's a fact of life.

STAHL: What do you tell Gore to do about it?

STROTHER: I would have Gore publicly ask Jesse Jackson to renounce Farrakhan.

HARRISON: I can't ask Simon to do that because Simon is competing with Jackson over who's going to be the party's conscience. If Jackson doesn't deliver a ringing denouncement of Farrakhan, I'm going to suggest Simon do two things.

First, let's tackle this issue of extremists in American politics and bring it into the open. Second, let's get on the phone with liberal fund-raisers who are especially sensitive to this issue to insure they understand just *who* is willing to stand up for the principles they believe in.

BECKEL: I would tell Dukakis that there's a bigger problem here. It's a *black* problem and it's huge. At the center is the candidacy of Jesse Jackson.

The problem with candidates such as Dukakis, Simon, Gephardt, Gore, and Babbitt is that none has a history in the black community. Mondale, for all his faults, was someone the black community could look to and remember: "Here's a man who fought with us during the civil-rights movement."

All these candidates are babes in the woods. They have no black support and that's the dilemma. If the Democrats are going to win any Southern states in the *general election*—and we've got to or we're not going to have a Democratic president—then we must have a large black turnout. But we need to win back the moderate white vote as well.

The intriguing part is to create a strategy that unites these two groups. What's really intriguing is that there isn't one. That is the problem the Democrats face and nobody is willing to talk about it. Nobody wants to talk about it because it's "The Black Problem," and Jesse Jackson—the man and the candidate—makes it an even larger problem.

New Hampshire: A Downpour of Money

STAHL: The Iowa caucus is over. It's Tuesday morning. Here are the results:

Gephardt	30%
Simon	20%
Dukakis	20%
Jackson	10%

The others are bunched at the bottom. The big story is that insurgent Paul Simon has come from nowhere. All of a sudden someone is winning. He's like Hart in '84, or like Carter in '76.

Simon was bleeding for funds, now suddenly he has $100,000 to spend in New Hampshire. But he has already spent within $2,000 of the New Hampshire ceiling allowed by the Federal Elections Commission. What do you do, Harrison?

HICKMAN: That's easy. I spend it anyway.

STAHL: But the law says you can't spend it.

HICKMAN: No, no, the law says if you get caught spending it you've got a real problem. There are ways to hide it.

First, it's going to be well into April or May before anybody—especially at the FEC—figures out we've exceeded the limit. Right now, I've found this wave out in the ocean. I'm going to climb on my surfboard and ride it. If I get caught later, I'll take my lumps then.

STAHL: You spend whatever you get.

HICKMAN: Absolutely.

STAHL: Ron, how do you spend it?

BROWN: One of your spending problems can be solved, at least partially, by spending money in *Massachusetts* media that play in New Hampshire as well.

HICKMAN: That's right. Simon can now occupy Gary Hart's position as the novelty candidate in New Hampshire. So follow Hart's '84 path. Buy Boston media but pour every ounce of energy and effort you can into New Hampshire. This is a chance for a real kill.

STROTHER: I'd say, "Senator Simon, you don't need the money right now. You've managed a miracle. You've come much closer than anyone expected. You're on the cover of *Time* and *Newsweek*. CBS is covering you every morning, every afternoon. You don't need the money now.

"Take the money and go South. Paid media can only jump-start a presidential campaign: they can't carry a campaign. So save your money.

"You have some wonderful new friends—the media—and they're going to do all the work for you. But be careful, because the media will be your friend only a few weeks—until they find a few flaws. Then you'll need the money."

HICKMAN: I disagree. I'd continue to spend money in New Hampshire. In a presidential campaign the next event is always the most important event.

STROTHER: It doesn't matter, Harrison. The media spigot doesn't get shut off in four days. It goes on and on. It will sweep you right into the South as it swept Hart in 1984.

STAHL: Ron, is all this illegal spending done because the FEC doesn't enforce the rules?

BROWN: It's not a question of lack of enforcement, but the *timeliness* of enforcement. They can't catch up with the expenditures until well after they've been spent.

BECKEL: In 1984 the limit in New Hampshire was $404,000. We, the Mondale campaign, spent $2.85 million.

STAHL: Were you penalized?

BECKEL: Yes, it was about a $400,000 fine. It wasn't a lot, and that's the whole point. You think George Bush has a wimp problem? The FEC is not one of the great enforcement agencies of modern politics. Face it, this is politics and you're going to take advantage of every loophole.

STAHL: Bob, Dukakis was supposed to win big in Iowa, but the press says Simon, who came in second, is the big winner. Now you are being played as the big loser. What do you say to Dukakis?

BECKEL: I say, "This is a huge dilemma we find ourselves in here. Let me tell you, Duke, I've been here before, and it ain't fun.

"Remember what happened to Mondale in New Hampshire in 1984? His voter base stood firm while Cranston, Hollings, Askew, Glenn, and the others fells apart. *Everyone else* collapsed around Mondale, and Hart absorbed that vote.

"But this is not a two-man race, so we can't allow any of the other guys to dominate. You've got a base in this state of, say, 34 percent. Let's figure out who—Gephardt or Simon—is on fire more, and let's take our money and take him on.

"Don't make the mistake Mondale made, which was to sit back and let Hart take off like a hula-hoop craze. Don't sit back while a lot of wimps say we shouldn't take him on for three weeks. Let's jump into the fray now and stop his free ride."

New Hampshire: A Scandal Breaks

STAHL: You're at your hotel in New Hampshire. The primary is just five days away, and your candidate says, "There's something I've been meaning to tell you. You know my résumé says I resigned my first job as assistant D.A. The truth is I was fired for padding my expense account. The D.A. pitied me and allowed me to resign. Yesterday I heard that the D.A.'s brother is working for one of the other candidates, and I'm worried. Harrison, what do you think we should do?"

HICKMAN: This is when being from Chicago may come in very handy. But my first reaction would be to curse.

We have to scope this thing out without tipping anybody off. First thing is to get a sense of the hostility level of the former D.A. and his brother.

STAHL: You can't find out anything, and you don't even know where the D.A. is.

HICKMAN: Then I'm going to think of the best possible explanation, have it ready, and pray this doesn't come out.

STAHL: Does anybody think he should preempt it?

STROTHER: No. Better to stonewall it and wait to see if it breaks. Often we're told of imminent disasters that are going to break in the next morning's newspaper that never break.

I'd be very cautious. I'd get my answer ready. When it did break, I'd call a press conference and say, "Fellows, I made a mistake and here it is. I was young, I was inexperienced, I made a mistake."

BECKEL: There's a cardinal rule in presidential politics: You don't create your own crisis. You've got enough crises already. A successfully managed crisis is limited to about four news cycles [a news cycle runs from the morning newspaper to the television evening news]. If it goes to six or eight news cycles, you're in serious trouble. What you *don't* want is to create it yourself. I'd figure out who the fall guy is, figure out who's to be pardoned, and then blame the campaign manager, as usual.

STROTHER: Or the media consultant.

STAHL: Ron, you're on the other side, working for the campaign where the D.A.'s brother works, and he tells you the story. He's got some documents to back it up. What do you do with that?

BROWN: It depends which candidate it's on, where he stands in the polls, and whether he's a threat.

STAHL: Say you're Gephardt's campaign manager and the story is on Simon.

BROWN: I'd leak it.

STAHL: Who would you leak it to?

BROWN: Some of my friends in the media who I talk to every night.

HICKMAN: Say he leaks it to you, Lesley. The first thing you're going to do is call me, the campaign manager of the aggrieved candidate and say, "What's going on here?"

I would give this story to an opposition newspaper, such as the Manchester *Union Leader*, so that I can direct my fire at such a conservative publication. Now I can diminish the credibility of the story because one source is the *Union Leader*.

BECKEL: It's a tough call. The day after Hart beat Mondale in New Hampshire, we got a flood of documents and anonymous calls and letters about Hart. I still have that file.

STAHL: Hmmm.

BECKEL: We had to make a decision. We never took it to Mondale.

STAHL: Supplying the boss with "plausible deniability"?

BECKEL: We'd never get him involved. The problem for the campaign manager is that Hart's taken off and suddenly we've got this stuff on him. And it's scurrilous stuff. Do we try to get it out?

Do I say, because I'm such a morally decent guy, "Oh, no, it would be wrong"? Of course not. I'm a campaign manager. I've got to decide what is in the best interest of my campaign.

The only time we would have smeared Hart was after we decided there was absolutely no other way to stop him. It's extremely dangerous. And my instincts are: If I leak this, it's going to be known that I leaked it. That will become a story in itself, and then I've got my own scandal on my hands.

BROWN: Bob, there are ways to leak a story without it being traced. You have enough media relationships that you could safely leak the story.

But if the scenario described was, say, a sexual indiscretion, it would be different.

STAHL: Say the story is about an affair then. The woman involved gives her story to *People* magazine.

STROTHER: I've just gone through this with Hart so I've thought about it a lot. It doesn't matter if it's a rumored story or whether it's in *People*. It depends on whether documentation exists, like pictures of the woman sitting on your lap or a videotape of y'all walking together outside your townhouse.

Until a sex scandal is proved beyond doubt, people are forgiving. Polls indicate that half the people in this country have committed adultery. So I think people are pretty forgiving about that. If there's no picture, I wouldn't even talk about it.

BROWN: If there is no proof, you don't have to do anything because it won't last.

BECKEL: I disagree. If there's any truth to the story, with or without documentation, I'd own up to it because I don't think it will go away. You'll be asked about it and asked about it, unless you own up to it. Incidentally, Dick Celeste did this, when he was considering running for president, and I thought he handled it pretty well because he brought his family into it right away.

STAHL: Bring the wife on television?

BECKEL: Yes, surrounded by your family you say, "Did I do it? Yes. Was it wrong? Yes. Am I going to answer any more questions about it? No." That's all I'd say.

The problem is that everybody tries to explain these things. I'd limit myself to "yes" and "no" answers. The press is going pretty far to ask you what *happened* during the affair. If it gets that kinky, the guy's in serious trouble.

HICKMAN: It depends on who it is and what the expectations are. I think Dukakis and Simon could probably escape it because I think they have a strong enough image to fight it. Other candidates suffer being "under suspicion" by the press. So when a particular suspicion is confirmed, the press bores in. If the suspicion was not already there, I think your image can withstand the assault.

Super Tuesday: The Black Vote

STAHL: We move down South. Ron, on the day you move down there, several black mayors hold a news conference. They say the man to lead America is not Jesse Jackson but Mike Dukakis. What is Jackson's strategy?

BROWN: He says he has taken his campaign to the people—not the mayors—from the beginning. It's not surprising that the political leadership doesn't support him.

It's not devastating at all. As Bob said, in 1984 you had a Walter Mondale whose civil-rights record gave him a legitimate claim to the black vote. You have no one with that strength now.

Jackson's candidacy will attract a much larger percentage of black voters this year than it did in 1984. As I recall, Jackson split the black vote evenly with Mondale in the early primaries. But toward the end Jackson got 70, even 80, percent of the vote in some places. This year Jackson will start off that high.

STAHL: Bob, do you think Jackson is going to get the black vote, period?

BECKEL: That's right.

STAHL: So you have to get the white vote.

BECKEL: That's right. These campaigns are all paying lip service to blacks. They've hired blacks on their staff, but they're not going to spend any time in the black community except to establish the *perception* that they're there.

There is no shaking Jackson's hold on the black vote. So you've go to fight in the South for white votes on Super Tuesday.

If I'm Dukakis, I pull back, pick two states I think I can do well in, and give up all the rest. Then expectations will come down. I'll go after, say, Alabama and North Carolina, and hope I'm still in it after Super Tuesday.

BROWN: The beauty of it, from the Jackson perspective, is he's the black candidate without having to run as the black candidate.

BECKEL: That's right, but for Jackson to get the turnout figures he got in '84, he's going to have to go home to his base—the black vote—and campaign hard.

His strategy centers on holding the black vote on Super Tuesday. Since one out of three Democratic primary voters in the South is black, Jackson can get 33 percent of the vote. His prayer is that the other three each get 22 percent and he comes out the winner.

STAHL: Ray, Gore's pollster comes to you and says, "Your only chance is to attack Jackson. It's the only prayer you have." The candidate doesn't want to do this. What do you tell him?

STROTHER: I'd tell him to look at Jesse Jackson not as a black candidate but simply as a candidate. I would even suggest to Albert Gore that he make this a two-man race. Make it an Al Gore versus Jesse Jackson.

STAHL: Are you going to stand strictly on the issues? What about the old Southern strategy of subtly tapping the old racism just beneath the surface? What about having Gore use the old code words: "welfare," "family," "traditional values"?

STROTHER: No. To be honest, I think those days are gone.

HICKMAN: You don't need code words here. With just a black-and-white TV you can figure it out if you're a Southern conservative. Any candidate who waits to attack Jackson until then has a big problem. Somebody who's perceived to have a Super Tuesday Southern strategy that includes attacking Jackson hard in order to pick up white votes will get caught.

News coverage nowadays is much more sophisticated about strategy and tactics. The real story will be a "character" story about a candidate who is creating differences for raw political advantage.

STROTHER: In the very beginning of this race, I said that Al Gore should use Iowa and New Hampshire as an arena. If he waits to engage Jackson, I agree, he's an opportunist and he appears a bit racist. But knowing that it's going to come to a showdown in the South between a white Southerner and a black Southerner, the earlier you start the dialogue the better.

BECKEL: Every candidate already has an anti-Jackson strategy—in their heads, if not actually on paper. No matter what it is, you had better do it early on and consistently because it's going to appear overtly racist to do it by the time you get to the South.

But I have a different strategy. I think you get a hell of a lot more votes by attacking Jackson in *New York* than you will attacking him in Mississippi. There's this notion that somewhere in the South a huge redneck vote is poised to descend on the Democratic primaries.

If you beat up on Jackson, so the thinking goes, all these conservatives from Tallahassee are going to run to the polls. But most of those voters are now Republicans. Look at the profile of the white Democratic voter in the South. These people are not a group of racists waiting to see who's going to be the toughest on Jackson.

BROWN: The strategists who pushed through Super Tuesday forgot *who* voted in Southern primaries. The folks they were looking for—conservative Democrats—don't vote in primaries, and possibly not at all. The Jackson campaign would like to be challenged on the issues because Jackson doesn't want to be peripheral. The way you are accepted as a serious candidate is if other candidates treat you as a serious candidate. All of these so-called moderate Southern Democratic strategies have an unintended consequence: They ultimately help Jackson.

STAHL: Are any of you thinking about the general election? Are you wooing Jackson to your side?

HICKMAN: I think someone like Paul Simon will woo him publicly. Simon, as the conscience of the Democratic Party, has to be seen *defending* Jackson at some critical point. He may attack him on the Farrakhan thing, but when a Gore or Gephardt takes him on, I think Simon might well have to defend him and say, "This is racism."

He has to turn up the heat to attract some of the liberal progressive vote. If he doesn't get that in the South, he has nothing in the South.

STAHL: What about some of the white candidates getting together in a back room and dividing up the South in order to stop Jackson?

STROTHER: No, we can't trust the other candidates.

BECKEL: I wouldn't believe what Strother told me five minutes after he walked out of the room.

But all this centers around Jackson again: There's not one candidate who doesn't wish Jackson wasn't in this race, including most of the Democratic leaders. Everybody says, "Isn't it nice Jackson's here?" The fact is everybody wishes Jackson would go away. The problem is that he won't. Jackson is the only candidate with a proven constituency. He is the only guy who can book hotel rooms in Atlanta for the convention and be sure he's going to be there to take them.

If I were Dukakis, I'd go to Jackson and say, "Jesse, I respect you. I may not like you, but I respect you. I'm going to fight with you. I'm going to take my shots at you wherever I can. But I want to keep this line of dialogue open. With Mondale, you could get away with running all over him because nobody thought Mondale could win. But this time we can win, and Jesse, I *need* you to win. We need black votes to win. But if the Democrats lose because you're being bad, the loss will be around your neck, friend, not mine. So let's cut this deal now."

STAHL: Do you offer him anything right then and there?

BECKEL: No, no, no.

HICKMAN: It's against the law.

BECKEL: That shouldn't hold you back.

STAHL: Suddenly it's against the law?

HICKMAN: I think what Jackson has just been offered is the most any candidate could expect: to be treated like a real presidential candidate—somebody who deserves respect.

Super Tuesday: A Surprise Candidate

STAHL: Ray Strother, you don't have a candidate anymore.

STROTHER: This has happened before.

STAHL: Actually, you haven't had one for the whole campaign. It's the day after Super Tuesday, and Jackson and two other candidates survive. In short, nobody won. The tabloids shout, *Seven Dwarfs Down, Three Stooges to Go.* The discontent is contagious and "Draft Bill Bradley" organizations have cropped up in most of the remaining states.

Bradley calls you on the phone, Ray. He tells you Paul Kirk, Bob Strauss, Ted Kennedy, even Mario Cuomo want him to run. The polls show that the people want him to run. He asks you if it's possible.

STROTHER: It's reminiscent of Scoop Jackson in 1976. Everyone told Scoop Jackson to get in and the world would beat a path to his door. It didn't.

You can get in late but you will need a national agenda with a purely national campaign.

BROWN: What you need is an extraordinary media candidate to do it and Bill Bradley is not one. One major problem is that many of the delegates are already committed.

STAHL: But some candidates have dropped out, and their delegates are no longer committed. They are floating around. Some of them have said, "We want Bill Bradley."

BROWN: Those who have dropped out have very few delegates. Those who are in have a lot of delegates. Once you pass Super Tuesday, it becomes increasingly more difficult.

STAHL: Harrison, what would be your advice to Bradley?

HICKMAN: I'd suggest he be Mario Cuomo's campaign manager.

STAHL: Would Cuomo make it different?

HICKMAN: He's much better known and has a much greater presence. You're going to run basically three strategies right now.

First, you need to get a current fix on any deadlines still open for you to get your name on a ballot. You need to try to win some delegates in those states.

Second, you're going to run a strategy to pick up delegates who are already committed to somebody else. You'll need the help of a good delegate counter and every politician you can muster.

Third, you're going to run a national media strategy to generate a grass-roots expectation that Cuomo may be the one guy who can win. This will make it easier to pull off the first two.

BROWN: I think Mario Cuomo is the only candidate who could pull it off after Super Tuesday. There's a base there and an image that he's a winner.

If the scenario holds, everybody will be desperately looking for a winner at that time. Everybody will be battered and bruised and bloody and broke. You do have all kinds of filing deadlines, plus delegate-selection and technical problems to overcome. But if, in fact, you blow them out in New York, Pennsylvania, and Ohio, and you go to California on June 7 and win big there, then you go to the convention with a chance.

BECKEL: If I were on Cuomo's side, I'd go to the second-place candidate and offer him the vice presidency and pick up his slates. That's the only way I can imagine it being done.

STAHL: Bob, as Dukakis's man, what do you do to stop Cuomo?

BECKEL: First, I assume the delegates I've earned by that point are mine. Realize that these delegates are your cousins, uncles, aunts, and assorted convicted felons and you've got their rap sheets. You are their parole officer. Those people *aren't* going to bolt. The myth that somehow you can shake loose committed delegates is silly.

If I'm Dukakis, I would go the second-place candidate, say, Gephardt, and say: "I'm number one; Dick, you're number two. Neither of us can get a majority of delegates if Cuomo starts to build momentum.

"The only way to stop this is to shake up the dynamic as much as it was shaken by Cuomo getting in. You accept the vice presidency, and we'll combine as a ticket. We'll combine our delegates and we'll stop Cuomo dead in the water."

Then we mount attacks on Cuomo as a Johnny-come-lately who didn't have the guts to face the American people with the rest of us. And we ask, "Why did you get in so late, Mario? Was there something you had to hide?"

STAHL: Ray, would you accept that deal if you were with Gephardt? Would you come on as vice president?

STROTHER: At that point probably so. I am marveling at Bob's impressive strategy.

STAHL: Ray, what does your anti-Cuomo media campaign look like?

STROTHER: I'd reduce Cuomo to a regional candidate. In my commercial, I'd have a map of America behind Dukakis and Gephardt, and I'd have New York as a little tiny place up in the corner. The voice-over would say, "You know me and you know my running mate who's from America's heartland. Our opponent—Mario Cuomo—is the guy from New York." Talk about code words. "New York" is an incredible code word.

HICKMAN: Cuomo will have to understand that a guerrilla war is about to break out; they will be firing heavy artillery at him. Cuomo should counter by getting on the air and dominating the interpretation of his quest. That's the secret to a late campaign: Direct communication with the American people.

STROTHER: My next commercial would say: "Until now, the insiders and the big money have felt shut out of the system. So now they have a candidate. He's from New York. Right now this campaign hinges on whether to hand over this country to the special interests and the insiders, or whether it belongs to us, the people."

HICKMAN: The problem with that, Ray, is what happens after America stops laughing at Dick Gephardt for accusing someone *else* of pandering. Cuomo's big advantage is that he's not scarred by this process like the other candidates.

Beckel hit on the most damaging strategy, which is not a specific charge but just an insinuation: "Mario, what have you got to hide?"

A Backward Look

STAHL: For the last several hours, you've been telling candidates what to do. What would you tell the American people about the system that creates their presidential nominees?

HICKMAN: There's nothing wrong with candidates convincing voters to support them. That's democracy. The problem is not Iowa and New Hampshire but that it's the same two states.

The caucus and primary are big industries for these states, and the voters there have become increasingly cynical. As far as having small states at the beginning—where you give a Jimmy Carter or a Gary Hart or a Dick Gephardt an opportunity to break out—it's a good system.

BECKEL: We're now facing the most dangerous selection process in the history of this country for either party. In the name of democracy, it has gotten completely out of hand.

This all came out of the reform movement after the 1968 election. It began as a supposedly pious movement to involve the people. Let's face it: The reform movement was a deliberate attempt to orchestrate a nomination. It worked.

We eliminated "brokers," because they supposedly have a bad name, and allowed a lot of people into the process. More importantly, we allowed the states to dictate the rules.

Worst of all, the winner of this brutal race emerges seriously compromised. These primaries don't enhance a candidate. They mold the public's opinion of a candidate and almost always mold it negatively. What I'm saying is we have no checks and balances in this system.

One of these candidates could explode out of New Hampshire, win big on Super Tuesday, and then three weeks later we could find out the new candidate has a serious problem.

This system has got to be overhauled, and we have to get this word "democracy" out of the way. We have to get back to selecting delegates in a rational way that gets us our best nominee with the least amount of fighting.

BROWN: I remember when the Hunt Commission wrote the rules for the 1984 election. Bob and I were on different sides then because everybody assumed the two candidates would be Mondale and Kennedy. We each tried to craft the rules that would help our candidate.

It is ridiculous for Iowa and New Hampshire to play the role they play—not because they're small states, but because they're really not representative of the American electorate. Every four years we make these same complaints, wring our hands, and make some modest attempt to change the rules. But we never go to the core problem, which is money and calendar.

STROTHER: The nomination process not only demeans the candidate, it demeans the presidency. We anguish over the lack of power and leadership of the presidency, yet we're contributing to it.

We force a man or woman to run for president of the United States as though he were a city-council candidate in Dubuque. There's really no difference.

This is the most important office on earth. The race for it should be nobler and larger. Then the person elected would be empowered to direct the policy of this country.

History is moved by momentous events and by people with great courage. Jimmy Carter made history in 1976 by writing his own rules, and we're still playing by them. But sooner or later we're going to have a candidate who says the process stinks. And this candidate will not play the state-by-state game.

He might announce his candidacy outside Iowa, bang his drum loudly, and say, "We've trivialized the presidency and done great damage to democracy. My candidacy is national, and I intend to run my campaign without once stepping foot inside Iowa or New Hampshire."

IV

Listening at the Margins

The trajectory of a new idea traced backward to its origins often winds up at the edge of polite society, among those most often dismissed as the lunatic fringe. When the mass media condescends to invite one of these cranks to present his thought, the etiquette of modern journalism (a.k.a. the standards of objectivity) requires that he be accompanied and surrounded by a phalanx of acceptable opinion. But sometimes it is worthwhile to hear them out—to discover what is incubating at the margins. In the past, *Harper's Magazine* has sat down with those deemed beyond the pale and turned on its tape recorder to hear the rage of Los Angeles gangs, the constitutional musings of animal rights advocates, or the arguments of computer hackers about electronic privacy.

To be sure, the lunatic fringe is mainly populated by lunatics. But it is important to search for those worth hearing. Consider that only a few years ago it was considered unpatriotic to discuss the withdrawal of American troops overseas. Now the Pentagon holds seminars to discuss the logistics of emptying Europe of an American presence. Consider the legalization of drugs—in 1985, the pipedream of potheads; for President Bush, a policy option. Or, think of Ronald Reagan in 1968. And again in 1980.

When You're a Crip (or a Blood)

The drive-by killing is the sometime sport and occasional initiation rite of city gangs. From the comfort of a passing car, the itinerant killer simply shoots down a member of a rival gang or an innocent bystander. Especially common among L.A.'s Bloods and Crips, the drive-by killing is the parable around which every telling of the gang story revolves. Beyond that lies a haze of images: million-dollar drug deals, ominous graffiti, and colorfully dressed marauders armed with Uzis. The sociologists tell us that gang culture is the flower on the vine of single-parent life in the ghetto, the logical result of society's indifference. It would be hard to write a morality play more likely to strike terror into the hearts of the middle class.

Many questions, though, go unasked. Who, really, are these people? What urges them to join gangs? What are their days like? To answer these questions, *Harper's Magazine* recently asked Léon Bing, a journalist who has established relations with the gangs, to convene a meeting between two Bloods and two Crips and to talk with them about the world in which the drive-by killing is an admirable act.

The following forum is based on a discussion held at the Kenyon Juvenile Justice Center in south central Los Angeles. Parole Officer Velma V. Stevens assisted in the arrangements. Léon Bing served as moderator.

LÉON BING
is a journalist living in Pasadena, California. She is the author of DO OR DIE: Voices from the Crips and Bloods.

LI'L MONSTER
was a member of the Eight-Trey Gangsters set of the Crips. He has served time for first-degree murder, four counts of attempted murder, and two counts of armed robbery.

RAT-NECK
was a member of the 107-Hoover Crips. He has served time for attempted murder, robbery with intent to commit grave bodily harm, assault and battery, burglary, and carrying concealed weapons.

TEE RODGERS
founded the first Los Angeles chapter of the Chicago-based Blackstone Rangers, affiliated with the Bloods. He is currently the resident "gangologist" and conflict specialist at Survival Education for Life and Family, Inc., and an actor and lecturer.

B-DOG
is a pseudonym for a twenty-three-year-old member of the Van Ness Gangsters set of the Bloods. After this forum was held, his telephone was disconnected, and he could not be located to supply biographical information.

186

Getting Jumped In

LÉON BING: Imagine that I'm a thirteen-year-old guy, and I want to get into a gang. How do I go about it? Am I the right age?

LI'L MONSTER: There's no age limit. It depends on your status coming into it. It's like, some people get jumped in, some people don't.

BING: Jumped in?

LI'L MONSTER: Beat up.

B-DOG: Either beat up or put some work in.

RAT-NECK: Put some work in, that's mandatory, you know, a little mis[misdemeanor]—small type of thing, you know. It's like this: say I get this guy comin' up and he says, "Hey, Cuz, I wanna be from the set." Then I'm like, "Well, what you *about*, man? I don't know you—you might be a punk." So I might send him somewhere, let him go and manipulate, send him out on a burg' or—

BING: —Is that a burglary?

LI'L MONSTER: Yeah. But then, you might know some person who's got a little juice, and, like, I might say, "You don't got to go through that, come on with me. You *from* the set."

TEE RODGERS: If you click with somebody that's already from a set, then you clicked up, or under his wing, you his protégé, and you get a ride in. Now, even though you get a ride in, there's gonna come a time when you got to stand alone and hold your own.

BING: Stand alone and hold your own? Does that mean I might have to steal a car or beat up somebody or commit a burglary?

187

RAT-NECK: Right.

BING: Is there another way?

RAT-NECK: You can be good from the shoulders.

LI'L MONSTER: Yeah. Fighting.

TEE: That's one of *the* best ways. A homeboy says:
I'm young and mean and my mind's more keen
And I've earned a rep with my hands
And I'm eager to compete with the bangers on the street
'Cause I've got ambitious plans.

LI'L MONSTER: See, when Tee was comin' up—he's *first* generation and we *second* generation. Now, if he saw me, he wouldn't be comin' from the pants pocket with a gat or a knife, he'd be comin' from his shoulders like a fighter. That's what it was established on. Then, later on, come a whole bunch of cowards that *can't* come from the shoulders, so they come from the pocket—

RAT-NECK: —he unloads!

BING: What's the most popular weaponry?

B-DOG: Whatever you get your hands on.

TEE: Keep in mind we don't have no target ranges and shit where we get prolific with these guns.

B-DOG: Shoot 'til you out of bullets, then back up.

RAT-NECK: Bullet ain't got no name, hit whatever it hit.

TEE: Wait a minute! That was a hell of a question, 'cause the mentality of the people that gonna read this be thinkin'—

LI'L MONSTER: —every gang member walks around with that type of gun—

TEE: —and I can hear the police chief saying, "That's why we need bazookas!" Look, put it on the record that everybody ain't got a motherfuckin' bazooka—or an Uzi. Okay?

BING: It's all on the record.

B-DOG: There *are* some people still believe in .22s.

TEE: Or ice picks. And don't forget the bat.

RAT-NECK: And the lock in the sock!

BING: Are there little peewees, say, nine- to ten-year-olds, in the sets?

RAT-NECK: Yeah, but we say "Li'l Loc" or "Li'l Homie" or "Baby Homie." We never use "peewee" because then people think you're a Mexican. Mexicans say "peewee."

TEE: If it's a Blood set, they use a *k* instead of a *c*. Li'l Lok with a *k*. See, Bloods don't say *c*'s and Crips don't say *b*'s. To a Blood, a cigarette is a "bigarette." And Crips don't say "because," they say "cecause."

BING: What prompted you to join, Li'l Monster?

LI'L MONSTER: Say we're white and we're rich. We're in high school and we been buddies since grammar school. And we all decide to go to the same *college*. Well, *we* all on the same street, all those years, and we all just decide to—

RAT-NECK: —join the gang.

TEE: What I think is formulating here is that human nature wants to be accepted. A human being gives less of a damn what he is accepted into. At that age—eleven to seventeen—all kids want to belong. They are un-people.

BING: If you move—can you join another set?

LI'L MONSTER: A couple weeks ago I was talking to a friend 'bout this guy—I'll call him "Iceman." He used to be from Eight-Trey, but he moved to Watts. Now he's a Bounty Hunter.

B-DOG: Boy, that stinks, you know?

BING: He went from the Crips to the Bloods?

LI'L MONSTER: Yeah. And he almost lost his life.

TEE: When you switch sets, when you go from Cuz to Blood, or Blood to Cuz, there's a jacket on you, and you are really pushed to prove yourself for that set. Sometimes the set approves it, and other time they cast you out. If you don't have loyalty to the *first* set you belong to, what the fuck makes us think you gonna be loyal to us? That's just too much *information*. Shit, we kickin' it, we hangin', bangin', and slangin'. But who the fuck are you, and where are you *really* at? Where your *heart* at?

B-DOG: Perpetrated is what he is!

BING: What does that mean?

TEE: A perpetrator is a fraud, a bullshitter.

BING: How can someone prove himself?

LI'L MONSTER: All right, like the cat Iceman. They might say, "To prove yourself as a Bounty Hunter you go hit somebody from Eight-Trey."

B-DOG: If you got that much love.

BING: Hit somebody from the very set he was in?

RAT-NECK: Yeah. Then his loyalty is there.

BING: But is it really? Wouldn't someone say, "Hey, he hit his homeboy, what's to say he won't hit us if he changes his mind again?"

TEE: Look, when he changes sets, he's already got a jacket on his ass. And when he goes back and takes somebody else out, that cuts all ties, all love.

B-DOG: Can't go to no 'hood. Can't go nowhere.

RAT-NECK: There it is.

TEE: The highest honor you can give for your set is death. When you die, when you go out in a blaze of glory, you are respected. When you kill for your set, you earn your stripes—you put work in.

RAT-NECK: But once you a Crip—no matter what—you can't get out. No matter what, woo-wah-wham, you still there. I can leave here for five years. Then I gets out of jail, I gets a new haircut, new everything. Then, "Hey, there goes Rat-Neck!" You can't hide your face. You can't hide nothin'! All that immunity stuff—that's trash. Nobody forgets you.

TEE: That's how it goes. Just like L.A.P.D.—once he retire and shit, that fool still the police! He's still strapped, carrying a gun. He's *always* a cop. Same with us. If you know the words, sing along: "When you're a Jet, you're a Jet all the way, from your first cigarette to your last dying day."

LI'L MONSTER: There you go.

Hangin', Bangin', Slangin'

BING: Once you're a Blood or a Crip, do you dress differently? We hear about guys with their jeans riding low, their underwear showing up top, wearing colors, and having a certain attitude.

TEE: See, a lot of that is media shit. A brother will get up, take his time, spray his hair, put his French braids in, fold his rag, press his Pendleton or his khaki top, put creases in his pants, lace his shoes, and hit the streets.

LI'L MONSTER: He's dressed to go get busy!

TEE: He's dressed, pressed, he's down!

BING: Is that the way you dress after you're in?

TEE: The reason a lot of brothers wear khaki and house slippers and shit like that is because it's cheap and comfortable.

B-DOG: Ain't no dress code nowadays.

LI'L MONSTER: Look, Rat-Neck got on a blue hat, I got on this hat, we Crips. B-Dog's a Blood: He got red stripes on his shoes, and *that* is that. Now I can be in the mall, look at his shoes, and know he's a Blood. He can look at *my* shoes— these B-K's I got on—and say, "He's a Crip."

RAT-NECK: But then again, might be none of that. Might just be ordinary guys.

BING: I've always thought that B-K stands for "Blood Killers" and that's why Crips wear them.

LI'L MONSTER: It stands for British Knights. I don't buy my clothes because they blue. My jacket and my car is red and white. I wear the colors I want to wear. I don't have no blue rag in my pocket. I don't have no blue rubber bands in my hair. But I can be walking down the street and, nine times out of ten, the police gonna hem me up, label me a gangbanger—

RAT-NECK: —or a dope dealer.

LI'L MONSTER: There's only one look that you got to have. Especially to the police. You got to look black. *That's* the look. Now B-Dog here's a Blood, and he doesn't even have to be gangbanging because if I'm in a mall with some of my homeboys, nine times out of ten we gonna look at him *crazy*. That's how you know. He don't have to have no red on, we gonna look at him crazy. *That's* the mentality.

TEE: Let me give up this, and you correct me if I'm wrong: police officers can recognize police officers, athletes can recognize athletes, gay people can recognize gay people. Well, we can recognize each other. It's simple.

BING: When someone insults you, what happens?

LI'L MONSTER: Depends on what he saying.

BING: Say he calls you "crab" or "E-ricket." Or, if you're a Blood, he calls you a "slob." These are fighting words, aren't they?

RAT-NECK: It's really just words. Words anybody use. But really, a lot of that word stuff don't get people going nowadays.

LI'L MONSTER: That's right.

TEE: There was a time when you could say something about somebody's mama, and you got to fight. Not so anymore.

LI'L MONSTER: Now just ignore the fool.

TEE: But if somebody say, "Fuck your dead homeboys," oh, *now* we got a problem.

LI'L MONSTER: Yeah, that's right.

TEE: Somebody call me "oo-lah" or "slob," fuck 'em. My rebuttal to that is "I'm a super lok-ed out Blood." There's always a cap back, see what I'm saying? But when you get down to the basics, like "Fuck your dead homeboy," and you *name* the homeboy, that is death. Oh man, we got to take *this* to the grave.

BING: Well, let's say you're with your homeboys and someone does say "Fuck you dead homeboys." What happens then?

B-DOG: That's it. The question of the matter is on, right there, *wherever* you at.

LI'L MONSTER: He's dead. And if he's not, he's gonna—

B-DOG: —wish he was.

BING: What does that mean?

TEE: I cannot believe the readers of this magazine are that naive. The point of the matter is, if he disrespects the dead homeboys, his ass is gonna get got. Period. Now let your imagination run free; Steven Spielberg does it.

BING: Why this intensity?

TEE: Because there's something called dedication that we got to get into—dedication to the gang mentality—and understanding where it's coming from. It's like this: there's this barrel, okay? All of us are in it together, and we all want the same thing. But some of us are not so highly motivated to be educated. So we have to get ours from the blood, the sweat, and the tears of the street. And if a homeboy rises up—and it is not so much jealousy as it is the fear of him *leaving* me—I want to come up *with* him, but when he reaches the top of the barrel, I grab him by the pants leg and I—

TEE AND LI'L MONSTER: —pull him back down.

TEE: It's not that I don't want to see you go home, but *take me with you!* As a man, I'm standing alone as an individual. But I can't say that to him! I got that manly pride that won't let me break down and say, "Man, I'm scared! Take me with you—I want to go with you!" Now, inside this barrel, we are in there so tight that every time we turn around we are smelling somebody's ass or somebody else's stinky breath. There's so many people, I got to leave my community to change my fuckin' mind!

RAT-NECK: Yeah!

TEE: That's how strong peer pressure is! It's that crab-in-the-barrel syndrome. We are just packed in this motherfucker, but I want to feel good. So how? By bustin' a nut. So I fuck my broad, she get pregnant, and now I got *another* baby. So we in there even tighter. In here, in this room, we can relax, we can kick it, we can laugh, we can say, "Well, shit—homeboy from Hoover's all right." Because we in a setting now, and nobody's saying, "FUCK HIM UP, BLOOD! FUCK HIS ASS! I DON'T LIKE HIM—*KICK* HIS ASS!" You know what I'm saying? That's *bullshit!* We can't just sit down and enjoy each other and say, "Are you a man? Do you wipe your ass like I wipe my ass? Do you cut? Do you bleed? Do you cry? Do you die?" There's nowhere where we can go and just experience each other as *people.* And then, when we *do* do that, everybody's strapped.

RAT-NECK: Seems like nothin' else . . .

BING: You make it sound inescapable. What would you tell someone coming along? What would you tell a younger brother?

RAT-NECK: I had a younger brother, fourteen years old. He's dead now, but we never did talk about it. He was a Blood and I am a Crip, and I *know* what time it is. I couldn't socialize with him on what he do. All he could do is ask me certain things, like, "Hey, bro, do you think I'm doing the right thing?" And, well, all I could say is, "Hey, man, choose what you wanna be. What can I do? I love you, but what do I look like, goin' to my mama, tellin' her I *smoked* you, *smoked* my brother? What I look like? But why should I neglect you because you from there? Can't do that. You my love." And if I don't give a fuck about my love, and I don't give a fuck about my brother, then I don't give a fuck about my mama. And then your ass out, when you don't give a fuck about your mama.

Like some people say, "I don't give a fuck, I'll *smoke* my mama!" Well, you know, that's stupidity shit.

BING: I realize that loyalty is paramount. But what I want to know is, if a rival set has it out for someone, does it always mean death?

LI'L MONSTER: Before anybody go shooting, it's going to be, "What is the problem?" Then we are going to find the root of the problem. "Do you personally have something against Eight-Trey?" You say, "No, I just don't like what one of your homeboys did." Then you all beat him up.

B-DOG: Beat him up, yeah.

LI'L MONSTER: Just head it up. Ain't nobody else going to get in this.

BING: Head it up?

LI'L MONSTER: Fight. One on one. You know, head up. And then it's over.

BING: Are you friends after that?

LI'L MONSTER: Well, you not sending each other Christmas cards.

BING: What if you just drive through another gang's turf? Are you in danger?

LI'L MONSTER: Yeah. I mean, I could be sitting at a light, and somebody say, "That's that fool, Li'l Monster," and they start shooting. That could be anywhere. Bam! Bam! Bam!

BING: Are you targeted by reputation?

LI'L MONSTER: Yeah. That's my worst fear, to be sitting at a light.

B-DOG: That's one of mine, too.

LI'L MONSTER: So I don't stop. I don't pull up right behind a car. And I am always looking around.

B-DOG: Always looking.

LI'L MONSTER: That's my worst fear because we did so much of it. You know, you pull up, man, block him in, and—

B-DOG: —that was it.

LI'L MONSTER: They put in work. That is my worst fear. And if you ever ride with me, you notice I always position myself where there is a curb. That middle lane is no-man's-land.

B-DOG: That's dangerous.

LI'L MONSTER: You know how they say, "Look out for the other guy"? Well, I *am* the other guy. Get out of my way. Give me the starting position. You know, because I can— phew! Claustrophobia. I seen that shit happenin', man. I *be* that shit happenin', man, and I don't *never* want that to happen to me, just to be sitting at the light and they take your whole head off.

BING: Say everybody's fired up to get somebody from an enemy set, but there's this young kid who says, "I can't do that. I don't feel right about it—this is a friend of mine." What's going to happen?

LI'L MONSTER: There's many ways that it can be dealt with. Everybody can disown him, or everybody can just say, "Okay, *fine*, but you gotta do something else." See what I'm saying?

B-DOG: But he's gonna be disciplined one way or the other.

RAT-NECK: 'Cause he know everything, man, and he think he gonna ride on up outta here?

LI'L MONSTER: So you go home and say, "Yeah, mama. I got out, mama. Everything's cool." And mama looking at *you* like—"Son, are you sure?" 'Cause she knows damn well those motherfuckers ain't gonna let you go that easy.

TEE: Now that's the flip side to those motherfuckers who say, "I smoke *anybody*—I'll smoke my mama!" We, as homeboys, look at him and say, "Your mama carried you nine months and shitted you out, and if you'll kill your mama, I know you don't give two shakes of a rat's rectum about me!"

RAT-NECK: He'll kill me. He'll smoke me.

BING: What's going to happen in 1989? Los Angeles has the highest body count ever. More deaths than in Ireland.

RAT-NECK: Not more than New York. In New York they kill you for just a penny. I took a trip to New York one time. This guy wanted me to see what it was like.

BING: You mean gang life in New York City?

RAT-NECK: No, to see how people live—gang life, the whole environment, the whole everything. I was there for two days, right? He took us to Queens, Harlem, the Bronx—everywhere. We talked about going out strapped. He said, "What the fuck, you can't go out there strapped! What's wrong with you?" But I say I gotta let 'em know what time it is and carry *something*, you know, 'cause we don't really know what's going on in New York. But we hear so *much* about New York, how they operate, how rough it's supposed to be. So, okay, we decide we gonna carry a buck knife—something. So we kickin', walkin', cruisin' the street, everything. And then I see a homeboy standin' right here next to me.

And he come up to us and do some shit like this: he take three pennies, shake 'em, and throw 'em down in front of his shoe. We, like, what the fuck is this? Is it, you got a beef? Like, he knew we weren't from there. So we not lookin' at him, but, like, why the fuck he throw three pennies down there? Like, was it, "Get off our turf"? But we didn't understand his language. Out here, it's like, "What's happenin'? What's up, Cuz? What's up, Blood?" But in New York, you lookin' at the damn pennies, and maybe he come back and hit you. Maybe if you pick up the pennies, then you got a beef with him. Maybe if you don't pick 'em up, then you supposed to walk off. But shit, we lookin' at the pennies, and lookin' at him, and it's like god*damn!* So we walks off and leaves the Bronx and goes to Harlem.

Oh, man—*that's* what you call a gutter. You get to lookin' around there and thinking, "God*damn*, these my people? Livin' like *this*? Livin' in a cardboard box?" I mean, skid row got it goin' *on* next to Harlem. Skid row look like *Hollywood* to them.

Kickin' It

BING: Did you vote in 1988?

TEE: Yeah, I voted. But look at the choice I had: Bush bastard and Dumb-kakis.

RAT-NECK: A bush and a cock.

BING: Why didn't you vote for Jesse in the primary?

TEE: I truly believe that shit rigged. Everybody I know voted for Jesse, but—

B-DOG: —Jesse was out.

RAT-NECK: It's different for us. Like, what's that guy's name shot President Reagan? What happened to that guy? *Nothin'!*

BING: He's in prison.

LI'L MONSTER: Oh no he's not. He's in a *hospital*.

TEE: They're *studyin'* him.

RAT-NECK: See, they did that to cover his ass. They say he retarded or something.

B-DOG: See, if I had shot Reagan, would they have put *me* in a mental facility?

RAT-NECK: They would have put you away right there where you shot him. Bam—judge, jury, executioner.

TEE: Why is it they always study white folks when they do heinous crimes, but they never study us? *We* got black psychiatrists.

BING: What about all this killing, then?

TEE: I'm gonna shut up now, because the way the questions are coming, you portray us as animals. Gangbanging is a way of life. You got to touch it, smell it, feel it. Hearing the anger, the frustration, and the desperation of all of us only adds to what the media's been saying—and it's worse, coming out of *our* mouths. There has to be questions directed with an understanding of our point of view. Sorry.

BING: All right. Ask one.

TEE: It's not my interview.

BING: I'm trying to understand your motives. Let me ask a different question: If a homeboy is killed, how is the funeral conducted?

TEE: You got four different sets here in this room, and each set has its own rules and regulations.

RAT-NECK: Okay, like, my little brother just got killed. You talkin' funeralwise, right? At this funeral, Bloods *and* Crips was there. But didn't nobody wear nothin', just suits. *Every* funeral you go to is not really colors.

TEE: Thank you! Yeah!

RAT-NECK: You just going to give your last respect. Like my little brother, it really tripped me out, the way I seen a big *"B"* of flowers with red roses in it, and one tiny *blue* thing they brought. And these were *Bloods*—goddamn! Like one of my homeboys asked me, "What's happenin', Rat?" and I said, "Hey, man—you tell *me.*" And I looked around, saw some other guys there, you know? They ain't *us,* but they came and showed respect, so—move back. Couple of them walked by us, looked at us, and said, "That's our homeboy, that's Rat-Neck's brother."

When he got killed, you know, I had a whole lot of animosity. I'd smoke any damn one of 'em, but one thing—one thing about it—*it wasn't black people who did it.* That's the one thing that didn't make me click too much. Now, if a black person woulda did it, ain't no tellin' where I'd be right now, or what I'd do, or how I'd feel. I'd be so confused I might just straight out fuck my job, my wife, my kid, whatever, and say, "I don't give a fuck about you—bro got killed!"

BING: How did he get killed?

RAT-NECK: I don't really know the whole rundown.

TEE: What Rat-Neck's saying is the respect. We buried three of our own yesterday, and for each one we went to the mother to see how *she* wanted it—

LI'L MONSTER: —how she wanted it! That's it!

TEE: 'Cause the mother carried that baby for nine months— that's her *child.* It's *her* family, and we're the extended family. She got the first rights on what goes on there. It's

A Gangbanger's Glossary

Baller: a gangbanger who is making money; also *high roller*

Cap: a retort

Click up: to get along well with a homeboy

Crab: insulting term for a Crip; also *E-ricket*

Cuz: alternative name for a Crip; often used in a greeting, e.g., "What's up, Cuz?"

Down: to do right by your homeboys; to live up to expectations; to protect your turf, e.g., "It's the job of the homeboys to be down for the 'hood"

Gangbanging: the activities of a gang

Gat: gun

Give it up: to admit to something

the respect factor that lies there, and if the mother says there's no colors, you better believe ain't no colors!

RAT-NECK: And no cartridges in the coffin.

TEE: If he went out in a blaze of glory, and his mama say, "You all bury him like you want to bury him"—oh, then we *do* it."

BING: How would that be?

TEE: If he was a baller—you know what I'm saying—then everybody get suited and booted.

BING: Do you mean a sea of colors?

EVERYONE: *NO!* Suits and ties! Shined shoes!

LI'L MONSTER: Jump in the silk!

TEE: We own suits, you know! Brooks Brothers, C and R Clothiers! And some of the shit is tailored!

BING: You mention your mothers a lot, and I sense a love that's very real. If you do love your moms so much and

---

Hangin', bangin', and slangin': to be out with the homeboys, talking the talk, walking the walk; slangin' comes from "slinging" or selling dope

Head up: to fight someone one-on-one

Hemmed up: to be hassled or arrested by the police

'Hood: neighborhood; turf

Homeboy: anyone from the same neighborhood or gang; a friend or an accepted person; in a larger sense, a person from the inner city; also *homie*

Jacket: a record or a reputation, both within the gang and at the police station

Jumped in: initiated into a gang; getting jumped in typically entails being beaten up by the set members

Kickin' it: kicking back, relaxing with your homeboys

you kill each other, then it has to be the mothers who ultimately suffer the worst pain. How do you justify that?

B-DOG: Your mother gonna suffer while you living, anyway. While you out there gangbanging, she's suffering. My mother's suffering right now. All my brothers in jail.

RAT-NECK: My mother's sufferin', sittin' in her living room, and maybe there's a bullet comin' in the window.

BING: What do you say to your mother when she says, "All your brothers are in jail, and you're out there in danger"?

B-DOG: We don't even get *into* that no more.

RAT-NECK: She probably don't think about that at all—just so she can cope with it.

B-DOG: Me and my mother don't discuss that no more, because I been into this for so long, you know. When me and

---

Loc-ed out: also *lok-ed out;* from "loco," meaning ready and willing to do anything

Make a move: commit a crime; also *manipulate*

Mark: someone afraid to commit a crime; also *punk*

O.G.: an abbreviation for Original Gangster; i.e., a gang member who has been in the set for a long time and has made his name

Oo-lah: insulting term for a Blood; also *slob*

Perpetrate: betray your homeboys; bring shame on yourself and your set

Put in work: any perilous activity from fighting to murder that benefits the set or the gang

Set: any of the various neighborhood gangs that fit within the larger framework of Bloods and Crips

Smoke: to kill someone

Top it off: to get along well with someone; reach an understanding

my mother be together, we try to be happy. We don't talk about the gang situation.

LI'L MONSTER: Me and my mother are real tight, you know? We talk like sister and brother. I don't try to justify myself to her—any more than she tries to justify *her* work or how she makes her money to me. What I do *may* come back to hurt her, but what *she* does may also come back to hurt me. Say I'm thirteen and I'm staying with my mother, and she goes off on her boss and loses her job—how does she justify that to *me*?

BING: Well, the loss of a job is not quite the same as an actively dangerous life-style in the streets, wouldn't you agree?

TEE: "An actively dangerous life-style"—that really fucks me up. Okay, here we go. "Woman" is a term that means "of man." Wo-*man*. My mother raised me, true enough. Okay? And she was married. There was a male figure in the house. But I never accepted him as my father. My mother can only teach me so much 'bout being a man-child in the Promised Land. If, after that, there is nothing for me to take pride in, then I enter into manhood asshole backwards, and I stand there, a warrior strong and proud. But there is no outlet for that energy, for me or my brothers, so we *turn on each other*.

So, Mom sends us to the show, and all we get is Clint Eastwood, *Superfly*, and *Sweet Sweet Bad Ass*. Now what goes up on the silver screen comes down into the streets, and now you got a homeboy. And mama says, "I don't want you to go to your grave as a slave for the minimum wage." So you say, "I am going to go get us something, make this better, pay the rent."

The first thing a successful athlete does—and you can check me out—is buy his mama a big-ass house. That's what we want. And if we have to get it from the streets, that's where we go.

BING: Why?

TEE: It's the same *everywhere*. A sorority, a fraternity, the Girl Scouts, camping clubs, hiking club, L.A.P.D., the Los

Angeles Raiders are all the same. Everything that you find in those groups and institutions you find in a gang.

BING: So are you saying there's no difference between the motives of you guys joining a gang and, say, a young WASP joining a fraternity?

RAT-NECK: You got a lot of gangbangers out there who are smart. They want it. They *got* what it takes. But the difference is they got no money.

TEE: I know a homie who had a scholarship to USC. But he left school because he found prejudice *alive* in America, and it cut him out. He said, "I don't have to stand here and take this. As a matter of fact, you owe my great-grandfather forty acres and a mule."

LI'L MONSTER: Forget the mule, just give me the forty acres.

TEE: So he took to the streets. He got a Ph.D. from SWU. That's a Pimp and Hustler Degree from Sidewalk University.

BING: If it went the other way, what would your life be like?

RAT-NECK: I'm really a hardworking man. I make bed mattresses now, but I would like to straight out be an engineer, or give me a daycare center with little kids coming through, and get me the hell away as far as I can. All I want to do is be myself and not perpetrate myself, try not to perpetrate my black people. Just give me a job, give me a nice house—everybody dream of a nice home—and just let me deal with it.

BING: And how do drugs figure into this?

LI'L MONSTER: Wait a minute. I just want to slide in for a minute. I want to set the record straight. People think gangs and drugs go hand in hand, but they don't. If I sell drugs, that make me a gangbanger? No. If I gangbang, does that make me sell drugs? No. See, for white people—and I am not saying for all white people, just like what I say about black people is not for all black people—they go for college, the stepping-stone to what they want to get. And some black people look to drugs as a stepping-stone to get the same thing.

B-DOG: They want to live better. To buy what they want. To get a house.

RAT-NECK: Not worry about where the next meal come from.

TEE: To live comfortable and get a slice of American Pie, the American Dream.

B-DOG: There it is.

TEE: The Army came out with a hell of a slogan: "Be all you can be." And that's it.

We want the same thing. We've been taught by television, the silver screen, to grow up and have a chicken in every pot, two Chevys, 2.3 kids in the family. So we have been taught the same thing that you have been taught, but there is certain things that we can hold on to and other things that—we see them, but we just cannot reach them. Most of us are dealing with the reality of surviving as opposed to, "Well, my dad will take care of it."

BING: Are you saying that gangbanging is just another version of the American Dream?

LI'L MONSTER: It's like this. You got the American Dream over there, and you reaching for it. But you can't get it. And you got dope right here, real close. You can grab it easy. Dealing with the closer one, you might possibly make enough money to grab the other one. Then you throw away the dope. That's a big *if* now.

BING: Seriously, does anybody ever stop dealing?

B-DOG: If you was making a million dollars off of drugs, you know what I'm saying, are you gonna give that up for a legitimate business?

TEE: This goes back to it. You started out for need, and now you stuck in it because of greed. That's when you play your life away. There comes a time when you have to stop playing, but as far as the streets go, you are a *street player*. Now there may come a time when you say, all right, I've played, I've had time in the gang, now I got to raise up. But if you is so greedy that you cannot smell the coffee, then you're cooked.

BING: But if you do get out, do you always have to come back when your homeboys call?

LI'L MONSTER: It ain't like you gonna be called upon every month.

B-DOG: But if you gets called, then you must be needed, and you must come.

LI'L MONSTER: It's like this—and I don't care who you are, where you started, or how far you got—you *never* forget where you come from.

TEE: That's it.

B-DOG: You *never* forget where you come from.

Just Like Us?

The relationship of man to
animal has long been one of sympathy, manifested in
such welfare organizations as the kindly Bide-A-Wee
or the avuncular ASPCA. In the last few years, the
politics of that relationship have been questioned by a
number of new and vociferous interest groups which
hold to the credo that animals are endowed with
certain inalienable rights.

Typically, when animal rights advocates are called
upon by the media to defend their views, they are
seated across the table from research scientists. The
discussion turns on the treatment of laboratory animals or the illegal efforts of fanatics who smuggle
animals out of research facilities via latter-day underground railroads to freedom.

Behind these easy headlines, however, stand serious philosophical questions: How should we treat
animals? Why do humans have rights and other animals not? If animals had rights, what would they be?
To address these questions, *Harper's Magazine* asked
two leading animal rights activists to sit down with a
philosopher and a constitutional scholar to examine
the logic of their opinions.

207

　◆　

The following forum is based on a discussion held at the Cooper Union for the Advancement of Science and Art, in New York City. Jack Hitt served as moderator.

JACK HITT
is a senior editor at Harper's Magazine.

ARTHUR CAPLAN
is director of the Center for Biomedical Ethics at the University of Minnesota.

GARY FRANCIONE
is a professor at Rutgers Law School. He frequently litigates animal rights cases.

ROGER GOLDMAN
is a constitutional law scholar and professor at Saint Louis University School of Law.

INGRID NEWKIRK
is the national director of People for the Ethical Treatment of Animals, in Washington.

Bunnies and Sewer Rats

JACK HITT: Let me ask a question that many readers might ask: Gary, why have you—a former Supreme Court law clerk and now professor of law at Rutgers—devoted your life to animal rights?

GARY FRANCIONE: I believe that animals have *rights*. This is not to say that animals have the same rights that we do, but the reasons that lead us to accord certain rights to human beings are equally applicable to animals. The problem is that our value system doesn't permit the breadth of vision necessary to understand that. We currently use the category of "species" as the relevant criterion for determining membership in our moral community, just as we once used race and sex to determine that membership.

If you asked white men in 1810 whether blacks had rights, most of them would have laughed at you. What was necessary then is necessary now. We must change the *way* we think: a paradigm shift in the way we think about animals. Rights for blacks and women were the constitutional issues of the nineteenth and twentieth centuries. Animals rights, once more people understand the issue, will emerge as *the* civil rights movement of the twenty-first century.

HITT: I want to see where the logic of your beliefs takes us. Suppose I am the head of a company that has invented a dynamite new shampoo. It gives your hair great body; everyone is going to look like the early Elizabeth Taylor. But my preliminary tests show that it may cause some irritation or mild damage to the eye. So I've purchased 2,000 rabbits to test this shampoo on their eyes first. Roger, do you find anything offensive about testing shampoo this way?

ROGER GOLDMAN: As someone new to the animal rights issue, I don't find it particularly offensive.

HITT: What if the only thing new about my shampoo is that it is just a different color?

GOLDMAN: If everything else is equal, then I would say the testing is unnecessary.

INGRID NEWKIRK: I think Roger hit the nail on the head. The public has absolutely no idea what the tests involve or whether they're necessary. I think Roger might object if he knew that there were alternatives, the human-skin patch test can be substituted for the rabbit-blinding test. If consumers were informed, then no compassionate consumer would abide such cruelty.

FRANCIONE: The problem is that we can use animals in any way we like because they are *property*. The law currently regards animals as no different from that pad of paper in front of you, Roger. If you own that pad, you can rip it up or burn it. By and large we treat animals no differently than glasses, cups, or paper.

ARTHUR CAPLAN: I know you lawyers love to talk about the property status of these little creatures, but there are other factors. We treat animals as property because people don't believe that animals have any moral worth. People look at rabbits and say, "There are many rabbits. If there are a few less rabbits, who cares?"

NEWKIRK: Not true. Many people, who don't support animal rights, *would* care if you stuck a knife in their rabbit or dog. They're deeply offended by acts of *individual* cruelty.

CAPLAN: Yes, but I suspect that if in your test we substituted ugly sewer rats for button-nosed rabbits, people might applaud the suffering. There are some animals that just don't register in the human consciousness. Rats don't, rabbits might, dogs and horses definitely do.

NEWKIRK: Not always. If the test were done to a sewer rat in *front* of a person, the average person would say, "Don't do that" or "Kill him quickly."

HITT: Why?

NEWKIRK: It's institutionalized cruelty, born of our hideous compartmentalized thinking. If the killing is done behind closed doors, if the government says it must be done, or if some man or woman in a white coat assures us that it's for our benefit, we ignore our own ethical good sense and allow it to happen.

HITT: If the frivolity of the original test bothers us, what if we up the ante? What if the product to be tested might yield a cure for baldness?

FRANCIONE: Jack, that is a "utilitarian" argument which suggests that the rightness or wrongness of an action is determined by the *consequences* of that action. In the case of animals, it implies that animal exploitation produces benefits that justify that exploitation. I don't believe in utilitarian moral thought. It's dangerous because it easily leads to atrocious conclusions, both in how we treat humans and how we treat animals. I don't believe it is morally permissible to exploit weaker beings even if we derive benefits.

GOLDMAN: So not even the cancer cure?

FRANCIONE: No, absolutely not.

CAPLAN: But you miss the point about moral selfishness. By the time you get to the baldness cure, people start to say, "I don't *care* about animals. My interests are a hell of a lot more important than the animals' interests. So if keeping hair on my head means sacrificing those animals, painlessly or not, I want it." It's not utilitarian—it's selfish.

FRANCIONE: But you certainly wouldn't put that forward as a justification, would you?

CAPLAN: No, it's just description.

FRANCIONE: I can't argue with your assertion that people are selfish. But aren't we morally obliged to assess the consequences of that selfishness? To begin that assessment, people must become aware of the ways in which we exploit animals.

Maybe I'm just a hopeless optimist, but I believe that once people are confronted with these facts, they will reassess. The backlash that we're seeing from the exploitation industries—the meat companies and the biomedical research laboratories—is a reaction of fear. They know that the more people learn, the more people will reject this painful exploitation.

HITT: But won't your movement always be hampered by that mix of moral utilitarianism and moral egotism? People will say, "Yes, be kind to animals up to a point of utilitarianism (so I can have my cancer cure) and up to a point of moral egotism (so I can have my sirloin)." There may be some shift in the moral center, but it will move only so far.

CAPLAN: I agree. Gary can remain optimistic, but confronting people with the facts won't get him very far. Moral egotism extends even into human relations. Let's not forget that we are in a city where you have to step over people to enter this building. People don't say, "Feed, clothe, and house them, and then tax me; I'll pay." We have a limited moral imagination. It may be peculiarly American, but you can show people pictures of starving children or homeless people or animals in leg traps, and many will say, "That's too bad. Life is hard, but I still want my pleasures, my enjoyments."

NEWKIRK: There are two answers to that. First, people accept the myth. They were brought up with the illusion that they *must* eat animals to be healthy. Now we know that's not true. Second, because of humankind's lack of moral—or even just plain—imagination, we activists have to tell people exactly what they *should* do. Then we must make it easier for them to do it. If we put a moral stepladder in front of people, a lot of them will walk up it. But most people feel powerless as individuals and ask, "Who am I? I'm only one person. What can I do?" We must show them.

HITT: Roger, I'm wondering whether your moral center has shifted since we began. Originally you weren't offended by my using 2,000 rabbits to test a new shampoo. Are you now?

GOLDMAN: I am still a utilitarian. But if the test is unnecessary or just repetitive, clearly, I'm persuaded that it should be stopped.

NEWKIRK: Precisely Gary's point. Armed with the facts, Roger opts not to hurt animals.

Enfranchising All Creatures

HITT: Art, what makes human beings have rights and animals not have rights?

CAPLAN: Some would argue a biblical distinction. God created humans in his image and did not create animals that way. That's one special property. Another philosophical basis is natural law, which holds that inalienable rights accrue to being human—that is a distinguishing feature in and of itself.

Personally I reject both those arguments. I subscribe to an entitlement view, which finds these rights grounded in certain innate properties, such as the ability to reason, the ability to suffer—

FRANCIONE: Let's take the ability to suffer and consider it more carefully. The ability to use language or to reason is irrelevant to the right to be free from suffering. Only the ability to feel pain is relevant. Logically, it doesn't follow that you should restrict those rights to humans. On this primary level, the question must be *who* can feel pain, *who* can suffer? Certainly animals must be included within the reach of this fundamental right.

If you don't, then you are basing the right not to suffer pain on "intelligence." Consider the grotesque results if you apply that idea exclusively to human beings. Would you say that a smart person has a right to suffer less pain than a stupid person? That is effectively just what we say with animals. Even though they can suffer, we conclude that their suffering is irrelevant because we think we are smarter than they are.

CAPLAN: The ability to suffer does count, but the level of thinking and consciousness also counts. What makes us human? What grants us the right to life? It is not just a single attribute that makes us human. Rather, there is a cluster of properties: a sense of place in the world, a sense of time, a sense of self-awareness, a sense that one *is* somebody, a sense that one is morally relevant. When you add up these features, you begin to get to the level of entitlement to rights.

FRANCIONE: And I am going to push you to think specifically about rights again. What must you possess in order to have a right to life? I think the most obvious answer is simply a *life*!

But let's play this question out in your terms. To have a right to life, you must possess a sense of self, a recollection of the past, and an anticipation of the future, to name a few. By those standards, the chimpanzee—and I would argue, the entire class of Mammalia—would be enfranchised to enjoy a right to life.

NEWKIRK: The question is, do they have an interest in living? If they do, then one has an obligation to recognize the natural rights. The most fundamental of these is a desire to live. They *are* alive, therefore they want to *be* alive, and therefore we should *let* them live.

The more profound question, though, is what distinguishes humans from other animals. Most scientists, at first, thought that what separates us from the other animals is that human beings use tools. So ethnologists went out into the field and returned with innumerable examples of tool use in animals. The scientists then concluded that it's not tool use but the *making* of tools. Ethnologists, such as Geza Teleki, came back with lots of different examples, everything from chimpanzees making fishing poles to ants making boats to cross rivers. One might think they would then elevate the criterion to making tools in *union* workshops, but they switched to "language." Then there was a discussion about what *is* language. Linguists, among them Noam Chomsky and Herbert Terrace, said language possessed certain "components." But when various ethnologists were able to satisfy each of these components, the Cartesian scientists became desperate and kept adding more components, including some pretty complicated ones, such as the ability to recite events in the distant past and to create new words based on past experiences. Eventually the number of components was up to sixteen! The final component was teaching someone else the language. But when Roger Fouts gave the signing ape, Washoe, a son, she independently taught him some seventy American hand-language signs.

CAPLAN: One of the sad facts of the literature of both animal and human rights is that everyone is eager to identify the magic property that separates humans from animals. Is it the ability to suffer? The ability to say something? The ability to say something *interesting*? I think the philosophers are all looking in the right place but are missing something. We have rights because we are *social*.

NEWKIRK: Since all animals are social, then you *would* extend rights to nonhumans?

CAPLAN: It's not just sociability. Of course, all animals interact, but there is something about the way humans need to interact.

Suppose we were little Ayn Rands who marched about, self-sufficient, proud, and arrogant. If we were able to chop our own wood, cook our own meals, and fend off those who would assault us, then we wouldn't need any rights. You wouldn't need to have a right to free speech if there was no one to talk to!

My point is that our fundamental rights are not exclusively intellectual properties. They are the natural result of the unique ways humans have come together to form societies, *dependent* on each other for survival and therefore respectful of each other's rights.

NEWKIRK: None of this differentiates humans from the other animals. You cannot find a relevant attribute in human beings that doesn't exist in animals as well. Darwin said that the only difference between humans and other animals was a difference of degree, not kind. If you ground any concept of human rights in a particular attribute, then animals will have to be included. Animals have rights.

CAPLAN: That brings up another problem I have with your entire argument. Throughout this discussion, I have argued my position in terms of *ethics*. I have spoken about our moral imagination and animal *interests* and human decency. Why? Because I don't want our relationship with animals to be cast as a battle of rights. Only in America, with its obsession for attorneys, courts, judges, and lawsuits, is the entire realm of human relationships reduced to a clash of rights.

So I ask you: Is our relationship with animals best conceived of under the rubric of rights? I don't think so. When I am dispensing rights, I'm relatively chintzy about it. Do embryos have rights? In my opinion, no. Do irretrievably comatose people have rights? I doubt it. Do mentally retarded people below some level of intellectual functioning have rights? Probably not.

There is a wide range of creatures—some of them human—for whom our rights language is not the best way to deal with them. I want people to deal with them out of a sense of fairness or a sense of humanity or a sense of duty, but not out of a claim to rights.

NEWKIRK: I don't like your supremacist view of a custodial responsibility that grants you the luxury to be magnanimous to those beneath you. The rights of animals are not peripheral interests. In this case, we are talking about blood, guts, pain, and death.

FRANCIONE: Art, when you start talking about obligations without rights, you can justify violations of those obligations or intrusions more easily by spinning airy notions of utility. The reason many of our battles are played out in rights language is because our culture has evolved this notion that a right is something that stands between me and an intrusion. A right doesn't yield automatically because a stronger party might benefit.

If a scientist could cure cancer—without fail—by subjecting me against my will to a painful experiment, it wouldn't matter. I have a right not to be used that way.

CAPLAN: Ironically, I agree with you. That's exactly the role that rights language plays. It defines the barriers or lines that can't be crossed. But if you hand out rights willy-nilly, you lose that function.

NEWKIRK: When should we stop?

CAPLAN: I'm not sure I know the answer, but if you cheapen the currency of rights language, you've got to worry that rights may not be taken seriously. Soon you will have people arguing that trees have rights and that embryos have rights. And the tendency would be to say, "Sure, they have rights, but they are not *important* rights."

NEWKIRK: Art, wouldn't you rather err on the side of giving out too many rights rather than too few?

CAPLAN: No.

NEWKIRK: So, according to your view, maybe we should take away some of the rights we've already granted. After all, granting rights to blacks and women has deprived society of very important things, such as cheap labor. That a society evolves and expands its protective shield should not daunt us. That's like saying, if I continue to be charitable, my God, where will it ever end?

CAPLAN: It may not be rights or bust. There may be other ways to get people to conduct themselves decently without hauling out the heavy artillery of rights language every time.

NEWKIRK: People have to be pushed; society has to be pushed. Those who care deeply about a particular wrong have to pressure the general population. Eventually a law is passed, and then adjustments are made to correct past injustices. You have to bring these matters to a head.

HITT: Roger, from a constitutional perspective, do you think that rights are cheapened when they are broadened?

GOLDMAN: When you put it in a constitutional context, you invite conflict. That's inevitable. If you have a free press, you're going to have fair trial problems. If you start expanding rights of liberty, you run up against rights of equality. I don't think expansion cheapens them, but by elevating animal rights to a constitutional issue, you certainly multiply the difficulties.

HITT: You could argue that conflict strengthens rights. If you had no conflict over free speech, would we have the solid right to free speech that we have today?

GOLDMAN: It depends on who wins. What would happen if free speech lost?

FRANCIONE: Roger, you will have conflict and difficulties whether you cast our relationship with animals as one of obligations *or* rights. The real question is, are those obligations enforceable by state authority? If they are, there will be clashes and we will turn to the courts for resolution.

CAPLAN: Gary, I would like those obligations enforced by the authority, if you like, of empathy, by the power of character. What matters is how people view animals, how their feelings are touched by those animals, what drives them to care about those animals, not what rights the animals have.

FRANCIONE: I agree that you don't effect massive social change exclusively through law, but law can certainly help. That's a classic law school debate: Do moral perceptions shape law or does law shape moral perceptions? It probably goes both ways. I have no doubt that we could effect a great change if animals were included within our constitutional framework.

NEWKIRK: Great changes often begin with the law. Remember the 1760s case of the West Indian slave Jonathan Strong. Strong's master had abandoned him in England after beating him badly. The judge in that case feared the consequences of emancipating a slave. But the judge freed Strong and declared, "Let justice prevail, though the heavens may fall."

Mojo, the Talking Chimpanzee

HITT: Meet Mojo, the signing chimpanzee. Mojo is female and has learned more words than any other chimpanzee. One day you're signing away with Mojo, and she signs back, "I want a baby." Roger, are we under any obligation to grant her wish?

GOLDMAN: Since I am not persuaded animals have any rights, I don't believe there is any obligation.

HITT: Doesn't it follow that if this chimpanzee can articulate a desire to have a child—a primal desire and one that we would never forbid humans—we have some obligation to fulfill it?

CAPLAN: You are alluding to a foundation for rights that we haven't yet discussed. Is the requirement for possessing a right the ability to *claim* it? That is, in order to hold a right to life, one must be able to articulate a claim to life, to be able to say, "I want to live."

There may be animals that can get to that level, and Mojo may be one of them. Nevertheless, I don't buy into that argument. Simply being able to claim a right does not necessarily entail an obligation to fulfill it.

FRANCIONE: But Mojo does have the right to be left alone to pursue her desires, the right *not* to be in that cage. Aren't we violating some right of Mojo's by confining her so that she cannot satisfy that primal desire?

HITT: Is this a fair syllogism? Mojo wants to be free; a right to freedom exists if you can claim it; ergo, Mojo has a right to be free. Does the ability to lay claim to a right automatically translate into a *possession* of such a right?

CAPLAN: You don't always generate obligations and duties from a parallel set of rights, matching one with another.

Look at the relationship that exists between family members. Some people might argue that children have certain rights to claim from their parents. But there is something wrong with that assumption. Parents have many obligations to their children, but it seems morally weird to reduce this relationship to a contractual model. It's not a free-market arrangement where you put down a rights chit, I put down an obligation chit, and we match them up.

My kid might say to me, "Dad, you have an obligation to care for my needs, and my need today is a new car." I don't enter into a negotiation based on a balancing of his rights and my duties. That is not the proper relationship.

NEWKIRK: But having a car is not a fundamental right, whereas the right not to be abused is. For example, children have a right not to be used in factories. That right had to be fought for in exactly the same way we are fighting for animal rights now.

CAPLAN: Gary, I want to press you further. A baby needs a heart, and some scientist believes the miniature swine's heart will do it.

FRANCIONE: Would I take a healthy pig, remove its heart, and put it into the child? No.

CAPLAN: I am stymied by your absolutist position that makes it impossible even to consider the pig as a donor.

FRANCIONE: What if the donor were a severely retarded child instead of a pig?

CAPLAN: No, because I've got to worry about the impact not only on the donor but on society as well.

FRANCIONE: Art, assume I have a three-year-old prodigy who is a mathematical wizard. The child has a bad heart. The only way to save the prodigy is to take the heart out of another child. Should we *consider* a child from a low socioeconomic background who has limited mental abilities?

CAPLAN: You're wandering around a world of slopes, and I want to wander around a world of steps. I have argued strongly in my writing that it is possible for a human being—specifically an infant born with anencephaly, that is, without most of its brain—to drop below the threshold of a right to life. I think it would be ethical to use such a baby as a source for organ transplants. I do not believe there is a slippery slope between the child born with most of its brain missing and the retarded. There are certain thresholds below which one can make these decisions. At some point along the spectrum of life—many people would say a pig, and I would go further to include the anencephalic baby—we are safely below that threshold.

FRANCIONE: You can't equate the pig with the anencephalic infant. The anencephalic child is not the subject of a life in any meaningful sense. That is to say, it does not possess that constellation of attributes—sense of self-awareness, anticipation of the future, memory of the past—that we have been discussing. The pig is clearly the subject of a meaningful life.

CAPLAN: But if it's a matter of saving the life of the baby, then I want a surgeon to saw out the pig's heart and put it in the baby's chest.

NEWKIRK: The pig can wish to have life, liberty, and the pursuit of happiness, and the anencephalic baby cannot.

CAPLAN: But you must also consider the effect on others. I don't think it's going to matter very much what the pig's parents think about that pig. Whereas the child's parents care about the baby, and they don't care about the pig.

FRANCIONE: Then you change their reaction.

CAPLAN: I don't want to change their reaction. I want human beings to care about babies.

NEWKIRK: Like racism or sexism, that remark is pure speciesism.

CAPLAN: Speciesism! Mine is a legitimate distinction. The impact of this transplant is going to be different on humans than on lower animals.

NEWKIRK: "Lower animals." There comes speciesism rearing its ugly head again. Look, Art, I associate with the child; I don't associate with the pig. But we can't establish why that matters *except* that you are human and I am human.

If a building were burning and a baby baboon, a baby rat, and a baby child were inside, I'm sure I would save the child. But if the baboon mother went into the building, I'm sure she would take out the infant baboon. It's just that there is an instinct to save yourself first, then your immediate family, your countrymen, and on to your species. But we have to recognize and reject the self-interest that erects these barriers and try to recognize the rights of others who happen not to be exactly like ourselves.

CAPLAN: I think you can teach humans to care about the pig. The morally relevant factor here is that you will never get the pig to care about *me*.

NEWKIRK: Not true, Art. Read John Robbin's new book, *Diet for a New America,* in which he lists incidents of altruism by animals outside their own species. Everybody knows about dolphins rescuing sailors. Recently a pig rescued a child from a frozen lake and won an award!

CAPLAN: To the extent to which you can make animals drop *their* speciesism, perhaps you will be persuasive on this point.

NEWKIRK: Art, if you don't recognize my rights, that's tough for me. But that doesn't mean my rights don't exist.

FRANCIONE: If blacks, as a group, got together and said, "We're going to make a conscious decision to dislike non-blacks," would you say that black people no longer had rights?

CAPLAN: No, but I would hold them accountable for their racism. I could never hold a pig accountable for its speciesism. And I am never going to see a meeting of pigs having that kind of conversation.

NEWKIRK: That happens when the Ku Klux Klan meets, and the ACLU upholds their rights.

CAPLAN: The difference is that there are certain things I expect of blacks, whites, yellows—of all human beings and maybe a few animals. But I am not going to hold the vast majority of animals to those standards.

NEWKIRK: So the punishment for their perceived defi-
ciencies—which, incidentally, are shared by the human
baby—is to beat them to death.

CAPLAN: I didn't say that. I am trying to reach for something
that isn't captured by the speciesist charge. The difference
between people and animals is that I can persuade people.
I can *stimulate* their moral imaginations. But I can't do that
with most animals, and I want that difference to count.

A World with No Dancing Bears

HITT: How would you envision a society that embraced animal rights? What would happen to pets?

NEWKIRK: I don't use the word "pet." I think it's speciesist
language. I prefer "companion animal." For one thing, we
would no longer allow breeding. People could not create
different breeds. There would be no pet shops. If people
had companion animals in their homes, those animals
would have to be refugees from the animal shelters and
the streets. You would have a protective relationship with
them just as you would with an orphaned child. But as the
surplus of cats and dogs (artificially engineered by centuries of forced breeding) declined, eventually companion
animals would be phased out, and we would return to a
more symbiotic relationship—enjoyment at a distance.

FRANCIONE: Much more than that would be phased out. For
example, there would be no animals used for food, no
laboratory experiments, no fur coats, and no hunting.

GOLDMAN: Would there be zoos?

FRANCIONE: No zoos.

HITT: Circuses?

FRANCIONE: Circuses would have to change. Look, right now
we countenance the taking of an animal from the wild—a
bear—dressing that bear in a *skirt* and parading it in front
of thousands of people while it balances a ball on its nose.
When you think about it, that is perverted.

HITT: Let's say that your logic prevails. People are sickened by dancing bears and are demanding a constitutional amendment. What would be the language of a Bill of Rights for animals?

NEWKIRK: It already exists. It's "life, liberty, and the pursuit of happiness." We just haven't extended it far enough.

GOLDMAN: I am assuming your amendment would restrict not only government action but private action as well. Our Constitution restricts only government action. The single exception is the Thirteenth Amendment, which prohibits both the government and the individual from the practice of slavery.

HITT: To whom would these rights apply? Would they apply among animals themselves? Does the lion have to recognize the gazelle's right to life?

NEWKIRK: That's not our business. The behavior of the lion and the gazelle is a "tribal" issue, if you will. Those are the actions of other nations, and we cannot interfere.

GOLDMAN: What if we knew the lion was going to kill the gazelle—would we have an obligation to stop it?

NEWKIRK: It's not our business. This amendment restricts only our code of behavior.

HITT: But what Roger is asking is, should the amendment be so broad as to restrict both individual and government action?

FRANCIONE: It should be that broad. Of course, it would create a lot of issues we would have to work out. First, to whom would we extend these rights? I have a sneaking suspicion that any moment someone in this room will say, "But what about cockroaches? Will they have these rights? Do they have the right to have credit cards?" Hard questions would have to be answered, and we would have to determine which animals would hold rights and how to translate these rights into concrete protections from interference.

NEWKIRK: The health pioneer W. K. Kellogg limited it to "all those with faces." If you can look into the eyes of another, and that other looks back, that's one measure.

So the amendment shouldn't be limited, as some animal rights advocates think, to mammals, because we know that birds, reptiles, insects, and fishes all feel pain. They are capable of wanting to be alive. As long as we know that they have these primal interests, then I think we need to explore down the line—if we think it is down.

GOLDMAN: Let me go up the line. What about humans?

NEWKIRK: They would be just another animal in the pack.

GOLDMAN: But your amendment would massively expand the reach of the Constitution for humans. For example, the Constitution does not require states to provide rights for victims of crime. Under your proposal, if a state decriminalized adultery, shoplifting, or even murder, the victim's *constitutional* rights would be violated.

CAPLAN: And if we take the face test, how is that going to affect the way we treat the unborn? Must we enfranchise our fetuses? That's going to be the end of abortion.

FRANCIONE: Not necessarily. I am fairly comfortable with the notion that a fetus does not have a right to life. But that is not to say that a fetus doesn't have a right to be free from suffering. Fetuses do feel pain and they *ought* to be free from suffering. But it doesn't make sense to talk about a fetus having a sense of the past, anticipation of the future, and a sense of interaction with others.

CAPLAN: But a mouse?

FRANCIONE: Sure.

CAPLAN: I guess we can experiment on and eat all the animal fetuses we want.

FRANCIONE: I didn't say you had a right to inflict pain on animal fetuses. I don't think you have a right to inflict pain on human fetuses.

CAPLAN: Are you suggesting that we can't inflict pain, but we can kill them?

NEWKIRK: You are talking about the manner in which abortions are currently performed, not whether they should be performed. Our standard of lack of suffering holds up if you apply it across the board, for human and nonhuman fetuses.

GOLDMAN: Let me see if I can bring together those who advocate animal welfare and those who believe animals hold rights. What about a different amendment, similar to the difference between the Thirteenth Amendment, which is an absolute ban on slavery, and the Fourteenth Amendment, which bans discrimination, but not absolutely. In fact, the Fourteenth allows us to take race into account sometimes, such as affirmative action. Do the animal rights activists see a role for a limited amendment similar to the Fourteenth? It would broadly protect animals from unnecessary suffering, but allow for some medical experiments.

FRANCIONE: Does your amendment simply expand the word "persons" in the Fourteenth Amendment to include animals?

GOLDMAN: No, but it is modeled on Fourteenth Amendment jurisprudence. It would not permit experimentation on animals unless necessary for a compelling need.

FRANCIONE: I would favor this approach if the experimenter had the burden to show the compelling need. I would have only one problem with adjudication under this compelling-need standard. My fear is that the balance would always favor the biomedical research community. Everyone agrees that no one should needlessly use animals in experimentation. Yet we all know that millions of animals are being used for frivolous purposes. That is because the biomedical researchers have persuaded enough people that their experiments are so important they have become "compelling" by definition.

GOLDMAN: Of course the difference with this constitutional amendment is that it wouldn't pass unless two-thirds of Congress and three-fourths of the states backed it. So if we're projecting a hundred years from now, you won't have the problem of science experts always prevailing.

FRANCIONE: Roger, I would retire tomorrow if I could get your amendment. The problem is that our society economically *benefits* from exploitation. The animal industries are so strong that they have shaped an entire *value* system that justifies and perpetuates exploitation. So I am not sure your compelling-need test would result in anything substantially different from what we have now. That's why I favor a hard rights notion, to protect the defenseless absolutely. As soon as you let in the "balancers," people such as Art Caplan, you've got trouble.

CAPLAN: The problem with your constitutional amendment is that, finally, it is irrelevant to human behavior. When the lawyers, the constitutional adjudicators, and the Supreme Court justices aren't there, when it's just me and my companion animal or my bug in the woods, where are the animal's rights then?

There was a time when I was a little boy running around in the woods in New England. It was just a bunch of Japanese beetles in a jar and me. The question was: How is little Art going to deal with those Japanese beetles? Pull their wings off? Never let them out of the jar? Step on them? What do I do with those bugs? What do I think of bugs? No Supreme Court justice is going to tell me what to do with them.

NEWKIRK: A lot of these conflicts of moral obligation result from the wide variety of *unnatural* relationships we have with animals in the first place—whether it's little Art with his jar of Japanese beetles, or the scientist in the lab with his chimpanzee, or any one of us at home with a cat. Just take the single issue of the sterilization of pets. We now have burdened ourselves with the custodial obligation to sterilize thousands of animals because we have screwed

up their reproductive cycles so much through domestica-
tion and inbreeding that they have many more offspring
than they normally would. What would happen if we just
left animals alone to possess their own dignity? You know,
you mentioned earlier that there is something cruel in the
lion chasing down and killing the gazelle. Well, nature *is*
cruel, but man is crueler yet.

Is Computer Hacking a Crime?

The image of the computer hacker drifted into public awareness in the mid-Seventies, when reports of Chinese-food-consuming geniuses working compulsively at keyboards began to issue from MIT. Over time, several of these impresarios entered commerce, and the public's impression of hackers changed: They were no longer nerds but young, millionaire entrepreneurs.

In this decade, the term has taken on a more felonious connotation. In January 1990, a graduate student named Robert Morris Jr. was convicted on a felony charge for releasing a computer program known as a worm into the vast Internet system, halting more than 6,000 computers. The subsequent public debate ranged from the matter of proper punishment for a mischievous kid to the issue of our rapidly changing notion of what constitutes free speech—or property—in an age of modems and data bases. In order to allow hackers to speak for themselves, *Harper's Magazine* recently organized an electronic discussion and asked some of the nation's best hackers to "log on," discuss the protean notions of contemporary speech, and explain what their powers and talents are.

The *following forum is based on a discussion held on the WELL,*
a computer bulletin-board system based in Sausalito, California.
The forum is the result of a gradual accretion of arguments as the
participants—located throughout the country—opined and react-
ed over an eleven-day period. Harper's Magazine *senior editor*
Jack Hitt and assistant editor Paul Tough served as moderators.

ADELAIDE
is a pseudonym for a former hacker who has sold his soul to the
corporate state as a computer programmer.

BARLOW
is John Perry Barlow, a retired cattle rancher, a former
Republican county chairman, and a lyricist for the Grateful
Dead, who currently is writing a book on computers and
consciousness entitled Everything We Know Is Wrong.

BLUEFIRE
is Dr. Robert Jacobson, associate director of the Human
Interface Technology Laboratory at the University of
Washington and a former information-policy analyst
with the California legislature.

BRAND
is Russell Brand, a senior computer scientist
with Reasoning Systems in Palo Alto, California.

CLIFF
is Clifford Stoll, the astronomer who caught a spy in a military
computer network and published an account of his investigation
entitled The Cuckoo's Egg.

DAVE
is Dave Huges, a retired West Pointer who currently operates
his own political bulletin board.

DRAKE
is Frank Drake, a computer-science student at a West Coast
university and the editor of W.O.R.M., *a cyberpunk magazine.*

EDDIE JOE HOMEBOY

is a pseudonym for a professional software engineer who has worked at Lucasfilm, Pyramid Technology, Apple Computer, and Autodesk.

EMMANUEL GOLDSTEIN

is the editor of 2600, *the "hacker's quarterly."*

HANK

is Hank Roberts, who builds mobiles, flies hang gliders, and proofreads for the Whole Earth Catalog.

JIMG

is Jim Gasperini, the author, with TRANS Fiction Systems, of Hidden Agenda, a computer game that simulates political conflict in Central America.

JRC

is Jon Carroll, daily columnist for the San Francisco Chronicle *and writer-in-residence for the Pickle Family Circus, a national traveling circus troupe based in San Francisco.*

KK

is Kevin Kelly, editor of the Whole Earth Review *and a cofounder of the Hacker's Conference.*

LEE

is Lee Felsenstein, who designed the Osborne-1 computer and cofounded the Homebrew Computer Club.

MANDEL

is Tom Mandel, a professional futurist and an organizer of the Hacker's Conference.

RH

is Robert Horvitz, Washington correspondent for the Whole Earth Review.

RMS

is Richard Stallman, founder of the Free Software Foundation.

TENNEY

is Glenn Tenney, an independent-systems architect and an organizer of the Hacker's Conference.

ACID PHREAK *and* PHIBER OPTIK

are both pseudonyms for hackers who decline to be identified.

The Digital Frontier

HARPER'S [Day 1, 9:00 A.M.]: When the computer was young, the word *hacking* was used to describe the work of brilliant students who explored and expanded the uses to which this new technology might be employed. There was even talk of a "hacker ethic." Somehow, in the succeeding years, the word has taken on dark connotations, suggesting the actions of a criminal. What is the hacker ethic, and does it survive?

ADELAIDE [Day 1, 9:25 A.M.]: The hacker ethic survives, and it is a fraud. It survives in anyone excited by technology's power to turn many small, insignificant things into one vast, beautiful thing. It is a fraud because there is nothing magical about computers that causes a user to undergo religious conversion and devote himself to the public good. Early automobile inventors were hackers too. At first the elite drove in luxury. Later practically everyone had a car. Now we have traffic jams, drunk drivers, air pollution, and suburban sprawl. The old magic of an automobile occasionally surfaces, but we possess no delusions that it automatically invades the consciousness of anyone who sits behind the wheel. Computers are power, and direct contact with power can bring out the best or the worst in a person. It's tempting to think that everyone exposed to the technology will be grandly inspired, but, alas, it just ain't so.

BRAND [Day 1, 9:54 A.M.]: The hacker ethic involves several things. One is avoiding waste; insisting on using idle computer power—often hacking into a system to do so, while taking the greatest precautions not to damage the system. A second goal of many hackers is the free exchange of technical information. These hackers feel that patent and copyright restrictions slow down technological

232

advances. A third goal is the advancement of human knowledge for its own sake. Often this approach is unconventional. People we call crackers often explore systems and do mischief. They are called hackers by the press, which doesn't understand the issues.

KK [Day 1, 11:19 A.M.]: The hacker ethic went unnoticed early on because the explorations of basement tinkerers were very local. Once we all became connected, the work of these investigators rippled through the world. Today the hacking spirit is alive and kicking in video, satellite TV, and radio. In some fields they are called "chippers," because they modify and peddle altered chips. Everything that was once said about "phone phreaks" can be said about them too.

DAVE [Day 1, 11:29 A.M.]: Bah. Too academic. Hackers hack. Because they want to. Not for any higher purpose. Hacking is not dead and won't be as long as teenagers get their hands on the tools. There is a hacker born every minute.

ADELAIDE [Day 1, 11:42 A.M.]: Don't forget ego. People break into computers because it's fun and it makes them feel powerful.

BARLOW [Day 1, 11:54 A.M.]: Hackers hack. Yeah, right, but what's more to the point is that humans hack and always have. Far more than just opposable thumbs, upright posture, or excess cranial capacity, human beings are set apart from all other species by an itch, a hard-wired dissatisfaction. Computer hacking is just the latest in a series of quests that started with fire hacking. Hacking is also a collective enterprise. It brings to our joint endeavors the simultaneity that other collective organisms—ant colonies, Canada geese—take for granted. This is important, because combined with our itch to probe is a need to *connect*. Humans miss the almost telepathic connectedness that I've observed in other herding mammals. And we want it back. Ironically, the solitary sociopath and his 3:00 A.M. endeavors hold the most promise for delivering species reunion.

EDDIE JOE HOMEBOY [Day 1, 4:44 P.M.]: Hacking really took hold with the advent of the personal computer, which freed programmers from having to use a big time-sharing system. A hacker could sit in the privacy of his home and hack to his heart's and head's content.

LEE [Day 1, 5:17 P.M.]: "Angelheaded hipsters burning for the ancient heavenly connection to the starry dynamo in the machinery of night" (Allen Ginsberg, "Howl"). I still get an endorphin rush when I go on a design run—my mind out over the edge, groping for possibilities that can be sensed when various parts are held in juxtaposition with a view toward creating a whole object: straining to get through the epsilon-wide crack between What Is and What Could Be. Somewhere there's the Dynamo of Night, the ultra-mechanism waiting to be dreamed, that we'll never get to in actuality (think what it would *weigh!*) but that's present somehow in the vicinity of those mental

A Hacker's Lexicon

Back door: A point of entry into a computer system—often installed there by the original programmer—that provides secret access.

Bomb: A destructive computer program, which, when activated, destroys the files in a computer system.

Chipper: A hacker who specializes in changing the programming instructions of computer chips.

Cracker: A hacker who breaks illegally into computer systems and creates mischief; often used pejoratively. The original meaning of *cracker* was narrower, describing those who decoded copyright-protection schemes on commercial software products either to redistribute the products or to modify them; sometimes known as a software pirate.

Hacker: Originally, a compulsive computer programmer. The word has evolved in meaning over the years. Among computer users, *hacker* carries a positive connotation, meaning anyone who creatively explores the operations of

wrestling matches. When I reemerge into the light of another day with the design on paper—and with the knowledge that if it ever gets built, things will never be the same again—I know I've been where artists go. That's hacking to me: to transcend custom and to engage in creativity for its own sake, but also to create objective effects. I've been around long enough to see the greed creeps take up the unattended reins of power and shut down most of the creativity that put them where they are. But I've also seen things change, against the best efforts of a stupidly run industry. We cracked the egg out from under the Computer Priesthood, and now everyone can have omelets.

RMS [Day 1, 5:19 P.M.]: The media and the courts are spreading a certain image of hackers. It's important for us not to be shaped by that image. But there are two ways that it can happen. One way is for hackers to become part of the security-maintenance establishment. The other, more subtle, way is for a hacker to become the security-breaking

computer systems. Recently, it has taken on a negative connotation, primarily through confusion with *cracker*.

Phone phreak: One who explores the operations of the phone system, often with the intent of making free phone calls.

Social engineering: A nontechnical means of gaining information simply by persuading people to hand it over. If a hacker wished to gain access to a computer system, for example, an act of *social engineering* might be to contact a system operator and to convince him or her that the hacker is a legitimate user in need of a password; more colloquially, a con job.

Virus: A program that, having been introduced into a system, replicates itself and attaches itself to other programs, often with a variety of mischievous effects.

Worm: A destructive program that, when activated, fills a computer system with self-replicating information, clogging the system so that its operations are severely slowed, sometimes stopped.

phreak the media portray. By shaping ourselves into the enemy of the establishment, we uphold the establishment. But there's nothing wrong with breaking security if you're accomplishing something useful. It's like picking a lock on a tool cabinet to get a screwdriver to fix your radio. As long as you put the screwdriver back, what harm does it do?

ACID PHREAK [Day 1, 6:34 P.M.]: There is no one hacker ethic. Everyone has his own. To say that we all think the same way is preposterous. The hacker of old sought to find what the computer itself could do. There was nothing illegal about that. Today, hackers and phreaks are drawn to *specific*, often corporate, systems. It's no wonder everyone on the other side is getting mad. We're always one step ahead. We were back then, and we are now.

CLIFF [Day 1, 8:38 P.M.]: RMS said, "There's nothing wrong with breaking security if you're accomplishing something useful." Huh? How about, There's nothing wrong with entering a neighbor's house if you're accomplishing something useful, just as long as you clean up after yourself. Does my personal privacy mean anything? Should my personal letters and data be open to anyone who knows how to crack passwords? If not my property, then how about a bank's? Should my credit history be available to anyone who can find a back door to the private computers of TRW, the firm that tracks people's credit histories? How about a list of AIDS patients from a hospital's data bank? Or next week's prime interest rate from a computer at the Treasury Department?

BLUEFIRE [Day 1, 9:20 P.M.]: Computers are everywhere, and they link us together into a vast social "cybernetia." The grand skills of the hackers, formidable though they may have been, are incapable of subverting this automated social order. The networks in which we survive are more than copper wire and radio waves: They are *the* social organization. For every hacker in revolt, busting through a security code, ten thousand people are being wired up with automatic call-identification and credit-checking machines. Long live the Computer Revolution, which died aborning.

JRC [Day 1, 10:28 P.M.]: We have two different definitions here. One speaks of a tinkerer's ecstasy, an ecstasy that is hard to maintain in the corporate world but is nevertheless at the heart of Why Hackers Hack. The second is political, and it has to do with the free flow of information. Information should flow more freely (how freely is being debated), and the hacker can make it happen because the hacker knows how to undam the pipes. This makes the hacker ethic—of necessity—antiauthoritarian.

EMMANUEL GOLDSTEIN [Day 2, 2:41 A.M.]: It's meaningless what we call ourselves: hackers, crackers, techno-rats. We're individuals who happen to play with high tech. There is no *hacker community* in the traditional sense of the term. There are no leaders and no agenda. We're just individuals out exploring.

BRAND [Day 2, 9:02 A.M.]: There are two issues: invariance and privacy. Invariance is the art of leaving things as you found them. If someone used my house for the day and left everything as he found it so that there was no *way* to tell he had been there, I would see no problem. With a well-run computer system, we can assure invariance. Without this assurance we must fear that the person picking the lock to get the screwdriver will break the lock, the screwdriver, or both. Privacy is more complicated. I want my medical records, employment records, and letters to *The New Republic* private because I fear that someone will do something with the information that is against my interests. If I could trust people not to do bad things with information, I would not need to hide it. Rather than preventing the "theft" of this data, we should prohibit its collection in the first place.

HOMEBOY [Day 2, 9:37 A.M.]: Are crackers really working for the free flow of information? Or are they unpaid tools of the establishment, identifying the holes in the institutional dike so that they can be plugged by the authorities, only to be tossed in jail or exiled?

DRAKE [Day 2, 10:54 A.M.]: There is an unchallenged assumption that crackers have some political motivation. Earlier, crackers were portrayed as failed revolutionaries;

now Homeboy suggests that crackers may be tools of the establishment. These ideas about crackers are based on earlier experiences with subcultures (beats, hippies, yippies). Actually, the contemporary cracker is often middle-class and doesn't really distance himself from the "establishment." While there are some anarcho-crackers, there are even more right-wing crackers. The hacker ethic crosses political boundaries.

MANDEL [Day 2, 11:01 A.M.]: The data on crackers suggests that they are either juvenile delinquents or plain criminals.

BARLOW [Day 2, 11:34 A.M.]: I would far rather have *everyone* know my most intimate secrets than to have noncontextual snippits of them "owned" by TRW and the FBI—and withheld from me! Any cracker who is entertained by peeping into my electronic window is welcome to the view. Any institution that makes money selling rumors of my peccadilloes is stealing from me. Anybody who wants to inhibit that theft with electronic mischief has my complete support. Power to the techno-rats!

EMMANUEL [Day 2, 7:09 P.M.]: Calling someone on the phone is the equivalent of knocking on that person's door, right? Wrong! When someone answers the phone, you are *inside* the home. You have already been *let* in. The same with an answering machine, or a personal computer, if it picks up the phone. It is wrong to violate a person's privacy, but electronic rummaging is not the same as breaking and entering. The key here is that most people are unaware of *how easy it is* for others to invade their electronic privacy and see credit reports, phone bills, FBI files, Social Security reports. The public is grossly underinformed, and that's what must be fixed if hackers are to be thwarted. If we had an educated public, though, perhaps the huge—and now common—data bases would never have been allowed to exist. Hackers have become scapegoats: We discover the gaping holes in the system and then get blamed for the flaws.

HOMEBOY [Day 2, 7:41 P.M.]: Large, insular, undemocratic governments and institutions need scapegoats. It's the first step down the road to fascism. *That's* where hackers play into the hands of the establishment.

DAVE [Day 2, 7:55 P.M.]: If the real criminals are those who leave gaping holes in their systems, then the real criminals in house burglaries are those who leave their windows unlatched. Right? Hardly. And Emmanuel's analogy to a phone being answered doesn't hold either. There is no security protection in making a phone call. A computer system has a *password*, implying a desire for security. Breaking into a poorly protected house is still burglary.

CLIFF [Day 2, 9:06 P.M.]: Was there a hacker's ethic and does it survive? More appropriately, was there a vandal's ethic and does it survive? As long as there are communities, someone will violate the trust that binds them. Once, our computers were isolated, much as eighteenth-century villages were. Little was exchanged, and each developed independently. Now we've built far-flung electronic neighborhoods. These communities are built on trust: people believing that everyone profits by sharing resources. Sure enough, vandals crept in, breaking into systems, spreading viruses, pirating software, and destroying people's work. "It's okay," they say. "I can break into a system because I'm a hacker." Give me a break!

BARLOW [Day 2, 10:41 P.M.]: I live in a small town. I don't have a key to my house. Am I asking for it? I think not. Among the juvenile delinquents in my town, there does exist a vandal's ethic. I know because I once was one. In a real community, part of a kid's rite of passage is discovering what walls can be breached. Drive 110 miles per hour on Main Street is a common symptom of rural adolescence, publicly denounced but privately understood. Many teenagers die in this quest—two just the night before last—but it is basic to our culture. Even rebellious kids understand that risk to one's safety is one thing, wanton vandalism or theft is another. As a result, almost no one locks anything here. In fact, a security system is an affront to a teenage psyche. While a kid might be dissuaded by conscience, he will regard a barricade as an insult and a challenge. So the CEOs who are moving here (the emperor of PepsiCo and the secretary of state among them) soon discover that over the winter people break into their protected mansions just to hang out. When systems are open, the community prospers, and teenage miscreants are satisfied to risk their own lives and little else. When the social contract is enforced by security, the native freedom of the adolescent soul will rise up to challenge it in direct proportion to its imposition.

HANK [Day 2, 11:23 P.M.]: Barlow, the small town I grew up in was much like yours—until two interstate highways crossed nearby. The open-door style changed in one, hard summer because our whole *town* became unlocked. I think Cliff's community is analogous to my little town—confronted not by a new locked-up neighbor who poses a challenge to the local kids but by a sudden, permanent opening up of the community to many faceless outsiders who owe the town no allegiance.

EMMANUEL [Day 3, 1:33 A.M.]: Sorry, I don't buy Dave's unlatched-window analogy. A hacker who wanders into a system with the ease that it's done today is, in my analogy, walking into a house without walls—and with a cloaking device! Any good hacker can make himself invisible. If housebreaking were this easy, people would be enraged. But we're missing the point. I'm not referring to accessing a PC in someone's bedroom but about accessing credit reports, government files, motor vehicle records, and the megabytes of data piling up on each of us. Thousands of people legally can see and use this ever-growing mountain of data, much of its erroneous. Whose rights are we violating when we peruse a file? Those of the person we look up? He doesn't even know that information exists, that it was compiled without his consent, and that it's not his property anymore! The invasion of privacy took place long before the hacker ever arrived. The only way to find out how such a system works is to break the rules. It's not what hackers do that will lead us into a state of constant surveillance; it's allowing the authorities to impose on us a state of mock crisis.

MANDEL [Day 3, 9:27 A.M.]: Note that the word *crime* has no fixed reference in our discussion. Until recently, breaking into government computer systems wasn't a crime; now it is. *Crime* gets redefined all the time. Offend enough people or institutions and, lo and behold, someone will pass a law. That is partly what is going on now: Hackers are pushing buttons, becoming more visible, and that inevitably means more laws and more crimes.

ADELAIDE [Day 3, 9:42 A.M.]: Every practitioner of these arts knows that at minimum he is trespassing. The English "country traveler ethic" applies: The hiker is always ethical enough to close the pasture gates behind him so that no sheep escape during his pastoral stroll through someone else's property. The problem is that what some see as gentle trespassing others see as theft of service, invasion of privacy, threat to national security—take your pick.

BARLOW [Day 3, 2:38 P.M.]: I regard the *existence* of proprietary data about me to be theft—not just in the legal sense but in a faintly metaphysical one, rather like the belief among aborigines that a photograph steals the soul. The crackers who maintain access to that data are, at this level, liberators. Their incursions are the only way to keep the system honest.

RMS [Day 3, 2:48 P.M.]: Recently, a tough anti-hacker measure was proposed in England. In *The Economist* I saw a wise response, arguing that it was silly to treat an action as worse when it involves a computer than when it does not. They noted, for example, that physical trespassing was considered a civil affair, not a criminal one, and said that computer trespassing should be treated likewise. Unfortunately, the U.S. government was not so wise.

BARLOW [Day 3, 3:23 P.M.]: The idea that a crime is worse if a computer is involved relates to the gathering governmental perception that computer viruses and guns may be related. I know that sounds absurd, but they have more in common than one might think. For all its natural sociopathy, the virus is not without philosophical potency—like a gun. Here in Wyoming guns are part of the furniture.

Only recently have I observed an awareness of their political content. After a lot of frothing about prying cold, dead fingers from triggers, the sentiment was finally distilled to a bumper sticker I saw on a pickup the other day: "Fear the Government That Fears Your Gun." Now I've read too much Gandhi to buy that line without misgivings, but it would be hard to argue that Tiananmen Square could have been inflicted on a populace capable of shooting back. I don't wholeheartedly defend computer viruses, but one must consider their increasingly robust deterrent potential. Before it's over, the War on Drugs could easily turn into an Armageddon between those who love liberty and those who crave certainty, providing just the excuse the control freaks have been waiting for to rid America of all that constitutional mollycoddling called the Bill of Rights. Should that come to pass, I will want to use every available method to vex and confuse the eyes and ears of surveillance. The virus could become the necessary instrument of our freedom. At the risk of sounding like some digital *posse comitatus*, I say: Fear the Government That Fears Your Computer.

TENNEY [Day 3, 4:41 P.M.]: Computer-related crimes are more feared because they are performed remotely—a crime can be committed in New York by someone in Los Angeles—and by people not normally viewed as being criminals—by teenagers who don't look like delinquents. They're very smart nerds, and they don't look like Chicago gangsters packing heat.

BARLOW [Day 4, 12:12 A.M.]: People know so little of these things that they endow computers and the people who *do* understand them with powers neither possesses. If America has a religion, its ark is the computer and its covenant is the belief that Science Knows. We are mucking around in the temple, guys. It's a good way to catch hell.

DAVE [Day 4, 9:18 A.M.]: Computers *are* the new American religion. The public is in awe of—and fears—the mysteries and the high priests who tend them. And the public reacts just as it always has when faced with fear of the unknown—punishment, burning at the stake. Hackers are like the early Christians. When caught, they will be thrown to the lions before the Roman establishment: The mob cheered madly when Robert Morris was devoured.

KK [Day 6, 11:37 A.M.]: The crackers here suggest that they crack into systems with poor security *because* the security is poor. Do more sophisticated security precautions diminish or increase the need to crack the system?

ACID [Day 6, 1:20 P.M.]: If there was a system that we knew was uncrackable, we wouldn't even try to crack it. On the other hand, if some organization boasted that its system was impenetrable and we knew that was media hype, I think it would be safe to say we'd have to "enlighten" them.

EMMANUEL [Day 6, 2:49]: Why do we insist on cracking systems? The more people ask those kinds of questions, the more I want to get in! Forbid access and the demand for access increases. For the most part, it's simply a mission of exploration. In the words of the new captain of the starship *Enterprise*, Jean-Luc Picard, "Let's see what's out there!"

ACID [Day 6, 8:29 P.M.]: CICIMS is pretty tough.

PHIBER OPTIK [Day 7, 2:36 P.M.]: Really? CICIMS is a system used by Bell operating companies. The entire security system was changed after myself and a friend must have been noticed in it. For the entire United States, there is only one such system, located in Indiana. The new security scheme is flawless *in itself*, and there is no chance of "social engineering," i.e., bullshitting someone inside the system into telling you what the passwords are. The system works like this: You log on with the proper account and password; then, depending on who you are, the system asks at random three of ten questions that are unique to each user. But the system *can* be compromised by entering forwarding instructions into the phone company's switch for that exchange, thereby intercepting every phone call that comes in to the system over a designated period of time and connecting the call to your computer. If you are familiar with the security layout, you can emulate its appearance and fool the caller into giving you the answers to his questions. Then you call the system yourself and use those answers to get in. There are other ways of doing it as well.

BLUEFIRE [Day 7, 11:53 P.M.]: I can't stand it! Who do you think pays for the security that the telephone companies must maintain to fend off illegal use? I bet it costs the ratepayers around $10 million for this little extravaganza. The cracker circus isn't harmless at all, unless you don't mind paying for other people's entertainment. Hackers who have contributed to the social welfare should be recognized. But cracking is something else—namely, fun at someone else's expense—and it ain't the folks who own the phone companies who pay; it's us, me and you.

BARLOW [Day 8, 7:35 A.M.]: I am becoming increasingly irritated at this idea that you guys are exacting vengeance for the sin of openness. You seem to argue that if a system is dumb enough to be open, it is your moral duty to violate it. Does the fact that I've never locked my house—even when I was away for months at a time—mean that someone should come in and teach me a good lesson?

ACID [Day 8, 3:23 P.M.]: Barlow, you leave the door open to your house? Where do you live?

BARLOW [Day 8, 10:11 P.M.]: Acid, my house is at 372 North Franklin Street in Pinedale, Wyoming. Heading north on Franklin, go about two blocks off the main drag before you run into a hay meadow on the left. I'm the last house before the field. The computer is always on. But do you really mean to imply what you did with that question? Are you merely a sneak looking for easy places to violate? You disappoint me, pal. For all your James Dean-on-Silicon rhetoric, you're not a cyberpunk. You're just a punk.

EMMANUEL [Day 9, 12:55 A.M.]: No offense, Barlow, but your house analogy doesn't stand up, because your house is far less interesting than a Defense Department computer. For the most part, hackers don't mess with individuals. Maybe we feel sorry for them; maybe they're boring. Institutions are where the action is, because they are compiling this mountain of data—without your consent. Hackers are not guardian angels, but if you think we're what's wrong with the system, I'd say that's precisely what those in charge want you to believe. By the way, you left out your zip code. It's 82941.

BARLOW [Day 9, 8:34 A.M.]: Now that's more like it. There is an ethical distinction between people and institutions. The law makes little distinction. We pretend that institutions are somehow human because they are made of humans. A large bureaucracy resembles a human about as much as a reef resembles a coral polyp. To expect an institution to have a conscience is like expecting a horse to have one. As with every organism, institutions are chiefly concerned with their own physical integrity and survival. To say that

A Brief History of Hacking

September 1970— John Draper takes as his alias the name Captain Crunch after he discovers that the toy whistle found in the cereal of the same name perfectly simulates the tone necessary to make free phone calls.

March 1975— The Homebrew Computer Club, an early group of computer hackers, holds its first meeting in Menlo Park, California.

July 1976— Homebrew members Steve Wozniak, twenty-six, and Steve Jobs, twenty-one, working out of a garage, begin selling the first personal computer, known as the Apple.

June 1980— In one week, errors in the computer system operating the U.S. air-defense network cause two separate false reports of Soviet missile launches, each prompting an increased state of nuclear readiness.

December 1982— Sales of Apple personal computers top one billion dollars per year.

they have some higher purpose beyond their survival is to anthropomorphize them. You are right, Emmanuel. The house analogy breaks down here. Individuals live in houses; institutions live in mainframes. Institutions are functionally remorseless and need to be checked. Since their blood is digital, we need to be in their bloodstreams like an infection of humanity. I'm willing to extend limitless trust to other human beings. In my experience they've never failed to deserve it. But I have as much faith in institutions as they have in me. None.

OPTIK [Day 9, 10:19 A.M.]: In other words, Mr. Barlow, you say something, someone proves you wrong, and then you agree with him. I'm getting the feeling that you don't exactly chisel your views in stone.

HANK [Day 9, 11:18 A.M.]: Has Mr. Optik heard the phrase "thesis, antithesis, synthesis"?

BARLOW [Day 10, 10:48 A.M.]: Optik, I do change my mind a lot. Indeed, I often find it occupied by numerous contra-

---

November 1984— Steven Levy's book *Hackers* is published, popularizing the concept of the "hacker ethic": that "access to computers, and anything that might teach you something about the way the world works, should be unlimited and total." The book inspires the first Hacker's Conference, held that month.

January 1986— The "Pakistani Brain" virus, created by a software distributor in Lahore, Pakistan, infects IBM computers around the world, erasing data files.

June 1986— The U.S. Office of Technology Assessment warns that massive, cross-indexed government computer records have become a "de facto national data base containing personal information on most Americans."

March 1987— William Gates, a Harvard dropout who founded Microsoft Corporation, becomes a billionaire.

November 1988— More than 6,000 computers linked by the nationwide Internet computer network are infected by a

dictions. The last time I believed in absolutes, I was about your age. And there's not a damn thing wrong with believing in absolutes at your age either. Continue to do so, however, and you'll find yourself, at my age, carrying placards filled with nonsense and dressing in rags.

ADELAIDE [Day 10, 6:27 P.M.]: The flaw in this discussion is the distorted image the media promote of the hacker as "whiz." The problem is that the one who gets caught obviously isn't. I haven't seen a story yet on a true genius hacker. Even Robert Morris was no whiz. The genius hackers are busy doing constructive things or are so good no one's caught them yet. It takes no talent to break into something. Nobody calls subway graffiti artists geniuses for figuring out how to break into the yard. There's a difference between genius and ingenuity.

BARLOW [Day 10, 9:48 P.M.]: Let me define my terms. Using *hacker* in a midspectrum sense (with crackers on one end

---

destructive computer program known as a worm and are crippled for two days. The worm is traced to Robert Morris Jr., a twenty-four-year-old Cornell University graduate student.

December 1988— A federal grand jury charges Kevin Mitnick, twenty-five, with stealing computer programs over telephone lines. Mitnick is held without bail and forbidden access to any telephones without supervision.

March 1989— Three West German hackers are arrested for entering thirty sensitive military computers using home computers and modems. The arrests follow a three-year investigation by Clifford Stoll, an astronomer at the Lawrence Berkeley Laboratory who began tracing the hackers after finding a seventy-five-cent billing error in the lab's computer system.

January 1990— Robert Morris Jr. goes on trial in Syracuse, New York, for designing and releasing the Internet worm. Convicted, he faces up to five years in prison and a $250,000 fine.

and Leonardo da Vinci on the other), I think it does take a kind of genius to be a truly productive hacker. I'm learning PASCAL now, and I am constantly amazed that people can spin those prolix recursions into something like Page-Maker. It fills me with the kind of awe I reserve for splendors such as the cathedral at Chartres. With crackers like Acid and Optik, the issue is less intelligence than alienation. Trade their modems for skateboards and only a slight conceptual shift would occur. Yet I'm glad they're wedging open the cracks. Let a thousand worms flourish.

OPTIK [Day 10, 10:11 P.M.]: You have some pair of balls comparing my talent with that of a skateboarder. Hmm . . . This was indeed boring, but nonetheless: *[Editors' Note: At this point in the discussion, Optik—apparently having hacked into TRW's computer records—posted a copy of Mr. Barlow's credit history. In the interest of Mr. Barlow's privacy—at least what is left of it—*Harper's Magazine *has not printed it.]* I'm not showing off. Any fool knowing the proper syntax and the proper passwords can look up a credit history. I just find your high-and-mighty attitude annoying and, yes, infantile.

HOMEBOY [Day 10, 10:17 P.M.]: Key here is "any fool."

ACID [Day 11, 1:37 P.M.]: For thirty-five dollars a year anyone can have access to TRW and see his or her own credit history. Optik did it for free. What's wrong with that? And why does TRW keep files on what color and religion we are? If you didn't know that they kept such files, who would have found out if it wasn't for a hacker? Barlow should be grateful that Optik has offered his services to update him on his personal credit file. Of course, I'd hate to see my credit history up in lights. But if you hadn't made our skins crawl, your info would not have been posted. Everyone gets back at someone when he's pissed; so do we. Only we do it differently. Are we punks? Yeah, I guess we are. A punk is what someone who has been made to eat his own words calls the guy who fed them to him.

Hacking the Constitution

HARPER'S [Day 4, 9:00 A.M.]: Suppose that a mole inside the government confirmed the existence of files on each of you, stored in the White House computer system, PROFS. Would you have the right to hack into that system to retrieve and expose the existence of such files? Could you do it?

TENNEY [Day 4, 1:42 P.M.]: The proverbial question of whether the end justifies the means. This doesn't have much to do with hacking. If the file were a sheet of paper in a locked cabinet, the same question would apply. In that case you could accomplish everything without technological hacking. Consider the Pentagon Papers.

EMMANUEL [Day 4, 3:55 P.M.]: Let's address the hypothetical. First, I need to find out more about PROFS. Is it accessible from off site, and if so, how? Should I update my 202-456 scan [a list of phone numbers in the White House's exchange that connect incoming calls to a computer]? I have a listing for every computer in that exchange, but the scan was done back in 1984. Is PROFS a new system? Perhaps it's in a different exchange? Does anybody know how many people have access to it? I'm also on fairly good terms with a White House operator who owes me a favor. But I don't know what to ask for. Obviously, I've already made up my mind about the *right* to examine this material. I don't want to debate the ethics of it at this point. If you're with me, let's do something about this. Otherwise, stay out of the way. There's hacking to be done.

ACID [Day 4, 5:24 P.M.]: Yes, I would try to break into the PROFS system. But first I'd have someone in the public eye, with no ties to hacking, request the info through the Freedom of Information Act. Then I'd hack in to verify the information I received.

DRAKE [Day 4, 9:13 P.M.]: Are there a lot of people involved in this antihacker project? If so, the chances of social engineering data out of people would be far higher than if it were a small, close-knit group. But yes, the simple truth is, if the White House has a dial-up line, it can be hacked.

EMMANUEL [Day 4, 11:27 P.M.]: The implication that a trust has been betrayed on the part of the government is certainly enough to make me want to look a little further. And I know I'm doing the right thing on behalf of others who don't have my abilities. Most people I meet see me as an ally who can help them stay ahead of an unfair system. That's what I intend to do here. I have a small core of dedicated hackers who could help. One's specialty is the UNIX system, another's is networks, and another's is phone systems.

TENNEY [Day 5, 12:24 A.M.]: PROFS is an IBM message program that runs on an operating system known as VM. VM systems usually have a fair number of holes, either to gain access or to gain full privileges. The CIA was working on, and may have completed, a supposedly secure VM system. No ethics here, just facts. But a prime question is to determine what system via what phone number. Of course, the old inside job is easier. Just find someone who owes a favor or convince an insider that it is a moral obligation to do this.

BARLOW [Day 5, 2:46 P.M.]: This scenario needs to be addressed in four parts: ethical, political, practical I (from the standpoint of the hack itself), and practical II (disseminating the information without undue risk).

Ethical: Since World War II, we've been governed by a paramilitary bureaucracy that believes freedom is too precious to be entrusted to the people. These are the same folks who had to destroy the village in order to save it. Thus the government has become a set of Chinese boxes. Americans who believe in democracy have little choice but to shred the barricades of secrecy at every opportunity. It isn't merely permissible to hack PROFS. It is a moral obligation.

Political: In the struggle between control and liberty, one has to avoid action that will drive either side to extreme behavior. The basis of terrorism, remember, is excess. If we hack PROFS, we must do it in a way that doesn't become a pretext for hysterical responses that might eventually include zero tolerance of personal computers. The answer is to set up a system for entry and exit that never lets on we've been there.

Practical I: Hacking the system should be a trivial undertaking.

Practical II: Having retrieved the smoking gun, it must be made public in such a way that the actual method of acquisition does not become public. Consider Watergate: The prime leaker was somebody whose identity and information-gathering technique is still unknown. So having obtained the files, we turn them over to the *Washington Post* without revealing our own identities or how we came by the files.

EMMANUEL [Day 5, 9:51 P.M.]: PROFS is used for sending messages back and forth. It's designed *not* to forget things. And it's used by people who are not computer literate. The document we are looking for is likely an electronic-mail message. If we can find out who the recipient or sender is, we can take it from there. Since these people frequently use the system to communicate, there may be a way for them to dial into the White House from home. Finding that number won't be difficult: frequent calls to a number local to the White House and common to a few different people. Once I get a dial-up, I'll have to look at whatever greeting I get to determine what kind of system it is. Then we need to locate someone expert in the system to see if there are any built-in back doors. If there aren't, I will social engineer my way into a working account and then attempt to break out of the program and explore the entire system.

BRAND [Day 6, 10:06 A.M.]: I have two questions: Do you believe in due process as found in our Constitution? And do you believe that this "conspiracy" is so serious that extraordinary measures need to be taken? If you believe in due process, then you shouldn't hack into the system to defend our liberties. If you don't believe in due process, you are an anarchist and potentially a terrorist. The government is justified in taking *extreme* action to protect itself and the rest of us from you. If you believe in the Constitution but also that this threat is so extreme that patriots have a duty to intercede, then you should seek one of the honest national officials who can legally demand a copy of the document. If you believe that there is no sufficiently honest politician and you steal and publish the documents, you are talking about a revolution.

ACID [Day 6, 1:30 P.M.]: This is getting too political. Who says that hacking has to have a political side? Generalizing does nothing but give hackers a false image. I couldn't care less about politics, and I hack.

LEE [Day 6, 9:01 P.M.]: Sorry, Acid, but if you hack, what you do is inherently political. Here goes: Political power is exercised by control of information channels. Therefore, any action that changes the capability of someone in power to control these channels *is* politically relevant. Historically, the one in power has been not the strongest person but the one who has convinced the goon squad to do his bidding. The goons give their power to him, usually in exchange for free food, sex, and great uniforms. The turning point of most successful revolutions is when the troops ignore the orders coming from above and switch their allegiance. Information channels. Politics. These days, the cracker represents a potential for making serious political change if he coordinates with larger social and economic forces. Without this coordination, the cracker is but a techno-bandit, sharpening his weapon and chuckling about how someday . . . Revolutions often make good use of bandits, and some of them move into high positions when they're successful. But most of them are done away with. One cracker getting in won't do much good. Working in coordination with others is another matter—called politics.

JIMG [Day 7, 12:28 A.M.]: A thought: Because it has become so difficult to keep secrets (thanks, in part, to crackers), and so expensive and counterproductive (the trade-off in lost opportunities is too great), secrets are becoming less worth protecting. Today, when secrets come out that would have brought down governments in the past, "spin-control experts" shower the media with so many lies that the truth is obscured despite being in plain sight. It's the information equivalent of the Pentagon plan to surround each real missile with hundreds of fake ones, rendering radar useless. If hackers managed to crack the White House system, a hue and cry would be raised—not about what the hackers found in the files but about what a threat hackers are to this great democracy of ours.

HARPER'S [Day 7, 9:00 A.M.]: Suppose you hacked the files from the White House and a backlash erupted. Congress-men call for restrictions, arguing that the computer is "property" susceptible to regulation and not an instru-ment of "information" protected by the First Amendment. Can we craft a manifesto setting forth your views on how the computer fits into the traditions of the American Con-stitution?

DAVE [Day 7, 5:30 P.M.]: If Congress ever passed laws that tried to define what we do as "technology" (regulatable) and *not* "speech," I would become a rebellious criminal immediately—and as loud as Thomas Paine ever was. Although computers are part "property" and part "prem-ises" (which suggests a need for privacy), they are su-premely instruments of *speech*. I don't want any congres-sional King Georges treading on my cursor. We must continue to have *absolute* freedom of electronic speech!

BARLOW [Day 7, 10:07 P.M.]: Even in a court guided by my favorite oxymoron, Justice Rehnquist, this is an open-and-shut case. The computer is a printing press. Period. The only hot-lead presses left in this country are either in museums or being operated by poets in Vermont. The computer cannot fall under the kind of regulation to which radio and TV have become subject, since computer output is not broadcast. If these regulations amount to anything more than a fart in the congressional maelstrom, then we might as well scrap the whole Bill of Rights. What I am doing with my fingers right now is "speech" in the clear-est sense of the word. We don't need no stinking mani-festos.

jimg [Day 8, 12:02 a.m.]: This type of congressional action is so clearly unconstitutional that "law hackers"—everyone from William Kunstler to Robert Bork— would be all over it. The whole idea runs so completely counter to our laws that it's hard to get worked up about it.

adelaide [Day 8, 9:51 a.m.]: Not so fast. There used to be a right in the Constitution called "freedom from unreasonable search and seizure," but, thanks to recent Supreme Court decisions, your urine can be demanded by a lot of people. I have no faith in the present Supreme Court to uphold any of my rights of free speech. The complacent reaction here—that whatever Congress does will eventually be found unconstitutional—is the same kind of complacency that led to the current near-reversals of *Roe v. Wade*.

jrc [Day 8, 10:05 a.m.]: I'd forgo the manifestos and official explanations altogether: Fight brushfire wars against specific government incursions and wait for the technology to metastasize. In a hundred years, people won't have to be told about computers because they will have an instinctive understanding of them.

kk [Day 8, 2:14 p.m.]: Hackers are not sloganeers. They are doers, take-things-in-handers. They are the opposite of philosophers: They don't wait for language to catch up to them. Their arguments are their actions. You want a manifesto? The Internet worm was a manifesto. It had more meaning and symbolism than any revolutionary document you could write. To those in power running the world's nervous system, it said: Wake up! To the underground of hackers, crackers, chippers, and techno-punks, it said: You have power; be careful. To the mass of citizens who find computers taking over their telephone, their TV, their toaster, and their house, it said: Welcome to Wonderland.

barlow [Day 8, 10:51 p.m.]: Apart from the legal futility of fixing the dam after it's been breached, I've never been comfortable with manifestos. They are based on the ideologue's delusion about the simplicity, the figure-out-ability, of the infinitely complex thing that is Life Among the Humans. Manifestos take reductionism for a long ride off a short pier. Sometimes the ride takes a very long time. Marx and Engels didn't actually crash until last year. Manifestos fail because they are fixed and consciousness isn't. I'm with JRC: Deal with incursions when we need to, on our terms, like the guerrillas we are. To say that we can outmaneuver those who are against us is like saying that honeybees move quicker than Congress. The future is to the quick, not the respectable.

RH [Day 8, 11:43 P.M.]: Who thinks computers can't be regulated? The Electronic Communications Privacy Act of 1986 made it a crime to own "any electronic, mechanical, or other device [whose design] renders it primarily useful for the purpose of the surreptitious interception of wire, oral, or electronic communication." Because of the way Congress defined "electronic communication," one could argue that even a modem is a surreptitious interception device (SID), banned by the ECPA and subject to confiscation. It's not that Congress intended to ban modems; it was just sloppy drafting. The courts will ultimately decide what devices are legal. Since it may not be possible to draw a clear bright line between legal and illegal interception devices, the gray area—devices with both legitimate and illegitimate uses—may be subject to regulation.

BARLOW [Day 9, 8:52 A.M.]: I admit with some chagrin that I'm not familiar with the ECPA. It seems I've fallen on the wrong side of an old tautology: Just because all saloon keepers are Democrats, it doesn't follow that all Democrats are saloon keepers. By the same token, the fact that all printing presses are computers hardly limits computers to that function. And one of the other things computers are good at is surreptitious monitoring. Maybe there's more reason for concern than I thought. Has any of this stuff been tested in the courts yet?

RH [Day 9, 10:06 P.M.]: My comments about surreptitious interception devices are not based on any court cases, since there have not been any in this area since the ECPA was enacted. It is a stretch of the imagination to think that a judge would ever find a stock, off-the-shelf personal computer to be a "surreptitious interception device." But a modem is getting a little closer to the point where a creative prosecutor could make trouble for a cracker, with fallout affecting many others. An important unknown is how the courts will apply the word *surreptitious*. There's very little case law, but taking it to mean "by stealth; hidden from view; having its true purpose physically disguised," I can spin some worrisome examples. I lobbied against the bill, pointing out the defects. Congressional staffers admitted privately that there was a problem, but they were in a rush to get the bill to the floor before Congress adjourned. They said they could patch it later, but it is a pothole waiting for a truck axle to rumble through.

JIMG [Day 10, 8:55 A.M.]: That's sobering information, RH. Yet I still think that this law, if interpreted the way you suggest, would be found unconstitutional, even by courts dominated by Reagan appointees. Also, the economic cost of prohibiting modems, or even restricting their use, would so outweigh conceivable benefits that the law would never go through. Finally, restricting modems would have no effect on the phreaks but would simply manage to slow everybody else down. If modems are outlawed, only outlaws will have modems.

RH [Day 10, 1:52 P.M.]: We're already past the time when one could wrap hacking in the First Amendment. There's a traditional distinction between words—expressions of opinions, beliefs, and information—and deeds. You can shout "Revolution!" from the rooftops all you want, and the post office will obligingly deliver your recipes for nitroglycerin. But acting on that information exposes you to criminal prosecution. The philosophical problem posed by hacking is that computer programs transcend this distinction: They are pure language that dictates action when read by the device being addressed. In that sense, a program is very different from a novel, a play, or even a recipe: Actions result automatically from the machine reading the words. A computer has no independent moral judgment, no sense of responsibility. Not yet, anyway. As we program and automate more of our lives, we undoubtedly will deal with more laws: limiting what the public can know, restricting devices that can execute certain instructions, and criminalizing the possession of "harmful" programs with "no redeeming social value." Blurring the distinction between language and action, as computer programming does, could eventually undermine the First Amendment or at least force society to limit its application. That's a very high price to pay, even for all the good things that computers make possible.

HOMEBOY [Day 10, 11:03 P.M.]: HACKING IS ART. CRACKING IS REVOLUTION. All else is noise. Cracks in the firmament are by nature threatening. Taking a crowbar to them is revolution.

V

Arguing from Principle

The destruction wreaked by what is called the sound bite can be heard in the data exchanges that today pass for what was once called public debate. Every television guest appears to have taken the typical advice of the media consultant: Ignore each question or comment and simply state your canned opinion. Thus, instead of argument—opinions clashing, changing one another, possibly creating a new idea—the television interview program is thirty minutes of contiguous, unrelated, staccato sound bites. To the audience, then, our society seems to skim from crisis to crisis, from one set of facts to another; and the discussion never digs into the underlying values that are being challenged by what's new.

On the issue of the environment, for example, we bob along amid oil spills, garbage recycling, toxic waste, and ozone holes. The debate is never left alone long enough to plumb the ephemera of headlines and address what is really changing: our definition of nature and our place in it. Likewise, arguments over birth control, in vitro fertilization, fetal brain implants, and embryonic surgery are restrained by brevity from arriving at the core question: How vigorously should we pursue the primal task of reproduction? In the debate over our very selves, we hear of organ transplants, genetic therapy, plundering of corpses, and the sale of parts. But what is really changing is not only the technology but the value we place on our bodies, both physically and metaphysically. On these three debates in particular—the environment, reproduction, and the body—where fundamental values are shifting, *Harper's Magazine* let the tape recorder run and allowed the sides to talk without a word from our sponsor.

Only Mankind's Presence Can Save Nature

The ongoing public conversation about the environment is grounded in the ancient dichotomy of man versus nature. So far we have sought to resolve the argument through a series of truces—either sequestering large tracts of wilderness in a state of imagined innocence, say, or limiting the ways in which man can domesticate nature's imagined savagery. A recent contribution to this conversation suggests that we have postponed too long a true settlement and that man is now talking to himself. Nature has ended.

But others say that we must radically change the conversation and begin to talk not of man *versus* nature but man *and* nature. This line of thinking suggests that we must discard what is, in fact, a false dichotomy and find new answers to old questions. What do we *see* when we look into a quiet stand of trees? Lumber? The planet's breathing apparatus? The habitat of animals? Home? In order to examine the rapidly changing metaphors that locate man's place into the world, *Harper's Magazine* recently asked five environmentalists with backgrounds in science, political activism, or philosophy to discuss the shifting definitions of nature and of ourselves.

---- ◆ ----

The following forum is based on a discussion held at the Ritz-Carlton Hotel in New York City. Michael Pollan served as moderator.

MICHAEL POLLAN
is executive editor of Harper's Magazine.

DANIEL B. BOTKIN
is professor of biology and environmental studies at the University of California at Santa Barbara and the author of Discordant Harmonies: A New Ecology for the Twenty-first Century.

DAVE FOREMAN
was chief lobbyist for the Wilderness Society and cofounded the environmental group Earth First! in 1980. He is the author of Ecodefense, The Big Outside, *and* Confessions of an Eco-Brute.

JAMES LOVELOCK
is an independent scientist who developed the Gaia theory, which regards our planet as a self-regulating system that behaves as if it were a living organism.

FREDERICK TURNER
is Founders Professor of Arts and Humanities at the University of Texas at Dallas and the author of the epic poem Genesis.

ROBERT D. YARO
is senior vice president of the Regional Plan Association in New York City, where he is preparing a new regional plan to manage future growth in the New York tri-state metropolitan region.

Beyond the Wilderness

MICHAEL POLLAN: Let us say we're in the town of Pineville, Connecticut. On the edge of town is a stand of virgin pine trees left to Pineville years ago with the stipulation that it be "kept in a state of nature." Known as the Tabernacle Pines, this forest is extraordinary, with trees more than 150 feet tall. A hurricane came through recently and devastated the forest. Seventy percent of the trees are down. The place is a mess, almost impassable. I am the curator of this forest, and I have to make a recommendation to the town. Do we leave it as it is—is that a state of nature?—or do we clear it out and replant pine, so that the next generation might enjoy some semblance of the old forest?

DAVE FOREMAN: Leave it as it is. Too often we think that nature is a snapshot in time. It's not. Nature is a continually evolving process. A large tree is often more important after it falls.

POLLAN: Important in what sense?

FOREMAN: A Douglas fir may stand for 800 years and provide various services to the life around it. After it falls, it provides even more services for the next 500 years—to beetles, termites, and fungi.

DANIEL BOTKIN: It's been shown that the shape and form of a stream and the life in it are often a function of the trees living and falling along the banks.

Forests are not static. They have a biography not unlike a human's. Their infancy is the open field or devastated forest. First, "pioneer species" begin to grow: herbs, grasses, and then shrubs. Afterward there are several stages of trees. These stages are dynamic and diverse. The forest's maturity is known as its "climax"—a more stable and less diverse mix of species that will persist for some time. In old age, a forest, such as the Tabernacle Pines, becomes susceptible to fire or hurricane. These stages of development, or forest succession, are quite interconnected. Take your fallen trees. Certain seeds regenerate best when they fall into the nest of a rotting log.

FOREMAN: Often you will see a "nurse log," with a series of trees growing out of it. After the log decays, you can sometimes see an archway in the roots. A forest will rejuvenate better if it's not replanted. When we try to jump-start the natural stages of forest development by replanting , we remove necessary nutrients, such as rotting logs, and the forests are crippled. Nature is not a pretty, manicured place maintained for human beings. It is a dynamic continuum, often a violent one.

JAMES LOVELOCK: If the land is surrounded by other forested areas, I agree. If the Tabernacle Pines were an *island* of trees, I think it would have been a kind of garden anyway. It might be more proper—even natural—to replant and rebuild.

FREDERICK TURNER: Leaving the land alone is attractive, but, as James Lovelock says, it might be *as* natural to do something with it. Certainly nature is not a manicured garden. Nature is a set of complicated feedback systems, constantly exchanging information. Some are self-duplicating—preserving the system as it is—and they are called homeostatic. Others are open-ended systems, constantly creating novel states and new ecologies. In an open-ended system, the most crucial element is the human species. So I would say that if the town is not involved in this question of leaving the forest alone or replanting it, one would then be violating nature, because absent from this process is the quintessential element of nature—us. Humankind is more *what nature is* than anything else.

POLLAN: Not just equal but more?

TURNER: More. Consider the fundamental tendency of evolution from the big bang to the higher animals. It is a tendency toward greater reflexivity, greater open-endedness, greater complexity, and greater "encephalization"—that is, a larger proportion of nervous tissue. Evolution in pre-living chemical systems occurs slowly and has no way of changing itself. Sexually reproducing life can record itself and then reshuffle and recombine the recordings. It can improve itself; that is evolution. Then you have organisms that thrive in societies, which is just another, perhaps more sophisticated, way of passing on information to another generation. Nature has had this tendency toward increasingly more complex ways of passing on information from the big bang all the way up. Humankind is what nature has been trying, all these millennia, "to be."

POLLAN: Are you saying that without man's intervention, nature doesn't know what is best for the planet?

TURNER: If one made the decision without human beings, then the decision would be, I think, unnatural.

BOTKIN: My problem is with the language "a state of nature." Nature does not exist in one state but in many states. If nature achieved a single *natural* state, then the answer to all environmental problems would be to let nature grow to that state. But once one knows that nature is dynamic, with changing states and different futures—and that these states range literally from fire to ice, with a variety of possible landscapes in between—then the choice becomes ours, mankind's, and that choice is "natural." So what is the nature we prefer? If you scratched beneath the assumptions of the average New Englander, you would discover that the idea of a "forest" is what the Pilgrims saw. It's as good a forest as any, so I would let the area grow back through the particular stages of succession that the Pilgrims saw. This means gardening the forest and weeding out the exotics—those species introduced by Europeans.

POLLAN: You would weed?

BOTKIN: Yes, the ailanthus, or tree of heaven; Japanese honeysuckle; the exotics. I'd do a little behind-the-scenes management.

ROBERT YARO: I would leave the land alone, but for a different reason. The landscape of Connecticut is as artificial as Central Park in New York City. It may not be as contrived, but the landscape of New England is a human creation. Unlike your England, Professor Lovelock, which is an over-tended "garden," New England is an under-tended garden. Early in this century, Massachusetts conducted an inventory of scenic landscapes and found a few remnants of forest in an otherwise open agricultural landscape. Fifty years later, when I conducted a similar inventory, I found that only 10 percent was agricultural and most of the rest was second-growth forest. Connecticut is quite similar. So I would leave Tabernacle Pines alone so that the people could learn the natural processes that shape their landscape. Dr. Botkin's goal of creating the forest succession of the Pilgrim era won't be useful on these few acres. I would turn to the larger canvas of the abandoned New England landscape. There are 130,000 acres of public land in Connecticut. Let's manage it and recreate a massive Pilgrims' forest.

LOVELOCK: The Tabernacle Pines were knocked down by a hypothetical hurricane. In fact, there have been many real hurricanes here, in England, and elsewhere. And we're getting more of them. I might follow E.F. Schumacher's maxim: Act locally, think globally. Thus, one wonders if it is sensible to plant the same kind of pines when the global climate is changing so much now.

POLLAN: What might be a good alternative?

LOVELOCK: Let nature select whatever would best survive under these new conditions.

BOTKIN: But the migration of the seeds is no longer possible from, say, the southern areas. So if you want to go that route, you would have to go to Virginia, collect the seeds, and then plant Virginia pine or southern pine

POLLAN: So aren't we really talking about *gardening* our state of nature, not leaving it alone?

FOREMAN: To a degree. First, we need to recognize that your Tabernacle Pines are tied not only to Connecticut and New England but to Central American rain forests. The songbird population—which needs all these habitats—is crashing right now because of the destruction of these forests.

Second, there is the opportunity for wilderness restoration on a grand scale in New England. One of the largest uninhabited areas in America is in northern Maine, 10 million acres without year-round inhabitants that stretch down to northern Vermont, New Hampshire, and the Adirondacks. Within my lifetime we could have a preserve in New England—with wolf, caribou, moose, and eastern panther—rivaling those in Alaska. We must use the ideas of conservation biology: core wilderness reserves, surrounded by buffer areas in which steadily decreasing human use is allowed as we get closer to the core, with biological corridors connecting the core preserves for the transmission of genetic material and wildness.

TURNER: The point about genetic material is critical. What might we want in our new forest? For example, should our goal be to maximize biomass—that is, the weight or mass of material? But how do you define "living"? What about most of a coral reef or heartwood, which is dead? Should the goal be to maximize the mass of DNA and RNA, the carriers of heredity? Should we farm the planet for genetic diversity? But one might think, Doesn't this idea slight other means of passing on information between generations—learning, rituals, libraries, this conversation, computers? Therefore, should we maximize nervous tissue—or the density of human culture—since that would maximize the amount of information getting passed on to other generations?

BOTKIN: The idea that we should find a single quantity to *maximize* is intellectual baggage from the nineteenth century. It is essentially the mechanical ideal, the metaphor of the engine with one peak of humming power. This metaphor coalesced with the ancient notion of a divine order—that nature was perfect. This union of ideas yielded the false view of nature as a single pristine state—undisturbed and without man. There is no such nature. Ecological systems have values other than "peak performance." The relationship between human beings and these natural systems is much more complex and more organic than the machine metaphor allows us to see. When we see ourselves as part of this *dynamism* of nature, we will have a more accurate metaphor and view of the world.

TURNER: Exactly my point. We're going to have to strive for all of these goals simultaneously.

POLLAN: I'm a bit alarmed that each of you is willing to interfere and make these decisions for nature. What is the measure of our actions? What is too much, too little?

FOREMAN: It's something we're going to be learning for the next thousand years. It's important to distinguish between native diversity—the life that has historical ties to a piece of land— and natural diversity—the life that will move on to a piece of land. Generally, those species that come in are "weed" species. We're finding out now, for example, that in the ancient forests of the Pacific Northwest, the marbled murrelet and the red-backed vole and the flying squirrel are losing habitat to the species adapted to disturbed ecosystems. For example, the white-tailed deer, in the North at least, is a weed species that has expanded its range as humans disrupt the environment, replacing caribou and moose.

LOVELOCK: I'm fascinated to hear Dave Foreman use the word *weed!* It's a dreadful word, isn't it?

TURNER: Isn't a weed a weed precisely because it's *good* at spreading itself around, and wouldn't it be *unnatural* to stop it from doing so? Why should we privilege the genetically less robust? Maybe weeds have a lot going for them.

BOTKIN: Maybe we should clarify what a weed is. A weed is to plants as dirt is to soil. A weed is a plant out of place. So a redwood tree in the desert is a weed. European weeds spread very well. They came over on the hosts of European ships, with cattle and hay. The most troublesome weeds arrive in the early stages of forest succession. If not weeded, for example, Japanese honeysuckle can overwhelm a sturdy hardwood stand in eastern North America.

FOREMAN: Spotted knapweed in Montana, tumbleweed in the Southwest, kudzu in the Southeast—all are weeds. But look at why they exist. I spent eight years locating the large roadless areas in the United States, and I found only 368 areas of more than 100,000 acres apiece in the West and 50,000 in the East. In other words, 92 percent of the lower forty-eight states has been developed. So we could try to reclaim some of the 92 percent. For example, the 10 million acres in Maine that I mentioned are owned by a few paper companies. The government could buy that land today for the price of a couple of Stealth bombers.

YARO: Dave, consider that the 10-million-acre forest in Maine is one of the last places in the Northeast where we have a resource-based economy. People work in the forest cutting trees and work in the mills turning the trees into paper—all of which relates to the people who pick up the *New York Times* in the morning. We shouldn't throw out the people and the economy to "save" the forest. Save both. A good example of this problem occurred in Cades Cove in the Smokies. The National Park Service came in sixty years ago to "preserve the Smokies" and threw out the local Appalachian people. To please the tourists, they have now hired costumed actors posing as Appalachians. We *can* introduce human use that isn't in conflict with preserving an intact ecosystem.

POLLAN: A preserve that includes *Homo sapiens?*

YARO: Yes. Last year I made trips to two similar landscapes—the Alps and Mount Rainier. In the Alps, I found beautiful landscapes that included villages, farms, factories, agriculture, and eventually wilderness. There was no national park and no artificial boundary between the natural and humanized area. Then, Mount Rainier. There's a line on the map. On one side of it, we've kicked out the local people. It's well kept inside the park but dull in comparison to its Swiss counterpart. Once you cross the line, all hell breaks loose. It's as though two alien cultures met at the national-park boundary. Outside of it are ticky-tacky signs, ski areas, and fast food. Now why can't we move the line of the park out but allow for certain human activity that reinforces what's there?

POLLAN: Let's return to Tabernacle Pines. There are houses bordering it. Forestry experts tell me that if I leave the drying, rotting logs, I can expect a major fire that would threaten the town, especially the property on the border.

BOTKIN: Tell them to go to Hartford and get fire insurance.

YARO: Insurance is a native industry in Connecticut, and we should respect it!

LOVELOCK: Without forest fires, you wouldn't have long-term oxygen regulation in the atmosphere. So if we stop all fires, we may harm ourselves in the long run.

POLLAN: Will you come with me and explain that to the fellow whose house is in danger?

LOVELOCK: Hard cases make bad law, don't they? Still, it's the only way, and somebody's going to be hurt.

FOREMAN: Why does nature always have to make the adjustment instead of people?

TURNER: Nature versus people again. I simply don't buy it. I want to register a protest about this and the 92 to 8 percent distinction. It is artificial. The Indians—the people who came across the Bering Land Bridge—changed the ecology of North America totally. And before that, the ice ages drastically altered these lands.

POLLAN: Is there a distinction between the changes wrought by humanity and the changes wrought by the ice ages?

BOTKIN: Yes. Essentially, the differences are the rate of change and man's introduction of novel actions. Trees migrate, but over thousands of years. In Michigan, Paul Bunyan's country, 19 million acres of white pine were logged in less than a hundred years. Plowing is a novel action, and we should avoid too much of it. Many chemicals are totally novel, so we should avoid them as well. Again, we shouldn't treat nature as if it's a machine—take it apart, rebuild it, and substitute new parts. The rule should be: Change nature at nature's rates and in nature's ways.

YARO: Our problem stems from a wilderness ethic that puts lines on maps and fences on the ground and says, "Keep your hands off." This ethic finds its complement in our land ethic, which says, "Take the money and run." This must end. We must manage our continent.

LOVELOCK: And that problem is made worse by agribusiness. We have plowed up so much more than we need. England is spending billions just to store its surplus grain. At one time, butter from my part of Britain was actually burned in German power stations.

POLLAN: Dave, are you sanguine when you hear all this optimistic talk about reconciling the interests of man and nature?

FOREMAN: No, I'm not. In studying evolution, we learn that the worst thing a species can be is too successful. That's the stage we're in. But we are living in a fool's paradise. We've ended a giddy drunk, and a nasty hangover awaits us. It might be AIDS, it might be something else. I want to make sure that we don't take everything with us. Believing this is the only thing that gives my life meaning.

Our problem is a spiritual crisis. The Puritans brought with them a theology that saw the wilderness of North America as a haunt of Satan, with savages as his disciples and wild animals as his demons—all of which had to be cleared, defeated, tamed, or killed. Opening up the dark forests became a spiritual mission: to flush evil out of hiding. If we are going to survive in North America, we have to go back, metaphorically, to that pilgrim shore again. Let's seek to learn from the land this time. I do believe that people are tied into nature. I don't want to separate humans from nature. But we must discover our proper place in that dynamic. Consider that Phoenix, Arizona, has one of the highest per capita water uses in the United States! People in Denver, Colorado, all have lawns requiring eleven inches of rain a week, just like English lords.

POLLAN: Are we threatening ourselves, the planet, or both?

FOREMAN: All of it. Ecologist Paul Ehrlich says that killing off species is analogous to taking rivets out of an airplane: Just one rivet, we can get by; but at some point, the airplane is no longer safe.

LOVELOCK: Paul Ehrlich propagates this notion of a fragile earth. It's not earth that's fragile; it's *we* who are fragile. Nature has withstood catastrophes far worse than what we've delivered. Nothing we do will destroy nature. But we can easily destroy ourselves.

Dave, we probably will experience a sudden drop in population, and comparatively soon. It won't happen here, of course, but in the tropical regions, where the sustaining forests are more gravely threatened. The humid, tropical forest regions house about a billion people. Once we've cleared 70 percent of the forests—which we are well on the way to doing—the remainder won't be able to sustain the region's climate. Without the rain, the trees will die. We may see this as early as 2000. And when that happens, a billion people will be facing death and starvation. We will have a refugee problem and political crisis as bad as a thermonuclear war.

FOREMAN: The naturalist Aldo Leopold said there are those who can live without wild things and those who cannot. I am one of those who cannot. I'm a product of the Pleistocene epoch, the age of large mammals. I am a large mammal. I *like* large mammals. I do not want to live in a world without jaguars and great blue whales and redwoods and rain forests, because this is my geological era, this is my family, this my context. I only have meaning *in situ*, in the age I live in, the late Pleistocene. I do not want to be the cause of a transition into a new era.

Designing Nature

POLLAN: Because of my brilliant disposition of the issue of Tabernacle Pines—suffice it to say I took *your* advice—I was elected mayor of neighboring Oakdale. Recently, an old women died and left a square mile of land on the edge of town to Oakdale. Her will stipulates that we use this land "for the benefit of Oakdaleans." The parcel has a moderate-size farm surrounded by second-growth oak forest. There's a bluff overlooking the farm and the famous Treaty Oak, where the Indians first made friends with the settlers. The bluff is where five generations of Oakdaleans have come to court; it has its *own* history. Now I am empowered to decide what happens to this land. I ran on a solid environmental ticket, and yet I also faced a 15 percent unemployment rate among the working class; pressure is building to develop on this land. What do I do?

TURNER: Allow limited development, but balance that by planting, *within* the town limits, indigenous species, thus extending their range. Erase the boundary between the urbanized area and nature. You might also offer property-tax exemptions for the number of species being preserved on your land. Lose species and you'd pay a higher tax.

YARO: He's assuming, Mr. Mayor, that you don't want to get reelected!

BOTKIN: I'd start with the Treaty Oak. That is history, so I'd leave it. I'd also take an acorn from it and plant it beside the old oak, so that there is a replacement. We always assume that trees, like nature, are permanent, and, of course, they're not. I would leave the farm alone and urge you to risk a push for conservation.

FOREMAN: I would turn it into an environmental education site for the town school system, basically maintain it as a natural area with trails, centers, environmental education. You could make the farm the headquarters, and you could employ some people that way.

YARO: Realize, right off that this is a sacred landscape. How many Oakdaleans were conceived in the backseats of Mustangs parked on the bluff? There are primal memories here. This place is a shrine. It will be very easy to muck things up if we aren't careful. You must keep the farm, because that's the vista seen from the bluff. You've got to manage it. To generate some money and jobs, I would consider limited development on the south end, built in a tight cluster tucked into the woods. It should look and feel like Oakdale instead of sprawl. Then, adopt new regulations that require similar land-conserving patterns of development throughout the Oakdale region.

BOTKIN: If you want to conserve it, I would avoid the pitfall that Central Park smartly avoided: letting people develop a little around the edges. You might try trading the southern land for additional northern land, especially the land upriver. Then you can make a statement about protecting the forest and the flood plain upriver.

LOVELOCK: If this were in Europe, one might consider "infilling." In other words, all development would happen *within* the town; the town's population density would be increased in order to spare the wilderness.

POLLAN: But I have to go to a town council meeting tomorrow night and I have to defend my decision.

YARO: Then you might want to keep your car engine running.

POLLAN: Exactly. So what do I say to the unemployed carpenter who will ask me how this decision will help get him a job?

FOREMAN: I don't really care what you say to him. Because I am going to organize people—birdwatchers, hikers, environmentalists, others—in such a way that you will fear them far more than an unemployed carpenter.

BOTKIN: Dave, don't give up completely on the carpenter and his sense of values. For example, the last uncut stand of virgin oak and hickory woodlands in New Jersey—the

Hutcheson Memorial Forest—was purchased and saved with funds from the carpenters' union, and it was named for a former president of the union. You can appeal to higher values, and the carpenters, among others, will respond.

POLLAN: Well, I have decided that you guys have your heads in the clouds. I am going to develop the entire square mile by selling five-acre plots. You've tried to stop me, but everything—petitions, lawsuits, protests—has failed. The political process is over. It's America. It's democracy. Do you go home now?

FOREMAN: I *never* go home.

POLLAN: What do you do?

FOREMAN: Conservationists have a fully equipped toolshed and use the proper tool for the proper job at the proper time.

YARO: Are hatchets in your toolshed?

FOREMAN: Lots of things are in there!

POLLAN: And after politics are exhausted?

FOREMAN: Oh, you might start by pulling up survey stakes. And you might want to engage in some paper monkey-wrenching, to slow things down.

YARO: Paper can be one of the most effective tools. You know, this society can't do things very quickly, but it is brilliant at slowing things down.

POLLAN: Suppose Dave called you the night before the bulldozers showed up. He's planning to pour something in the gas tanks. Will you help him?

TURNER: People do what they are best equipped to do. I'm not a politician. My inclination would be to use art, theater, poetry, and song. The power of a good song, like the coal miners' strike songs, is terrific.

BOTKIN: I agree with Fred. What I bring to the environmental arena is my reputation as an objective scientist who can evaluate the land. To pour something in a gas tank—

FOREMAN: —grinding compound—

BOTKIN: —would destroy my credibility. We all must play different roles.

LOVELOCK: Dave, it just so happens that my main line of work is as an inventor. I can think of a lot of things I could do to those bulldozers.

FOREMAN: Let's talk.

LOVELOCK: See, if I really felt strongly about this issue, I would be obliged to act—even at the risk of losing credibility.

POLLAN: Is there a limit to what you'd do?

FOREMAN: There are certain issues I feel so strongly about that I will plant my spear in the ground and stand there, regardless. For example, during the demonstrations in Oregon to save old-growth forests, I was run down and pushed for a hundred yards by a truck full of loggers. They were trying to kill me and I knew it, but I couldn't get out of the way because I had made a commitment that I was going to stand there. My larger commitment is that I'm going to be nonviolent toward living things. I am willing to die for what I believe in. I am not willing to *kill* for what I believe in—although if I were an Indian in Amazonian Peru and my land was being invaded by oil companies, I might use my blowgun or my bow and arrow. But this is a real problem I continually run into with the yippie type who believes in revolution for the hell of it. I'm a very reluctant radical.

YARO: Sometimes, though, we have to lose a place in order to galvanize public attention. Sometimes the most effective way of preventing future damage is to let the damage occur. And record it, publicize it. The Glen Canyon Dam is one of the most horrible things to occur on this continent. It's what's known as a cash-register dam—built for no good reason except to finance even more pork-barrel programs. Now it is a symbol and has inspired a conservation movement across the country.

Speaking for Wolf

POLLAN: Because of my brilliant management of this problem, I have moved on to a higher office. I am President of the United States. I am a *real* environmental President, and I want to do something dramatic. What actions—both political and symbolic—would you advise me to take in order to motivate the nation?

TURNER: As I mentioned earlier, I would reform the tax system to penalize species loss and encourage ecological diversity. And, since the U.S. Forest Service has done such a rotten job with the land, it would be better to sell it to private owners with the kind of tax structure that would encourage them, pridefully and profitably, to care for the land. State control of the economic system failed in Eastern Europe. Why should state control of the ecosystem work any better than private ownership here?

BOTKIN: As long as we thought nature was "one state," we didn't need to monitor it. Now that we know that nature is always changing, we must track its conditions. We need global-research institutes—one research center per continent—to study the atmosphere and the dynamics of Earth. I would revise the national park system so that the parks were connected in such a way that natural migrations might occur. As a symbolic action, I would honor the treaty with the Sioux, return the Black Hills to them to run buffalo and manage the ecology. You could get a lot of press for this; you'd be the next Teddy Roosevelt.

FOREMAN: Let's recognize that 1992 is the 500th anniversary of the European economic discovery of America and then seek a new covenant with the land. As President, you should invite the leaders of native peoples to the White House to apologize for what we've done and to seek their advice on how to live on Turtle Island. I, too, would return the Dakota prairie to the Sioux. Use 1992 as a symbolic time to launch these initiatives.

To manage the human population, offer every woman in the world free access to family planning, abortion, and sterlization—at home and abroad. Don't impose it, just offer it. Finally, announce national goals to cut by 50 percent America's consumption of paper, wood, minerals, energy, and water by the year 2000.

YARO: I would start by having you roll out of bed one morning at Pennsylvania Avenue and walk to Union Station and hop on the Metroliner to Philadelphia—one of America's first planned cities. There you would announce a 25-cents-a-gallon increase in the oil-import duty for each of the next ten years. This will bring U.S. oil prices in line with the rest of the world. With the revenue you can retire a big chunk of the national debt and announce a national program to rebuild the metropolitan transportation systems.

LOVELOCK: We are in a similar position to that of Europe in 1938. In those days one knew that a war was looming, but nobody had the slightest idea what to do about it. One group was saying, Fight Nazism; another was saying, Disarm. There were a few sensible people who prepared for the war. Well, we are in for the equivalent of a war in the next five or ten years, and it would be sensible to prepare people's minds for that.

The destruction of the tropical rain forests and the greenhouse effect are so serious—they're not just the doom stories of scientists—that the consequences will be upon us within five to ten years. They will come in the form of surprises: storms of vastly greater severity than anything we've ever experienced before, disruptions in the ozone layer, events for which no amount of expensive computer simulation could possibly prepare us. As is the essence of surprises, we can't know what they will be. We have an enemy out there, and it will play some dirty tricks and hit us with some new weapons.

POLLAN: Do we have to wait for a Pearl Harbor before we can act?

LOVELOCK: That gets to my suggestion. As President, you should go to Pearl Harbor and give a nationwide televised speech to prepare the people.

BOTKIN: Jim is right. Our projections on global warming suggest that by the year 2000, we will begin to see rapid changes over vast areas. In parts of the North, we expect to see stately old trees beginning to die back. The warmer temperature will make many trees vulnerable to insect attacks and different blights. Hikers will increasingly find themselves among dead trees. Loggers will have to choose between harvesting the dead timber and glutting the lumber and paper industries. And the diebacks will affect water supply and erosion rates. It's really overwhelming.

So your policies to curb global warming should be yoked to symbolic actions in order to motivate people. For example, I might have the President create an environmental trail beginning at the front door of the White House, going out of President's Park, down to the Mall, into Rock Creek Park, on to the Appalachian Trail, all the way to the Blue Ridge Mountains. I've checked this out. It can be done.

TURNER: I am bothered by the model of war. I am not a scientist, but I gather that there is much scientific data to the effect that the changes wrought by human beings in the ecosphere are still within the range of changes that have been going on anyway. Isn't the climate of the world on a kind of random wave into which these changes fit comfortably? I think the war model, by which we try to get everybody anxious, leads to despair and to a point where people act out of guilt and fear. The motivations of guilt and fear are as damaging to one's capacity for creativity as they are to sex: If you're in an acute state of guilt and fear, you will not be very good at sex or at coming up with good ideas.

I would look for ways to use hope, expectation, adventure, and curiosity as motivators. I want to see the destruction of the rain forests and the ozone layer and the greenhouse effect as occasions for international cooperation. We are at the beginning of the greatest period of human history. To motivate us in a positive way, I have two suggestions:

First, let us recognize that nature is a process of reproduction, of inaccurate self-copying—a series of "flaws" that account for evolution. And that human reproductions of nature are not substitutes for authentic nature but *are* authentic nature. Humankind's efforts are a continuation and extension of that reproduction, evolution, and improvement. Since only about 5 percent of the genetic material of any species is expressed, the other 95 percent is an archive of evolutionary history. Thus we may be able to *reconstruct* lost species. We should do so, and we should think of these efforts as positive accomplishments. We are promoting nature because *we are nature.* We are the leading edge, the sensitive tip, the cambium of nature. And we are charged with its promotion.

Second, this world, this universe, is a chaotic, self-organizing, dissipative system that never repeats itself. If we believe that we must maintain nature at a particular point of arcadian or pastoral perfection, then we are doomed. We must see ourselves as part of a universe whose divine drama has only begun. So let us recover our ritual sense of evolution. I would establish a Presidential Prairie and create two festival days in the year. The first would be seed-collecting day for the president, his family, kids, the Girl Scouts—all of us—to go to old graveyards, railroad rights-of-way, and the like and collect the seeds to be planted in the prairie. Since prairies have to be burned, the second festival would be in the spring, and there would be a great burning. It would be a ritual performance, and TV would be there. You would see it. It would be photogenic. It would be great footage. It would be a beautiful thing.

LOVELOCK: Fred, I just want to return to my wartime language. I remember 1938 very clearly, and it was not a time of despair at all. The threat of war stirs a feeling of adventure. If you had lived in London then, you would have found it was a very pleasant place. The threat of war didn't cause misery or a lack of creativity. Art and writing flourished in those heady times. Far more paralyzing than the threat of war is the foolish suburban contentment in which many people now languish.

YARO: Since this is the decade of turning ICBMs into plow-shares, I propose two post-Cold War initiatives for the president. Make "America the Beautiful" the nation's anthem. Instead of contemplating the "rockets' red glare," let's reflect on "thine alabaster cities" and "purple mountain majesties." Then, let's reclaim that song's images and vistas by bringing home the 300,000 soldiers from Europe and dedicating the resulting savings to repairing our lands and cities.

BOTKIN: And let's turn our coastal military bases into maritime research centers and convert our land bases into environmental stations.

LOVELOCK: As we make these changes, we shouldn't neglect technological advances. Shell Oil in Europe, for example, has a scheme for burning coal in pure oxygen that eliminates pollution. I am not one of those environmentalists who say we should go back to the land and burn candles to light our homes. It's like passengers on a ship deciding they loathe ironware technology and jumping off the ship to swim the rest of the way.

POLLAN: Dave, are you as confident about our ability to solve our problems?

FOREMAN: I guess I disagree with everybody. We are foolish to believe that all our problems are solvable, especially by technology or sociology. The technological fix often creates twice as many problems as it solves. We need fewer solutions and more humility. Our environmental problems originate in the hubris of imagining ourselves as the central nervous system or the brain of nature. We're not the brain, we are a cancer on nature.

The Oneida Indians tell an old story about the tribe discovering a new, perfect place. After they moved, they found that the area had many wolves. They considered slaughtering the wolves but then thought, What kind of people would we become if we killed them? They stayed, but, to deal with this problem in the future, they appointed one man to attend the council meetings and "speak for wolf." We must overcome our hubris and learn to speak for wolf.

TURNER: There may be limits to technology, but I've seen blackened and polluted sections of England made rich with life. Technology is not necessarily bad, and neither are we. I deeply object to the metaphor of humankind as a cancer. My parable, Dave, is that early on, when life first appeared, the crystals and chemical organisms must have thought, What is this thing that keeps reproducing itself? It keeps on changing. It's messing up the atmosphere. It keeps transforming itself. It's full of hubris, life. For what is life but a cancer upon the purity of the inorganic? If we are a cancer, if life is a cancer, then I am for it. The nervous system is a glorious cancer that has evolved, and I stand with it. I am that cancer.

FOREMAN: And I am the antibody.

Ethics in Embryo

Soon after the introduction of a controversial technology—nuclear energy, say, or the test-tube baby or the artificial heart—something goes very obviously wrong. A baby dies, a circulatory system fails, a radioactive cloud escapes on an easterly wind.

The event sets in motion an anguished debate between those who believe in what they are pleased to call progress and those who argue unprincipled science will subvert the moral order and diminish the value of human life. The two sets of apologists agree on only one point—that the public debate began only after the damage had been done. In anticipation of this familiar complaint, *Harper's Magazine* assembled a small group of people associated with various aspects of the current discussion about the uses of genetic engineering. No subject excites stronger emotions or opens more doors into a brave new world.

Presented with three proposed techniques—not yet practicable but entirely plausible within the bounds of current laboratory research—the participants were invited to address the embryonic moral questions implicit in the biotechnologies.

*T*he following forum is based on a discussion held at the Cooper Union for the Advancement of Science and Art in New York City. Lewis H. Lapham served as moderator.

LEWIS H. LAPHAM
is editor of Harper's Magazine.

NANCY NEVELOFF DUBLER
is the director of the Division of Legal and Ethical Issues in Health Care at the Montefiore Medical Center in New York City. She has written widely about medical dilemmas in contemporary health care.

THOMAS H. MURRAY
is the director of the Center for Biomedical Ethics at the School of Medicine of Case Western Reserve University.

JEREMY RIFKIN
is president of the Foundation on Economic Trends in Washington, D.C. He is the author of Biosphere Politics: New Consciousness for the New Century.

LEE SALK
is clinical professor of psychology in psychiatry and pediatrics at Cornell University Medical Center and professor of child development at Brown University. He is the author of nine books on the parent-child relationship.

Fetal Brain Implants

PROPOSED TECHNOLOGY

Scientists discover that fetal brain implants restore mental lucidity in Alzheimer's disease patients.

LEWIS LAPHAM: Let's say the breakthrough of using fetal brains to reverse Alzheimer's was announced this morning. Now almost everyone will have a grandfather or grandmother who could benefit. Nancy Dubler, do you think there's a problem with the widepread use of fetal brains as a routine therapy?

NANCY DUBLER: That depends on the restrictions applied, the assumptions about the fetus, and the context. Fetuses deserve respect. I don't think that principle conflicts with the right of a woman to an abortion. But it would demand that nothing demeaning or repugnant be done with the fetus.

Let us assume a woman opts for an abortion and the fetus that is removed has brain tissue which could be effectively transplanted. If the mother had no objection, then it could be used. There should be a requirement that the arrangement not be commercial. The woman should not profit from the procedure. The issue of profit to the physician is slightly more complicated.

LEE SALK: I agree with Nancy that the context is important. What would make it repugnant would be if a woman became pregnant in order to sell the aborted fetus.

LAPHAM: Tom Murray, why is the profit motive repugnant? We sell blood.

THOMAS MURRAY: Actually we sell very little blood in this country. The overwhelming majority is donated. We used to think that you had to pay people to get them to give

285

blood. But that turns out not to be true. The American public is overwhelmingly against a commercial system for blood. They would probably feel the same repugnance to a market in fetal brains.

One of the primary reasons we donate blood, organs, and other kinds of tissues is to affirm our ties with the strangers among whom we live. It is one of the few ways left open for us, in a mass bureaucratic society, to minister to their needs, particularly their health needs.

LAPHAM: I really don't understand the objection to the profit motive. We're talking about a waste product here: thousands of fetuses are discarded every day.

DUBLER: We would not want to live in a society where women became pregnant for the purpose of making money.

LAPHAM: For Mary Beth Whitehead, we already do live in that kind of society.

DUBLER: That's different. And some of us want to see that practice halted.

But if you go back to blood donation—and I think Tom is right, that is the closest analogy—we discovered that to maintain the highest quality blood supply it was unwise to have people sell their blood. The profit motive, it turns out, encourages blood donations from hepatitis carriers. But more than that, you don't want to encourage commerce in human parts. That's a bad idea.

LAPHAM: Let's say there's no commercial motivation: Should you use discarded fetal brains to treat Alzheimer's?

DUBLER: In organ donations, when someone dies, we approach the family. We say, "Now that this person is dead, someone else may benefit from what remains physiologically of this person." We ask the family for their consent. That seems to me to be the closest analogy we have.

LAPHAM: So that you would ask women coming into abortion clinics routinely to sign a waiver allowing the fetal tissue to be used?

DUBLER: Yes. It would be a two-step process. First, society reaches a judgment, either through its legislative process or through a combination of political and administrative processes, that this is good for society and should be encouraged. Step two, the individual involved—the gestational mother—can refuse or consent to have those fetal parts used.

LAPHAM: Jeremy Rifkin, do you agree?

JEREMY RIFKIN: There's a broader question that needs to be looked at. For the last hundred years in Western medical science, there has been a shift toward utilitarianism, toward short-term benefits to individuals. However, utilitarianism has thrived at the expense of a gradual desacralization of the life process. In this kind of procedure, two different values conflict: the short-term utilitarian value to the individual versus the long-run systematic desacralization of human life itself.

Science and technology in Western civilization have increasingly reduced living things to dead material for manipulation. We need to ask ourselves: Is life more than the chemicals that make it up? Is life more than tissues and cells and nucleic acid sequences?

MURRAY: I don't think utilitarianism or reductionism is the issue here. In fact, if you consider how the theologians have approached organ transplantation—theologians such as Paul Ramsey—they can, in the end, justify organ transplantation precisely because they believe in the sacredness of life.

DUBLER: I am a bit surprised, Jeremy, by your answer. When you sign an organ-donation card, or when a family agrees to an organ transplant after a person is brain-dead, that is a benefit to others and not a detriment to the individual. I would argue it enhances the sanctity of life by permitting others to enjoy a better quality of life.

RIFKIN: Let me try to place this in another time context. I'm not talking about the immediate moment because one could advance very good arguments for each immediate moment over the last fifty to seventy-five years of medical advances in Western culture. I'm arguing abut a longer time span. If we look at this period anthropologically, we find that, step-by-step, we are reducing life to the chemical components that make it up. And we're doing it in the name of good, in the name of providing benefits for our fellow human beings. But we're going to have to look at the long-term implications of doing that. I think they are profound and disturbing, and again they get to the heart of our world view.

In public policy in Washington, ethical concerns always play a secondary role to commercial considerations. By the time the ethics of a new technology are debated, it's generally too late to change course. The technology is already ensconced in the marketplace. The religious community, the social philosophers, and the ethicists—much to my chagrin—have been edged out of public deliberation in any meaningful way on these technologies.

MURRAY: You could make those arguments about almost any earlier technology. Penicillin was a new technology once; it was discovered in 1928 and made available in the '40s. At the same time you could have said: We don't know all the effects—more children will survive childhood and that will affect housing markets; more old people will live longer because we can now cure them of pneumonia at age seventy-three instead of just letting them die. We could have faced exactly the same questions.

SALK: Take the case of diabetes: Insulin treatment has allowed millions of people to reach reproductive age who have a diabetic tendency. Insulin has introduced into the population a high incidence of people prone to diabetes.

My own research on adolescent suicide suggests that complications during pregnancy, labor, and delivery seem to increase the likelihood of suicide during adolescence and perhaps later in life. Now that we can save more babies, we might be, in a sense, tampering with nature's quality control.

Thirty years ago we did not engage in heroics in the delivery room. Newborns were allowed to die if there were any complications. Today those same babies survive and seem to be at risk for problems later. Maybe we're introducing certain weaknesses into the species. That's the disadvantage and it suggests a much larger question.

Survival of the fittest in the evolutionary process and natural selection may no longer be the only factors influencing the course of life. We have reached the point where we can control our evolution and change the world we live in without waiting for natural forces to operate. We have become the force that can control our evolution. The problem is *how* we are going to shape it. We will indeed be doing that and manipulating things that were once considered totally unacceptable. Implanting fetal brains in adults' brains is only the beginning.

Sex Determination Before Conception

PROPOSED TECHNOLOGY

A spermicide that kills either male- or female-producing sperm and provides near statistical certainty in determining the sex of the child.

LAPHAM: Let's suppose that this spermicide—let's call it Sexselex—can determine at intercourse the sex of the child.

MURRAY: I suppose it comes in pink and blue tubes?

LAPHAM: Exactly. Now, I'm the father of, say, three sons, and I want to have a daughter. I want to buy Sexselex. What do you tell me?

DUBLER: You can't buy it. I tell you to read all the pertinent literature and to arrange intercourse at that time and in that position recommended by the literature to produce the boy or girl you want.

LAPHAM: What's the difference? I can buy it for $5 in a blue or pink tube. Otherwise it could take ten years and I could miss. Maybe I'm not athletic enough.

DUBLER: I'm telling you there are certain technologies which could be disruptive to the basic fabric of society that we will say they are excluded from the marketplace. Whatever shadow of that technology you can achieve through more natural processes, you're welcome to do.

Given the ongoing problem of female infanticide in China and India, it seems clear that the technology would be used to discriminate mainly against females.

SALK: I have no doubt that we will use this technology, but I have real problems with it. If we begin to manipulate the existing balance between genders in any society we will have a major disruptive effect on society.

If a man and a woman want to bring a child into this world only if it is a certain gender, they shouldn't have a child in the first place. When it comes to French poodles, they can choose. But the nurturing of a child should not depend on its gender.

LAPHAM: Wait. I'm allowed to take an aspirin. I'm allowed to take penicillin. I'm allowed to take all kinds of products that are not natural. But now you're telling me that to conceive a child I must return to the state of nature.

DUBLER: You're also allowed to take medication that will prevent conception. But there are certain parts of the reproductive process that properly lie beyond individual manipulation by scientific technology.

LAPHAM: Do you think you have any chance explaining that to a desperate father?

DUBLER: I think that there are some plights of the human condition for which there are impermissible answers. This is one. I'm sorry that you have only three sons. I agree that daughters are highly valuable. But it is not a problem to which society permits a specific and effective solution.

LAPHAM: Even though I can buy it in the drugstore?

DUBLER: No, no. I'm not letting you buy it in the drugstore.

SALK: You're not going to be able to stop him.

DUBLER: I would make every effort to keep it out of the drugstore by having the FDA refuse to license it.

LAPHAM: If you pass that law, I'll make a fortune. I'll make much more with Sexselex on the black market than I could over the counter.

RIFKIN: This example forces us to address what's really happening here. As we move out of the Industrial Age into the Biotechnical Age, we're increasingly able to manipulate living things for our own advantage. What we're really talking about is engineering the life process. So let's begin by understanding what engineering is.

We are introducing technological principles into reproduction. We are exploiting living things with the same methodology used during the Industrial Age to exploit inanimate things.

Engineering is about quality controls, design, and building predictability into the product.

SALK: It is disruptive to any culture to interfere with the balance of male and female. But it's inevitable; it's going to happen. With so many new technologies, we look back and wonder "How did we ever adapt?" Well, we did adapt.

LAPHAM: But would you try to legislate this technology out of existence?

SALK: If we did, we would indeed make some people rich by creating a black market. My approach would be for public education to convince people it's unwise to do this. It may be better to develop a conscience than to develop legislation. People may act on their conscience.

MURRAY: We shouldn't let this product on the market. The reason Lee Salk and Nancy Dubler offer is cogent, but it's not the only reason.

If we let you choose your child's sex, we're saying it is socially legitimate to get pregnant, test the fetus, and decide whether to keep it or not.

LAPHAM: Don't we do that already?

MURRAY: We do for certain limited purposes. We use amniocentesis to look for certain serious detectable disorders.

Should we also use it to screen for gender? I think not.
Look what the baby becomes—a commodity just like
your car. You want it with air-conditioning? This one
doesn't have air-conditioning, so you return it to the man-
ufacturer.

LAPHAM: Our society already treats its citizenry like commodities.

MURRAY: Do you really believe we can buy and sell each
other?

LAPHAM: That's exactly what we do every day.

DUBLER: This sounds like Sweeney Todd's London.

LAPHAM: No, it sounds like Donald Trump's New York.

Genetic Profiles of Test-tube Babies

PROPOSED TECHNOLOGY

*The woman takes fertility drugs, or is "superovulated," to produce around
thirty eggs. These are fertilized and genetically profiled to determine
whether the embryo has diseases, such as Huntington's chorea; afflictions,
such as Down's syndrome, or even simple astigmatism; and finally for
characteristics such as eye color, skin color, and physical imperfections.*

LAPHAM: I've got thirty fertilized eggs here. Ms. Dubler, am I
allowed to throw out the embryos with Down's syndrome
or serious disorders?

DUBLER: Yes. We look to find out if there is Down's syndrome or any other affliction that we recognize as excep-
tionally painful and difficult, those that are not a "good"
in human beings.

LAPHAM: How do we know which traits are "not a good in
human beings"?

RIFKIN: Exactly. Every year we locate more and more genetic
markers for single-gene diseases. When the technology
exists to remove them, there will be parental pressure to
do so. Soon parents are going to have a genetic readout of
all the traits they can potentially pass on to their children.

Parents will become statisticians. They're going to ask, "Do I want to burden my child with a particular trait?"

Where do you draw the line? There are several thousand recessive traits. Leukemia can kill your child at three, heart disease at thirty, and Alzheimer's at fifty. At what point do you say no? Society might even legislate or compel parents not to pass on certain traits because of the health costs likely to be incurred.

We're forcing a profound change in the parent-child relationship. As we introduce predictability, we create more pressure for perfect eggs, perfect sperm, and perfect embryos.

MURRAY: Let's make a distinction. With a disease, a child is sick and in pain. And there are a relative handful of genetic disorders that cause great suffering. But with a recessive trait the gene is not expressed, so the child is not ill. There are thousands of those, so why remove them?

LAPHAM: Let's get back to my petri dish. You've got thirty fertilized eggs. You're going to allow me to take out Down's. What else are you going to let me take out?

DUBLER: Tay-Sachs, Huntington's. If we have the same information about early-onset Alzheimer's as we do about Tay-Sachs, I would include early-onset Alzheimer's.

LAPHAM: I'm down to twenty-six. Now let's suppose the twenty-fifth one has got a harelip. Am I allowed to take that one out?

DUBLER: You're not going to test for that, so you're not going to know.

LAPHAM: As soon as I get the technology I'm going to test for that. Mr. Rifkin is right. Once you let me take out Tay-Sachs, there's no stopping.

DUBLER: I don't agree with that at all. There is a fundamental assumption in this discussion with which I disagree profoundly: that we as a society cannot make and enforce decisions. We as a society could have a reproductive policy which stated that we could test for those conditions that burden life to such a degree that it is permissible to exclude them. The number of conditions would be limited. Aside from those, you would not gather the information. It would be regulated the same way we now regulate research.

RIFKIN: How do you determine "the conditions that burden life"? What about a disease that kills at age five or one that kills at age thirty?

DUBLER: Dying of Huntington's is a terrible death, and I think that society has a shared perception on certain diseases. We can draw lines. We are human beings; we deal with difficult problems all the time.

MURRAY: Jeremy, you lack faith in our ability to make judgments, yet we make judgments all the time. We decide what is a disease and what is not a disease, what's a deformity and what's not a deformity. For example, society says: "If you have a harelip, that's a deformity, and it's enough of one to warrant trying to correct it. We'll even help you pay for it."

That's a social consensus. Whereas if you want a tummy tuck because you don't like your paunch, we say we'll let you do it, but we sure as hell won't pay for it. We draw that line. You may want to argue with me about how to draw it, but we draw it nonetheless.

LAPHAM: But our "society" is defined by the marketplace. And a capitalist ethic does not allow the state to say: Do this, do that.

DUBLER: Sure it does. Let me give you an example. On the black market, you can buy or sell anything. You can torture people. You can pay to have them killed. You can sell human flesh. I don't want to argue that criminals don't exist. On the open market, though, what society professes to believe guides our behavior.

Over the last decade we as a society have said there are certain values in medical research which we will support and ones we will prohibit.

For example, you can't do research on children where there is more than a "minimal risk to the child" unless there is an overwhelming compensating benefit. So we've taken medical research, which is also driven by the marketplace, by gain, by ego, by position, and we've said, *no*, there are certain things that you can't do.

Let me come back to our petri dish. There are certain things you can't do. You can take out Huntington's and you can take out early Alzheimer's and then you are left with a certain number of fertilized eggs. Here's what you do: You will line them up, you will take the first one in line, and you will implant it. I don't think that's any more difficult than regulating research. The black market will exist, but that doesn't invalidate my argument.

RIFKIN: What we're really talking about is eugenics. Professional ethicists keep looking out the front door saying, "I hope this technology isn't abused by a particular government or a particular ideological system. I hope another Adolf Hitler doesn't come along."

Meanwhile a new eugenics has quietly slipped in the back door. You can hear it in our conversation today. We're talking about commercial eugenics. We want perfect babies. We want perfect plants and animals. We want a better economy. There's no evil intent here. The road to the Brave New World is paved with good intentions.

Step-by-step, we are deciding to engineer parts of the genetic code of living things. Two important questions emerge: If we're going to engineer the genetic code, what criteria does this society establish for determining good and bad, useful and dysfunctional genes? And I would like to know whether there is an institution anyone here would trust with the ultimate authority to decide the genetic blueprints for a living thing?

MURRAY: Wait. You asked me to come up with a criterion for a disease everyone thinks should be engineered out. Here it is: a disease that causes a prolonged, painful, and undignified death. How does that sound?

RIFKIN: Would you feel qualified to be on the President's Commission set up to advise on this?

MURRAY: You never answer a question.

RIFKIN: Would you feel qualified to give advice and consent as to what genetic changes in the biological code of human beings are permissible?

MURRAY: Yes. I wouldn't feel qualified to make the ultimate judgment, but I would feel qualified to become part of the discussion. The alternative is to do nothing. Again, Jeremy, you hold no faith in our ability to make any distinctions, any reasonable judgments.

RIFKIN: I have faith in humanity's ability to make reasonable judgments. The question is who is making the judgments and on behalf of whom? What are the preconceptions and central assumptions that we're using?

SALK: Let's look for a moment at a technology developed two decades ago and see where that's taken us. Neonatology, the medical science devoted to troubled newborns, emerged as a subspecialty around 1965 and created a new breed of physicians. Have we made any reasonable judgments in this field? What I see is a technology driving these doctors to save babies at the lowest birth weight possible. Today I see babies born in our hospital with multiple handicaps. We can save a 600-gram baby, but I don't think the doctors are as concerned with the quality of life as they should be.

DUBLER: I disagree with that entirely. They're very concerned, although puzzled as to how to determine it. They're very aware that it would be unethical to save a 200-gram infant.

SALK: But I'm not sure it's ethical to save a 1,000-gram infant with multiple handicaps.

DUBLER: Many neonatologists would agree.

SALK: But no one is setting up any criteria that they can abide by. Thirty years ago, when a baby was born with respiratory distress, other than giving it oxygen, they would just put it in the corner and let nature take its course. Mothers were told, "This is God's will. You would have had a multiply handicapped child. It's better to let it go." And people accepted that. They had no problems with that at all.

DUBLER: I disagree with almost every one of your statements. There are some babies who are so clearly in intractable pain that they cannot lead any sort of reasonable life. At that point they are let go. Those decisions are made carefully and adequately on moral bases by the medical team and the parents.

Neonatology is a good example where principles—incorporating both science and ethics—have provided real guideposts for caregivers. Similarly, I think a standard for genetic decisions could be developed along the lines of Tom Murray's criterion: when suffering and disease and an undignified death are inevitable.

MURRAY: It's hard to imagine a culture that would not spare people suffering and painful death, as long as it didn't come at a terrible moral price.

LAPHAM: What I hear Nancy and Tom saying is that you are prepared to breed out pain or death in our petri dish but you're not prepared to breed anything in.

DUBLER: Correct.

MURRAY: Right.

LAPHAM: Why not breed in? We could solve the problem of racism, for instance. Let's take out skin color in my petri dish. Why won't you let me do that?

MURRAY: Is that the way to respond to a social problem like discrimination?

LAPHAM: You let me prevent hideous death, but you won't let me put in any "positive" traits.

RIFKIN: When the day comes that we can make these decisions, we will probably be less tolerant of the disabled because we will perceive them as defective *products*.

Also, we're likely to see the beginning of a prejudice based on genetic type, on genetic readout, which is likely to be just as virulent as prejudice based on race or ethnic background.

Should your employer know that you have a tendency toward Alzheimer's? Should your school system know the genetic readout of your child? Should a government have these records? I suspect we're going to see the beginning of a biological caste system in the next two to three centuries. We may be seeing the gradual emergence of eugenics in civilization.

MURRAY: You're using the word "eugenics" a little too cavalierly here. Eugenics means the management of the genetic stock of a population.

RIFKIN: To improve it.

MURRAY: To "improve" it, as if we know what that means.

RIFKIN: That's the problem with engineering for improvement. Do you know of any engineer who only wants to make technology *somewhat* efficient but not *perfectly* efficient? Do you know of any engineer who stops midway through the process and decides to accept less than the most efficient solution? I don't. Engineers want to continue the process until they have *perfected* the technology. Why would it be any different in genetic engineering than it is in mechanical or electrical or nuclear engineering?

DUBLER: Because people are not bolts of steel.

RIFKIN: But we are beginning to perceive living things as indistinguishable from bolts of steel.

DUBLER: I don't accept that judgment.

RIFKIN: It depends on what your highest value is. If your highest value is respect for life, then I would agree that we've got a fighting chance here. If, however, the highest value in civilization is efficiency, expediency, and engineering values, then I would say we're in trouble.

MURRAY: If that's the way the values line up, we're in deep trouble. I think fortunately the values don't line up that way.

RIFKIN: The problem with these different values is that they are being developed into a new sociology, one that goes hand-in-hand with genetic engineering. Increasingly we open up the newspaper and find articles saying we have located the newest gene governing personality or social behavior (a good example is the much celebrated but recently discredited "depression" gene).

We're beginning to believe that our social behavior is a direct result of our genetic typing. Social biologists don't come right out and say, "It's all genetics; it's all inheritance." What they do say is more subtle: That genetic inheritance is the *broad determinant* of your personality. Environment, institutions, and values play some role, they say, but it's a smaller role than we had thought.

What happens in a society that has both the technology to manipulate the genetic code and a social biology that suggests that we are no more or less than the genes that make us up? It's a dangerous combination, moving us ever closer to a eugenic civilization.

MURRAY: This is not the first sweeping intellectual change that mankind has experienced. I think Jeremy is right in saying that this challenges the way we think about ourselves. But then again so did Copernicus, so did Darwin, so did Freud. They challenged us to think about ourselves in entirely new ways—in ways at least as profound as those imposed by the genetic-engineering revolution. We still look at ourselves as creatures capable of dignity, capable of meaning, capable of morality.

DUBLER: One example of individual choice—and a simple form of genetic engineering—is choosing your spouse. If you think, for example, that sociological characteristics are linked to behaviors that are determined by genes, then you ought not to choose someone to reproduce with who has a history of assaults or burglaries or murders.

LAPHAM: You're allowing me free choice with my spouse but not my child.

DUBLER: Yes, absolutely. Even though over 50 percent of us in this country make bad decisions in our choice of a spouse, we will not limit that foolishness even when it's repetitive foolishness. That's because there are values inherent in individual choice.

LAPHAM: I don't understand what value system anybody at this table lives by. You'll allow me free choice with a spouse, but not with a child.

SALK: We'll allow you free choice about whether or not to have children.

LAPHAM: And you'll allow me to design my child with enormously expensive neonatal care, private schools, child psychiatrists, Yale University.

DUBLER: That's coping with your decisions.

LAPHAM: No. It's trying to imprint on my descendant a certain set of traits.

DUBLER: You get to rear your child, that's all.

LAPHAM: I get to rear—not design—my child?

DUBLER: Yes.

RIFKIN: But wait a minute. What I gather from you is that some design is permissible and some isn't.

DUBLER: To manipulate for a good—such as ruling out Huntington's—is different than designing.

RIFKIN: To plan in advance the outcome of something: That's what design is. So what you really want is to eliminate the word "design."

DUBLER: Because language helps us distinguish among processes even when they are similar.

RIFKIN: Haven't you introduced design by eliminating one gene? It seems to me you're not taking full responsibility for this. You're saying you are willing to design for some things but not others. It's not semantics. It's a question of whether you're willing to plan any part of the genetic makeup of your offspring in advance.

MURRAY: I'm willing to spare my offspring the horrors of a few terrible diseases.

RIFKIN: It's interesting how we use language. Scientists used the term "genetic engineering" up until the late 1970s. When the controversy over genetics emerged, the word was changed from "engineering" to "therapy." Suddenly we're talking about gene therapy. What's the difference between engineering and therapy?

LAPHAM: From this discussion it seems obvious. Therapy connotes taking away the negatives, and engineering connotes putting in the positives. The sentiment here is that it's okay to take away the negatives; that's therapy. It's not okay to put in the positives; that's engineering.

RIFKIN: So when an engineer takes a defect out of a machine, that's not engineering—that's therapy.

MURRAY: We're not talking about engineering; we're talking about eliminating a disease.

RIFKIN: You're talking here about changing the blueprint of life itself.

MURRAY: When a physician cures a disease, is that engineering?

RIFKIN: Yes, if the physician engineers changes into the genetic blueprint. When an engineer eliminates a defect in the design of a tool, that's engineering. Because you're going right to the heart of the actual technology that you've created. Remember, just because something can be done doesn't mean it inevitably should be done. Throughout history many more technologies have been rejected by various cultures than accepted. It's only in the last 200 years of the Western world view that we have come to believe that if it can be done, it's inevitable—a fait accompli. As if new technologies come here in some mysterious way, by the gods, and we just stumble across them and therefore have to live with them as we do the changing seasons. That view allows us not to take responsibility. I don't assume that any of these things is a fait accompli.

DUBLER: It's a wonderful moment: Jeremy and I agree. There is no technological imperative. That's exactly what I've been arguing. Simply because a technology exists is no reason that we must use it or that we can use it.

RIFKIN: But what are you going to do? You have to have a change in world views to deal responsibly with this technology. You can't use this world view to critique this technology because this world view is the architect of this technology.

DUBLER: I believe that scholarly discussion serves as the basis for public discussion and that is how our society should proceed. Ideas are addressed by scholars, which are then discussed by legislators, which then become the subject of articles in the public press. Eventually, but not without great difficulty, this debate will produce a consensus on what our overriding values should be.

Sacred or for Sale?

The urgent arrival of technological change over the last twenty years has forced society to rethink the truths it once assumed to be as absolute as they were precious. The beginning of life itself has been relocated from a point in time to a process over time. This new understanding provoked the rancorous debate over abortion, a debate that quickly degenerated into cries of murder and freedom. More recently, the singular clarity of death has become a similarly murky discussion of process, and the same twin shouts can be heard from both sides.

Now this kind of brutal reckoning will be brought to bear upon democracy's fundamental component—the individual. The body is rapidly becoming the raw material for the inchoate industry of biotechnology, which stands to earn millions of dollars from products derived from a freak spleen cell or an efficacious gene. Familiar questions must be asked: Do we own our bodies, to do with them as we like, including selling them off? Or is the body a sacred vessel that must be protected? Before technology propels us into hasty decisions, *Harper's Magazine* asked a philosopher, a lawyer, a doctor, and an ethicist to trace the shifting boundary between the sacred and the profane.

---- ◆ ----

*T*he *following forum is based on a discussion held in th*e *Rainbow Room at Rockefeller Plaza. Jack Hitt served as moderat*or.

JACK HITT
is a senior editor of Harper's Magazine.

LORI ANDREWS
is a research fellow with the American Bar Foundation and a senior scholar at the Center for Clinical Medical Ethics at the University of Chicago. She is the author of Between Strangers: Surrogate Mothers, Expectant Fathers, and Brave New Babies.

JACK KEVORKIAN
is a retired pathologist and the inventor of the Thanatron™ *—a device that allows for a doctor-assisted suicide.*

ANDREW KIMBRELL
is an attorney and the policy director for the Foundation on Economic Trends in Washington, D.C., and the author of Second Genesis.

WILLIAM MAY
is the Cary M. Maguire Professor of Ethics at Southern Methodist University. He is the author of The Physician's Covenant *and* The Patient's Ordeal.

The Value of Life

JACK HITT: In the 1980s, according to the United States Patent and Trademark Office, nearly a third of all the patent requests from medical-research facilities involved human tissue. Is it fair to assume that the body is becoming one of our great contemporary resources?

Consider John Moore. This man entered UCLA Medical Center in 1976 for a routine operation: the removal of a cancerous spleen. While examining Moore, his physician discovered that Moore's spleen cells contained peculiar and useful properties. From these cells he developed the "Mo" cell line, and UCLA was awarded a patent in 1984. The researchers went into business with Genetics Institute Inc. and Sandoz Pharmaceuticals Corporation to make a protein that battles various bacteria, even cancer. Estimates of the potential sales of this protein run into the hundreds of millions of dollars. When Moore found out what had happened to him—during the development of the cell line the researchers kept bugging him for more blood samples—he sued. Should he be awarded money?

LORI ANDREWS: The California Supreme Court argued, unpersuasively I thought, that he couldn't sue on property grounds, because his body wasn't his property, but that he *could* sue for damages, because the researchers had a "fiduciary" obligation to inform Moore of their intent. So he may end up getting money anyway.

ANDREW KIMBRELL: The court was in a peculiar position, because it had to consider Moore's property claim alongside *Diamond* v. *Chakrabarty*. In that notorious 1980 decision, the Supreme Court held, by only a 5-4 vote, that you could patent a microorganism, that you could patent *life*, by applying the same law that allows you to patent toasters or tennis rackets. That's exactly how the researchers seized

305

the advantage here. They patented Moore's cells and claimed the profits as their own. With *Diamond*, we have sanctioned the unholy alliance of the biotechnology industry and academia, of profits and science. And now people like John Moore will ask, "Why shouldn't I get my share?"

ANDREWS: I agree. It seems unjustified to keep the patients out of the profit. People like to focus on the changes in biotechnology and the novelty of the science, but really, these possibilities have been around for years. People have sold blood. The first cell line, similar to John Moore's, was created in 1951. In the 1960s, Italian nuns donated their urine so that Pergonal, a fertility drug, could be made to help women have babies. The body has been a "factory" for quite a while. What's different now is the potential for commercialism. We're seeing it throughout medicine: the evolution of hospitals into profit centers and the increasing fees paid to certain physicians. Leon Rosenberg, dean of the Yale University School of Medicine, has observed that medical schools have moved from the classroom to the boardroom, from *The New England Journal of Medicine* to the *Wall Street Journal*, and, in my view, it's unfair to cut out the person who is contributing the most to this process.

KIMBRELL: Lori, the body is not a factory. The body is not a machine. That is the "pathetic fallacy" in reverse. The original pathetic fallacy had the unruly passions of the human spirit inhabiting stones, trees, and rivers. Now we seem to believe that nothing has soul: We are all *inanimatta*, analogous to machines or factories, and can be treated as such.

ANDREWS: I'm the first to admit that the body is more than the sum of its parts. But my ability to sell certain parts of my body doesn't diminish dignity any more than my ability to sell the "intellectual products" of my body—as I do when I write an article. My ability to control—even to the point of sale under certain circumstances—enhances rather than diminishes dignity.

HITT: Dr. Kevorkian, do you think that John Moore should get money?

JACK KEVORKIAN: It's his body. He has the primal right of ownership. First of all, the word "soul" has no place in this discussion. No invented human abstraction of a theological nature will solve anything. It only obscures the issue. You mention a soul, but no one knows anything about it; it's absolutely ethereal. Body parts are property. The person owns them and has the absolute right over what will be done with them in, every situation.

KIMBRELL: Including the right to sell one's whole self into slavery?

KEVORKIAN: Absolutely. The absolute right.

HITT: Yet our Constitution—

KEVORKIAN: Jack, our Constitution is morally arbitrary.

KIMBRELL: But in today's brave new world, it would offer some protection. You know, in 1987, when the Patent Office announced that you could patent animals, including animals with human genes, they said they weren't *certain* you could patent human beings because the Thirteenth Amendment forbids human slavery. But, Dr. Kevorkian, this secular myth—that we live as autonomous individuals, as islands unto our selves, without rights balanced by duties—is absurd. Every decision you may make, whether it be to sell yourself into slavery or to sell yourself into prostitution, adds to and creates the *telos*— the purpose—of community you inhabit. You do not exist as an island. The obligations and duties we owe one another are reflected in our laws, including laws that protect the environment, prevent exploitation in the workplace, and ban discrimination. These are community values. To break those down into libertarian terms is absurd.

ANDREWS: Do you think that John Moore should be able to get money?

KIMBRELL: The existence of one evil—the patenting of life forms—is not remedied by the sanction of a second one— allowing individuals to sell their body in the marketplace. Given the facts before them, however, the Supreme Court of California made a judicious decision by giving John

Moore an economic remedy that satisfies the problem of economic justice but without breaking the new moral ground that Dr. Kevorkian would have us travel into the brave new world of selling ourselves as commodities.

KEVORKIAN: I'm not recommending anything. It's an individual's right to choose what he will do with his body. If I want to destroy my body, I will.

KIMBRELL: Dr. Kevorkian, you are not responsible for your own birth. You owe that to another, don't you?

KEVORKIAN: That's right.

KIMBRELL: You're not responsible for your nourishment or your education. You owe that to the entire community and to the educational system of this society. Correct? So, at some late date to excavate yourself from the community that created you and to locate yourself in some kind of existential void is unrealistic.

ANDREWS: But, Andy, if you push communitarian values too far, you come to the other conclusion: that the state should have the right of eminent domain. Why should all these people on the kidney waiting list die when the community—i.e., the government—could come in and seize my body parts after death? Sandoz Pharmaceuticals, which manufactured the product in the Moore case, actually argued that the University of California—the location of the operation—had the right of eminent domain and should have been allowed to take whatever they wanted from Moore without even asking him.

WILLIAM MAY: I find it strange to solve a problem of justice and inequity in this case by extending property rights. Just because the doctors are making a lot of money and the institutions are making a lot of money, I'm not sure the solution is to cut the patient in. You only create another injustice. The desperately ill will cure their ailments by exploiting the desperately poor. You will convert poor patients into the equivalent of Third World people. Instead of selling bananas, coca, or poppy, they will sell body parts. I abhor the solution. There are other means of redress: Why should health care be built on a free-lance, piecework system? Why can't physicians go on salary like academics and others who serve an important community good?

ANDREWS: I would love to see doctors put on salary. What I fear is that we talk up a storm and never better the situation for the exploited or the poor. Another concern of mine is that in this era when the Supreme Court is chipping away at the right of privacy and when many of us must entrust parts of our body to our physicians—embryos in vitro, semen, blood for people who want to avoid AIDS and have surgery—we don't really have a way for a person to maintain control over what happens to his or her body parts after they've been removed.

I think property is a place to start. The problem with the property label is the implication that everything's for sale under any circumstances. Owning property doesn't necessarily mean that you can do anything you want with it. A lot of property is sold or traded under various restrictions. You can sell, but you can't give away, your holdings if you're in bankruptcy. You can give away, but you can't sell, items made from endangered species. So among the many limits I would impose would be that only the person, himself or herself, can engage in sales. And all of those sales would be revocable by the owner. So you couldn't have the tax man putting a lien on your body. That way we avoid the situation of the poor man who, in 1890, sold his body to an institute in Sweden for research purposes, to commence upon death. When he regained his wealth, he tried to buy it back, but they wouldn't let him. In fact, they fined him for having two teeth missing— he'd diminished the value of the product.

MAY: Could the family of a notorious celebrity—say, Al Capone—sell his body to a carnival?

ANDREWS: No. That would fit into one of my categories of restrictions. No sales for entertainment or cosmetics. And for live sales, no one would be allowed to put himself at a higher risk than he normally would be at in his daily life.

You couldn't sell your heart, for example, but you could sell a kidney.

HITT: Wasn't the body of the poet John Dryden seized upon his death?

ANDREWS: Yes, his body was "arrested"—during the funeral procession—for nonpayment of loans. But I wouldn't have any of that.

KEVORKIAN: What's wrong with that?

KIMBRELL: Under your scheme we will create a breeder class of the poor who produce cells, tissues, kidneys, and children for those who can afford the price. That's taking the natural inequities of the marketplace and translating them into a new form of exploitation that is horrifying. Lori, you don't even distinguish between something that's replenishable and something that's unique. You don't distinguish between selling hair and selling kidneys.

ANDREWS: Because I'm looking at risk.

KIMBRELL: No difference between hair and children?

ANDREWS: Andy, right now the people who donate are richer, white, and better educated than others. So the real question is: Should we allow poor people to take an action—for money—that we heartily encourage everyone to take by donation? I understand the potential for exploitation, and I think you can circumvent it by allowing sale upon death so that nobody's paid during his or her life. Money will go to the estate, and then there'll be a system in which we distribute the organs by a lottery or by medical need so that organs and tissue can be parceled out more fairly.

HITT: Under our current donor system, we have a situation in which, in one period in Washington, D.C., in the early Eighties, 25 percent of the donated organs went to foreigners, mainly Arabs. Is it grotesque to assume that rich oil barons are "buying" the healthy organs of our capital's poor?

KEVORKIAN: Jack, you prove my point. You cannot legislate morality when there's such a tremendous demand. There *will* be a market.

MAY: Dr. Kevorkian, the marketplace is a wonderful mechanism for generating and distributing *certain* goods; ties, refrigerators, wrenches—

KEVORKIAN: —spleens.

MAY: No. If I buy a judge's verdict, I corrupt the meaning of justice.

KEVORKIAN: True.

MAY: If I buy a Nobel Prize, I corrupt the meaning of the Nobel Prize. If I buy an exemption from the draft, which was permitted in the Civil War, I corrupt the meaning of citizenship. If I buy and sell children, I corrupt the meaning of parenthood. And if I sell myself, I corrupt the meaning of what it is to be human.

KEVORKIAN: What does it mean to you to be human?

MAY: I find it passingly strange that you, who elevate autonomy above all other virtues, would permit anyone to annihilate that precious autonomy through slavery. The human body is not analogous to a machine with parts. It's an organism with organs. I not only have a body; I *am* my body. It is my means of self-presentation to the world, and if, in response to some need, I act to contribute part of it, the appropriate form should be giving, not selling.

ANDREWS: I think much of the case in this discussion against my core position hangs on the assumption that there's only exploitation and coercion when there's payment involved. The current system for organ and tissue donation often exerts enormous pressure on family members to be donors. One study, for example, shows that the black sheep of the family often donates, hoping it will make the rest of the family love him or her more. Does a mother have a choice when asked to donate for her child?

KIMBRELL: Lori, I think it's far from a proven point that parents are coerced to donate their organs to their children. Most parents, including myself, would give up their lives for their children. That's not called coercion. It's called love.

ANDREWS: But isn't it love when someone sells his organs to benefit his children?

MAY: Not every act of commerce is a tawdry act. A poor mother who sells her organs in order to save her child is acting nobly. But that noble act does not redeem the tawdriness of a social system that would force a poor parent to help her child that way. The facts that there would be virtue under a system of buying and selling and that there can be coercion under a system of giving and receiving don't get to the cumulative issue of what kind of society you would create: The rich would buy and the poor would sell.

KIMBRELL: Anyone who has survived a Christmas knows that gifts can definitely be coerced. But gifts are essentially uncoerced. The gift relationship strengthens the bonds between people and the members of a community. It brings out the best in us and goes far beyond the shallow relationships of the marketplace.

ANDREWS: What's wrong with the sale upon death, in order to gather organs in a way not coercive to the poor, coupled with a lottery system or a medical necessity criterion to dispense them, which is not disposed toward the rich?

MAY: The price of funerals would go up, because the funeral directors would know that the poor have a new way of paying for them.

KIMBRELL: The other problem with commercialization is that research proceeds only when there is a buck in it.

ANDREWS: For years, about 80 percent of the blood used routinely during operations was purchased. Today, nearly all the blood—except rare types—is donated. I think the existence of the market and the donation system side by side in the Sixties accounted for much of that giving. A person does not feel more virtuous for performing a particular act when the alternative is forbidden by law. John Milton once said, "I cannot praise a fugitive and cloistered virtue . . . that never sallies out and sees her adversary."

KIMBRELL: I am against the unfettered market, because it's gotten us into so much trouble. Did it curb our abuse of industrial and chemical technology? No, it led to global warming, ozone depletion, and a global environmental crisis. Did the market limit nuclear technology to its beneficial purposes? Left alone, did we limit child labor? The unregulated market does not control technological abuse; it encourages it.

HITT: I hear us coming to a slippery-slope argument. Andy, every decision is a slippery slope. Humankind dwells on a slippery slope. But we set limits all the time. True, for too long we allowed grotesque child labor, but we did finally pass laws that sought to stop it. In fact, every realm of development you mentioned was rigorously debated, fought over, and finally limited in some ways. Lines were drawn.

MAY: Our environmental problems, as Andy has said, have emerged because we have become obsessively oriented to *product* and have neglected issue of *process*. The phrase "gross national product" aptly describes this obsession. Now we have a shortage of organs and tissue. To argue that the free market is the best way to get this larger amount of product fails to question *how* we get it. There are four systems. The first is eminent domain or automatic salvaging. Society has a right—presumed consent, as it's known—to take all the organs it needs when you die unless you carry a card forbidding it.

ANDREWS: Let's talk about presumed consent. They adopted it in France and found that it didn't increase the number of donated organs, because physicians were still reluctant to intrude on someone else's body. That's why I give the nexus of control to the individual.

MAY: The second system is the appeal to individual giving, which is by and large the system in which we now operate. The third is buying and selling, which we've spent most of our time on here. The fourth is organized giving, which has been largely unexplored at this table and throughout this debate. Who handles funerals? It is religious communities. Consider Christianity's central act of worship, in which Jesus says, "This is my body, this is my blood," and gives it to others. The central liturgy of the Christian faith is the giving of body and blood in the form of bread and wine. From the pulpit, Christians might be persuaded to understand that the central symbol of their faith makes it fitting and appropriate to donate.

KEVORKIAN: Sort of brainwashing the family is what you're doing.

MAY: Oh, come on. Is there no difference between brainwashing and education?

KIMBRELL: All right. Then it's persuading the family, which is a form of coercion.

MAY: Not quite. Persuasion and coercion differ; and the two ancient societies of Sparta and Athens symbolize that difference. Sparta was a military society built upon the bark of command and the grunt of obedience. Athens depended upon *logos*, the word. There's a difference between the act of education and the act of commanding, between persuasion and coercion.

KEVORKIAN: Education's a form of coercion. You are what you are because of the culture you grew up in. What you say and do is often foreign to, say, an Afghani or a Shintoist. To you, hara-kiri is ugly, even evil, but to one who has been properly "educated," it's holy and sacred.

KIMBRELL: Dr. Kevorkian, the ethicist Tom Murray writes about *sacra*—objects or ceremonies that any particular culture finds sacred or reveres. We may find the *sacra* of other cultures barbaric and repulsive. Yet despite their apparent barbarism—and this is true of hara-kiri—the act itself always seeks to increase dignity, self-respect, and honor.

Despite such differences, all cultures share the belief that the body is a *sacra*, a unique and venerable aspect of the human person. Why, then, should we allow the commodification of the human body—the enclosure of the genetic commons, if you will—when we are now trying to reverse the vast destruction resulting from adopting the same attitude toward the earth?

ANDREWS: The examples you have been citing, Andy, are inappropriate. We don't want anyone to *give* themselves into slavery. We don't even want children laboring for *free*. We don't want havoc wreaked on the environment *without* payment. But with the human body, there is consensus that organ donation is good. Professor May even wants our religious traditions to encourage it. The issue is not that payment harms us as a society but rather the risk of living without the organ or the risk of potential coercion and so on. Your examples are issues we've legislated against because we wouldn't want them under any circumstances.

KIMBRELL: Lori, you see too much benevolence in capitalism. I'm making no secret here that I think the capitalist economy is often a terrible and destructive force. It's destroyed our natural resources, our spiritual life, and our relations in the workplace. So I'm obviously not too enthusiastic about its invasion of my body.

MAY: I'm not inclined to pronounce a global repudiation of capitalism. I just think it has its appropriate sphere, following the arguments that Michael Walzer made in *Spheres of Justice*. He held that different principles of distribution apply in different spheres. And it seems to me that the right system of distribution with regard to the human body, given its relationship to human dignity, is not the marketplace.

ANDREWS: The same argument about *sacra* and dignity was made against autopsy in the nineteenth century, abdominal surgery in this century, and even artificial insemination.

KIMBRELL: That returns us to Dr. Kevorkian's point: Science and medicine are culturally based. For instance, there's a good reason why thousands of years of Chinese medicine gave us interrelated therapy like acupuncture, which understands the interconnectedness of the self and its environment. Western medicine, on the other hand, still struggles under the metaphor of the Cartesian clockwork universe, with its interchangeable parts—a medicine that may have reached its mechanistic zenith with the attempt to install a baboon heart into a baby in Loma Linda, California. This is a highly intrusive, highly capital-intensive type of medicine that ignores preventative medicine, nutrition, the environment, and gross statistics such as our infant-mortality rate.

Our gee-whiz attraction to organ transplants, to genetic engineering and television-spectacular operations is *culturally* determined. Much of the supply and demand for organs and tissues Lori talks about comes from the fact that our science has promised us we can know everything, our technology has promised us we can do everything, and our advertisers have promised us we can have everything. But it just ain't so. The supply and demand the medical community tries to support are culturally determined. There's nothing objective here. Many of us are revulsed at the idea of an open sale of body parts. It's what I call the "yuck factor." It's healthy. As Professor Leon Kass points out, autopsy was offensive two centuries ago when people protested, and today—despite its acceptance—it is *still* offensive.

ANDREWS: Since we really are talking about drawing lines and the yuck factor, why *is* it acceptable to cut someone up because they've signed a donor card? Why doesn't it desecrate the temple of the body to peel off the skin of others for burn victims or to remove any of the fifteen salvageable organs, leaving this husk?

The Value of Death

HITT: Let's consider the Gaylin scenario, based on an article written by Dr. Willard Gaylin in this magazine in 1974. Then, it was satire. Today, it's potential public policy: I can write a living will saying that if I become brain-dead, others may either maintain me on life support or let me die. It's *my* choice. But I have written my living will with a slight twist: Should I become brain-dead, I wish to be maintained on life support and to have my organs taken *as they are needed*. This is how I want to donate my body to science.

MAY: I don't have a major problem with that.

ANDREWS: Really? I am troubled by the idea of "bioemporiums" with 200 bodies—I believe Dr. Gaylin called them "neomorts"—lying around. Frankly, I find this much less dignified than selling tissue or organs.

MAY: There is the problem of the family coming to terms with your death. If this period of donating your body goes on for an indefinite time, it would seem rather insensitive.

KIMBRELL: Look. Ideas have consequences. The idea that we are biological machines has consequences. Consider: What rights adhere to a biological machine? What duties and obligations are owed a biological machine? What dignity and love should be given to a biological machine? The whole constitutional system of rights, duties, and respect is based on the old-fashioned idea that we are reverable persons, not machines. Moreover, the idea of an emporium with dozens or thousands of these neomorts all over the country—what does this do to our view of the dignity of death?

Is this really advancement? You're going forward. But going forward to what?

You can't know what going forward means unless you have a future vision, one that requires us to judge all of the possibilities we all talk about these days: a future that permits the sale of fetal parts, that subcontracts out having a baby, that creates a breeder class to sell tissues and organs, and that allows us to change the definition of death so that we will have a regular harvesting of organs. Let's not review these developments one at a time or in a vacuum. We may end up like the frog that's put in a pot of water heated up one degree at a time: He never gets alarmed enough to jump out before he's boiled to death.

HITT: Andy, I wonder if what we are edging up to is not a brave new world but a new ethic of the body. Don't some of these developments seem inevitable? Doesn't it seem likely—as more and more medical treatments and products are created from tissue samplings of the human body—that some kind of limited property right to oneself will prevail? Is the body, in a sense, the new farm? Might there be some way that the community will ponder the multitude of curious new uses of the body, embrace these changes, and come up with a new way to define human dignity? Dr. Kevorkian?

KEVORKIAN: I don't know what you mean by "ethic of the body." A body's a body. A dog's a body. Any mammal is a body. And when you cut, you bleed. When you die, you stink. That's all we know about it. Is there sacredness in all this?

My idea of the human body is that it's a living organism like any mammal. You want to know what to do with it? Then you must consider: What are the exigencies of the spatial and temporal situation you're in at the time? Then you apply your reason, which is uniquely human and often abused—and most often by ethicists—and you use your common sense and logic and try to arrive at a solution to the problem *you are in*, not some preconceived idea that you're trying to fit reality into.

You've got to see what humans are and how they behave. Prohibition proved you can't legislate morality. We've legislated against commercialization of organs without any real insight into the problem. We've rammed it through, but wait until the demand increases over time. We will *have* a black market in organs. You're not going to solve the problem with all this moralizing. You've got to discover a motivation for people to donate. It isn't going to be education or implied consent or required request. They aren't going to do it. It's been proven! There's only one thing that motivates humanity. Self-interest. Profit. Tell me I'm wrong.

MAY: You're wrong.

ANDREWS: Dr. Kevorkian, self-interest takes many forms. Some say that altruism is a kind of self-interest: You give to others so that you will have good feelings about yourself, a sense that you are noble and above others.

KEVORKIAN: You know, these old arguments aren't going to solve anything.

KIMBRELL: *You* have the oldest argument of them all, and that's your problem. You adhere to a theology that began to develop 400 years ago that believes the natural world is devoid of any sacred meaning, that it is just a collection of resources to be consumed. That's not some essential "truth"—it's the theology of the marketplace, the faith for those who have no faith. Its God is the aptly named "invisible hand" and its greatest good is efficiency—a term borrowed from the lexicon of the machine, on which the market system is based. Now, if I told you I had two children and treated them "efficiently" or that I had a friend or a pet and I treated him or it "efficiently," wouldn't you properly think I was mad? No one treats anything they care about based on efficiency. We have applied this kind of thinking to nature, and now we seek to apply it to our bodies. We can look at the destruction of the earth as a model of what we will do to ourselves.

ANDREWS: Every time we take an action of any kind we change nature. And when we go too far we correct ourselves by outlawing certain kinds of action. We *can* think prospectively about the boundaries we set.

MAY: Let me clarify something. What happens in the relationship of the human being to his body over a lifetime—and this is where we differ from an amoeba or even a dog—is that we bond, become friends, with our own body. This is the crucial distinction that troubles us in questions of neomorts and surrogacy and the rest. That's why manufacturing is the wrong metaphor. Manufacturing insists upon the separation of product from process. In fact, it is wrong for workers to bond to refrigerators or monkey wrenches, or at least it is odd. Artists do form this kind of relationship with their work, a feature that distinguishes art from commerce.

ANDREWS: But do you want me to bond to my kidney? I think it would be strange if I were too fetishistic about my kidney.

MAY: It seems wrong to me for the mother to alienate herself from that "product" to which she has bonded, whereas it seems right for workers to be alienated from those refrigerators. Laborers don't gather weepily on the docks on the day of shipping; there shouldn't be rituals of grief for the monkey wrenches.

HITT: But, Professor May, in my case no one is doing this to me. I am simply exercising my freedom. I am pro-choice, as it were. But since many of you are troubled by the image of my body lying on a table for a long period of time, let me change the scenario a bit. I am brain-dead, but I want to donate my body immediately, with respirators going, to a medical school to allow surgeons to practice surgery on my functioning body. As I'm sure you are all aware, surgeons do not emerge from their anatomy textbooks any more capable of precise surgery than a music student who has read a dozen scores can sit down to a piano and play Chopin. So here's a body that bleeds to practice on. May I make this donation?

ANDREWS: I'd need strong evidence that you wanted this. I am concerned about coercion.

MAY: Would you allow the family veto power?

HITT: There is no family, and there's been no coercion. There is only me and my living will, which sets out my wishes unambiguously. All my life I have been told that organ donation is a good thing. Well, here's a fully working set of them.

KIMBRELL: Given the changes in public policy, why couldn't he? This is the result of switching the whole definition of death. And, frankly, it was very suspicious. The whole brain-dead concept is based on a desire for efficiency, and —I don't think too many people will disagree with me—it was drawn up to fulfill the need to harvest organs.

HITT: Wasn't it to allow relatives to unplug a brain-dead patient so he or she wouldn't have to linger on life support?

MAY: No. That's allowing someone to die.

ANDREWS: Andy's right, actually. You could still make a decision to allow your relative to die without having to change the definition of death. We all know that the change was made to facilitate organ harvesting. And it is by a similar "coincidence" that hospitals designated as trauma centers tend to be ones that have transplantation teams on the premises.

KIMBRELL: Now, *this* is a slippery slope.

MAY: We reviewed this very issue at The Hastings Center. We had approved much of the criteria currently used to determine death, but we specifically refused to include a need for organs. After all, if it is permissible to change death because you need organs, then you can move death back earlier and earlier. The only reason for declaring people dead is that they're dead. Leon Kass drew a distinction between the death of an *organism as a whole* and the death of the *whole organism*. Throughout human history, death has never been defined as the death of the whole organism, because life continues in the body's parts—the hair and the nails, for example, continue to grow. But brain death entails the death of the organism as a whole, a state that modern technology merely obscures by keeping the heart and lungs pumping and the body warm.

But your hypothetical case is a tough one. In a way, this gift, for educational purposes, is more beneficial than a single organ donation because it would make that surgeon more capable of *successful* transplantation of dozens of organs down the road. It would, of course, make gross anatomy grosser, with the body actually bleeding. I don't know how I come out on this one. I wonder what the reaction of young physicians would be?

KIMBRELL: They should be revulsed—the way children are when you first tell them where the meat in the grocery cooler comes from. There they are, nicely packaged little frankfurters, little patties. But every parent who's not a vegetarian has experienced that moment when you tell a child, "Well, that is actually a pig" or "This is a cow." And the kid freaks. When you chop things up, they immediately lose their sacramental worth, that *sacra*. What has every civilization had to do to outsiders before it exploited them or practiced genocide on them? Dehumanize them. Call them subhuman. Remove their *sacra*. That's what we did to the natural world before we moved in to destroy it. Unless we heed our revulsion, we are poised to do it to our own bodies.

MAY: I am reminded of the Grimm's fairy tale about the young boy who was unable to shudder. He visited the hangman's tree and saw seven dead men. Instead of being afraid, he cut them down and played with them, arranging them around a campfire as if they were guests. Another time he was found playing ninepins with two skulls and nine dead men's legs. His parents despaired. And before they would admit him into the family and before society would count him as one of its own, he wandered the land, trying to learn this uniquely human characteristic—to shudder at the sight of the dead.